PRAISE FOR **Teach For America Counter-Narratives**

"Finally, a detailed indictment of one of the most nefarious organizations to attack teachers and public education in over a generation. TFA has long enjoyed support from corporations and politicians (and a duped public) who know little to nothing about the intricacies and nuances of good teaching and quality education. This volume peels back the arrogant veneer of assumption and misinformation that characterizes the real TFA. For anyone interested in understanding the importance of critical scholarship in public life, this work is a long-overdue, much-needed, and insightful counter-narrative to the lies TFA continues to propagate. It's a must-read for anyone who cares about public schooling in the U.S."

Deron Boyles, Professor of Philosophy of Education, Georgia State University

"This collection provides a timely and much-needed critical analysis of Teach For America (TFA) from the perspective of a diverse set of former corps members. For those seeking to move beyond narratives that are distilled through TFA's public relations arm, or the often simplistic, back-and-forth debates about TFA, this book provides first-person, nuanced, and thoughtful analyses and reflections of teaching and education reform. Readers will walk away with a more complex understanding of TFA's role in teaching, educational policy, and educational leadership."

Janelle Scott, Associate Professor, Graduate School of Education &
African American Studies Department, University of California at Berkeley

Teach For America Counter-Narratives

ALUMNI SPEAK UP AND SPEAK OUT

Edited by T. Jameson Brewer and Kathleen deMarrais

PETER LANG
New York • Bern • Frankfurt • Berlin
Brussels • Vienna • Oxford • Warsaw

Library of Congress Cataloging-in-Publication Data

Teach for America counter-narratives: alumni speak up and speak out /
.   edited by T. Jameson Brewer, Kathleen deMarrais.
pages cm. — (Black studies and critical thinking; vol. 9)
Includes bibliographical references and index.
1. Educational equalization—United States.
2. People with social disabilities—Education—United States.
3. Teach for America (Project) I. Brewer, T. Jameson. II. deMarrais, Kathleen.
LC213.2.T43   379.2'6—dc23   2015008441
ISBN 978-1-4331-2877-6 (hardcover)
ISBN 978-1-4331-2876-9 (paperback)
ISBN 978-1-4539-1556-1 (e-book)
ISSN 1947-5985

Bibliographic information published by **Die Deutsche Nationalbibliothek**.
Die Deutsche Nationalbibliothek lists this publication in the "Deutsche
Nationalbibliografie"; detailed bibliographic data are available
on the Internet at http://dnb.d-nb.de/.

© 2015 Peter Lang Publishing, Inc., New York
29 Broadway, 18th floor, New York, NY 10006
www.peterlang.com

Dedication

TJB: *for Mallory*
KD: *for Jamie*

Contents

Introduction

TEACH FOR AMERICA: HISTORICAL AND CURRENT CONTEXT

The idea for Teach For America (TFA) was originally proposed in Wendy Kopp's (1989) senior thesis, *An Argument and Plan for the Creation of the Teacher Corps*, presented to the faculty of the Woodrow Wilson School of Public and International Affairs, Princeton University. In that document, Kopp outlined the need for alternatively certified teachers to ameliorate the national teacher shortage of the late 1980s, while putting forward an argument for "smarter" teachers in the profession—those who Kopp labeled the "best and brightest." From its inception, TFA has relied heavily on ties to corporate and venture philanthropic organizations for its funding (deMarrais, 2012; deMarrais, Lewis, & Wenner, 2011) as well as extensive federal funding.

And while the first 20 years of TFA were billed as working toward a viable solution for addressing teacher shortages, the organization has slowly transformed into acting on Kopp's second assumption, that traditionally trained teachers are not as qualified or intelligent as they should be; her cadre of Ivy League, predominantly White, and affluent corps members are innately better suited to become teachers because education majors have low SAT scores (Goldstein, 2014). This change is evident in the organization's recent shift away from rhetoric about teacher shortages to an argument that the 145 hours of training corps members receive during TFA's Summer Institute—only 18 hours of which are "teaching" hours (Brewer, 2014)—is superior to the traditional 4-year college degree and student teaching semester.

A more recent shift in TFA's strategy has been exemplified by its push to create "educational leaders" by way of principals and elected policy officials (e.g., school board members, state representatives, etc.). The organization has moved from its early focus on teacher shortages toward an effort to influence educational policies and practices. To facilitate these efforts, TFA created its 501(c)4 spin-off organization, Leadership for Educational Equity (LEE), which promotes and supports the political campaigns of TFA alumni (Cersonsky, 2012; Simon, 2013) and assists candidates in attracting significant financial contributions (Magan, 2014). What is troubling about TFA's involvement in propping up TFA candidates, all of whom are former TFA corps members, is that those individuals largely support pro-reform policies that TFA supports (Jacobsen & Wilder Linkow, 2014). In addition to the organization's goal of installing alumni into policy positions, TFA has also focused on installing alumni as school principals. Accordingly, with TFA's "Principal Pipeline," alumni with just 2 to 3 years teaching experience are sent to a partnering university (Columbia University was the first) for coursework in administration, and the end result is a job back in a TFA region as a principal—ultimately, with hiring power to expand the number of TFA teachers. TFA's organizational focus has strayed from seemingly humble and benign aspirations of contributing to the profession to seeking outright control of the profession by way of TFA's circle of influence (see Figure 1).

In addition to its U.S.-based programs, TFA has expanded its efforts to export its brand of pedagogical and education reform internationally by way of Teach For All (TFAll). Launched at the Clinton Global Initiative in 2007 (Dillon, 2011), TFAll has now expanded into 34 countries in addition to the United States (Teach For All, n.d.).

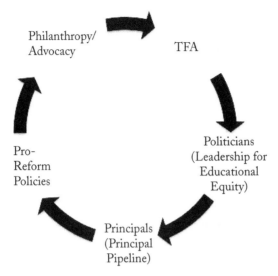

Figure 1. TFA Circle of Influence.

AIM OF THIS BOOK

TFA has been, without doubt, very successful in growing its brand of alternative teacher certification since its inception in 1990. And while TFA did not invent behavioristic classroom management styles or test-focused pedagogy, part of TFA's success—particularly in garnering millions of dollars from private venture philanthropists—is grounded in its adoption of such classroom practices. TFA is not the only alternative certification program that exists, but it certainly garners the bulk of attention, because

> the debate TFA opened up about teacher preparation and quality teaching, while often rancorous, has been deeper and more evidence-based than any the nation has had since the inception of common schooling in the nineteenth century. In part, this is because so many TFA alumni have written frankly about their experiences and have had the connections to amplify their critiques and defenses of the program through magazine articles, books, and op-eds. (Goldstein, 2014, p. 195)

And, although the debate surrounding TFA has become rancorous in recent years through anti-TFA events (Black, 2013), the trending Twitter hashtag #resistTFA (Strauss, 2014a), calls by student activist organizations for universities to break ties with TFA (Strauss, 2014b), and an increase in academic critique (Kovacs & deMarrais, 2013), TFA has historically enjoyed a largely positive image in the media (Brewer & Wallis, in press). Yet, TFA has actively responded to this growing tide of criticism in an effort to salvage its reputation. The article "This Is What

Happens When You Criticize Teach For America" (Joseph, 2014) was published in *The Nation* just as our authors were submitting their final chapters for this project. That article not only highlights the uniquely oppressive nature of TFA's public relations team when dealing with dissent, it also illustrates the realities that alumni face when seeking venues for critique of the organization.

The inspiration for this book sprang from an increase in the number of emails that Jameson Brewer (a Metro-Atlanta corps member from 2010–2012 and a 2011 Atlanta Institute school operations manager) received from active TFA corps members, recent alumni, and those who recently had quit TFA prior to the end of their 2-year teaching commitments. Many of the authors of those emails expressed their thanks to Brewer for putting into words (Brewer, 2012, 2013) the feelings that they felt on a daily basis, and also their utter dismay at their experiences with TFA. This project has, of course, had the usual obstacles associated with organizing chapters into a cohesive volume. However, the process was made more problematic by the nature of the relationship TFA has with its dissenters.

During the course of our active call for chapter proposals, we received numerous emails and phone calls from corps members and alumni interested in the opportunity to share their stories, perspectives, and insights. What was surprising was the percentage of those individuals who asked if it would be okay to use a pseudonym (for fear of reprisal from TFA or its far-reaching corporate associations), or ultimately decided either that their story was too difficult for them to share or that the use of a pseudonym would not be enough to shelter them from retaliation. This, to us, constitutes a great concern about the culture of control and fear that TFA instills into its corps members. If TFA is, in fact, interested in hearing and considering critique—as they claim (Villanueva Beard, 2013)—the experiences of many corps members and alumni who fear reprisal contradicts TFA's claim of openness.

We hope this volume provides a unique and unfettered glance into TFA and provides some answers for those asking "Should I join TFA?" "Should my child join TFA?" "Should I hire a TFA corps member?" or "Should our district work with TFA?"

THE ROLE OF NARRATIVES IN TFA'S HISTORY

TFA has a well-established history of highlighting stories of "successful" corps members and alumni that, while admitting the difficulties of being a classroom teacher, serve largely as the primary foundation of organizational marketing, recruiting, and fundraising. In fact, Wendy Kopp's most recent book (Kopp & Farr, 2011) makes a point of highlighting just a handful of anecdotal "stories" to prove that TFA is a force for good. And while there does exist a collection of corps members' vignettes that cast TFA in positive light (Ness, 2004), until now there has not been a collection of counter narratives that not only provide relevant and valuable critique of the organization but also serve as balance in the conversation about corps members' experiences in the organization. It is with this aim that we have collected counter narratives from alumni who represent a broad range of time periods, geographic regions, race/ethnicities, and genders. We have intentionally compiled a collection of narratives because

> narratives, storytelling, and counter-stories can be transformative and empowering for educators, students, and community members. These methods can make public what many already know but have not spoken out loud: There are futures and lives at stake in the process we call *education*. (Fernández, 2002, p. 60) [Emphasis in original]

Because TFA has enjoyed more than 2 decades of positive rhetoric and financial support, the time has come when the voices of dissenters and critics can be heard. Based on the content of the chapters submitted for inclusion in this book, we have organized them into three main sections: (1) TFA's Recruitment, Training, and Support Structure; (2) TFA's Approach to Diversity; and (3) TFA's Approach to Criticism and Critics (see Table 1). Authors in the first section share their early experiences with TFA as they were recruited and inducted into the organization. These narratives clearly demonstrate issues associated with a brief and ineffective teacher education, the lack of support structures as the corps members moved into their own classrooms, and the long-term impacts these experiences have had on their professional and personal lives. The chapters in the second section focus on their authors' experiences of diversity within TFA, and the colonizing, racist, classist, and heteronormative values and practices that made their experiences in TFA difficult. Finally, the third section's narratives focus on TFA as an organization that for years has relied on its belief in its own philosophy, resisting and attempting to silence its critics. To counter TFA's successful public relations machine, we offer these narratives to inform potential corps members and their parents, philanthropic and corporate funders, and the policy makers who continue to support and finance TFA.

T. Jameson Brewer and Kathleen deMarrais

Table 1. Key Issues in Chapters.

Author	TFA Placement & Dates	Key Concepts
SECTION I: TFA'S RECRUITMENT, TRAINING, AND SUPPORT STRUCTURE		
1. Jessica Millen	New Orleans, June–October 2013	• Bait-and-switch recruitment vs. reality • Corporate culture, prestige, career opportunities, financial incentives • Description of Summer Institute—inadequate preparation, behaviorist management strategies, scripted curriculum
2. Erin Nolan	St. Louis, 2007–2008	• TFA able to communicate overall vision but unable to prepare corps members for classrooms culturally different from their own backgrounds • Lack of experience of TFA staff • TFA was "soul-killing for me and unproductive for my students"
3. Brendon Jobs	Philadelphia, 2005	• Experience of dismissal from TFA during Institute • TFA's core values—Big Goals and data • Lack of comprehensive diversity training • Deficit of mentoring models for supporting preservice teachers • Use of inconsistent, inadequate feedback
4. Michael J. Steudeman	Greater New Orleans, 2010–2012	• Lack of preparation; narrow pedagogy • Absence of theoretical expertise • Experience as a corps member advisor • TFA pedagogy as the *only* pedagogy • Devalued school faculty advisors' expertise • TFA's structural rigidity • Limited mentoring and staff support
5. Laura Taylor	Houston, 2007–2009	• Shift from TFA champion to opponent • Role of theory in teacher education • TFA staff with little experience • TFA's limited, narrow perspectives on teaching • No tools for reflection on teaching

Author	TFA Placement & Dates	Key Concepts
SECTION I: TFA'S RECRUITMENT, TRAINING, AND SUPPORT STRUCTURE, Continued		
6. Matthew Lynde Chesnut	San Antonio, 2011–2013	• Disillusionment with TFA narrative • Institute experiences • Inexperienced TFA staff • Resistance to behavior management, testing, and data-tracking regime • Critique of TFA's philanthropic funding • Recommendations for TFA
7. Ian Scott	Los Angeles, 2011–2013	• Inadequate training program • TFA as neoliberal reform for privatization of education • Special education—"the gap within the achievement gap" • Clear explanation of history/concepts of neoliberalism • Philanthropy behind TFA • Inconsistent/inexperienced support for corps members across regions • Mentoring from university rather than TFA staff
SECTION II: TFA's APPROACH TO DIVERSITY		
8. Sarah Ishmael	Baton Rouge, 2010–2013	• Critical race theory • Personal narrative of institutional racism • TFA ignores underlying racial and class dynamics and perpetuates institutional racism in classrooms • Need for TFA to interrogate beliefs about non-White people and their children, and racist roots of educational inequity
9. Amber Kim	Metro Atlanta, 2001–2003	• TFA perpetuated and cultivated colorblind racism • TFA Institute as a culture of compliance • Promoted deficit views of parents • Urges TFA to partner with teachers, families, and students

Author	TFA Placement & Dates	Key Concepts
SECTION II: TFA's APPROACH TO DIVERSITY, Continued		
10. Jay Saper	Philadelphia, Summer 2013 (dismissed from Institute)	• Teaching for obedience • Summer Institute—resistance to curriculum • Lack of involvement in community and with children's lives • Community organizing in Philadelphia • TFAers replaced laid-off teachers • Charter schools options as bribes for families
11. Anne Martin	Metro Atlanta, 2008–2010	• TFA recruitment strategies focused on elitism • Impressed with TFA's sophisticated corporate culture • Recognized and resisted TFA's colonizing perspective • TFA CMs enjoy credibility excess in educational policy despite limited classroom experience • Dissonance between TFA's narrative of urban schools and reality of her school placement • Inadequate preparation in Institute vs. quality mentoring from school colleagues/mentors • TFA placements where no teacher shortage exists
12. Monica Chen	BIA School, Navajo Nation, New Mexico, 2012–2014	• Role of regional TFA offices • Rural, isolated TFA placements • Safety issues and lack of support • "Teaching as Leadership" Evaluation • Lack of preparation and mentoring • Conflict between imposed curriculum and testing regime and students' needs
13. Summer Pennell	Eastern North Carolina, 2009–2011	• TFA ignores gaps it creates with corps members and between corps members • Cultlike Institute • Lack of support of TFA staff • Heavy recruitment efforts • Heteronormative culture • Savior mentality • No policy/training on LBGTQ issues

Author	TFA Placement & Dates	Key Concepts
SECTION III: TFA'S APPROACH TO CRITICISM AND CRITICS		
14. Wendy Chovnick	Houston Summer Institute, 1998; Bronx Summer Institute, 2001; Washington, D.C. corps member, 2001–2003; Phoenix staff member, 2009–2012	• TFA's philanthropic funding and endowment • TFA as a failing organization o Management structures and layers are barriers to consistent, quality support of corps members o Recent changes in core values not appropriate for new teachers o Limited patience/stark criticism of struggling staff and corps members o TFA's suppression of criticism o Calls for TFA to earn public's trust
15. Walt Ecton	Metro Atlanta, 2010–2012	• "I'm doing TFA" vs. "I'm becoming a teacher" • TFA's positives: recruits are elite students who would not consider teaching; innovative program • Critiques TFA's ability to sway corps members' opinions on education reforms • Limited role of faculty advisors in Summer Institute • Test-prep teaching through data-driven systems • Promotes unsustainable approach to teaching, leading to intense burnout • TFA urged to act as a learning organization
16. Ryan Garza	Chicago, 2011–2013	• TFA's role with charter schools • Placement of corps members in charter schools • TFA's support from Joyce Foundation, and the foundation's anti-union, pro-charter initiatives

Author	TFA Placement & Dates	Key Concepts
SECTION III: TFA'S APPROACH TO CRITICISM AND CRITICS, Continued		
17. Derrick Houck	Philadelphia, 2010–2012	• 2013 TFA Alumni *Free Minds, Free People* Conference—growing dissent from within TFA
		• TFA's public relations work for image control
		• Penn-TFA partnership—differences in approaches to teacher education, and TFA's responses to dissenting voices
		• TFA's listening tour
		• TFA's entrepreneurial leadership vs. democratic input and reform within communities
		• Commitment to image vs. commitment to social justice
		• TFA as part of neoliberal agenda for nonunionized privatization of schools
18. Terrenda White	Los Angeles, 2002–2004	• TFA's construction of corps members as "superheroes"
		• TFA's silencing of views of critical members
		• Individualistic and market-driven reform/restructuring of public schools
		• Education entrepreneurial networks push neoliberal principles
		• TFA's lack of racial diversity within the corps—organization steeped in White privilege
		• No teacher shortage
19. Barbara Veltri	Researcher (not a TFA corps member)	• TFA's singular voice and message
		• Various corps members' response to the messaging
20. Gary Rubinstein	Houston, 1991–1995	• TFA as a lying organization
		• Trying to improve TFA for over 20 years

REFERENCES

Black, C. (2013). Teach For America alumni organize "resistance." Community Media Workshop. Retrieved from http://www.newstips.org/2013/07/teach-for-america-alumni-organize-resistance/

Brewer, T. J. (2012). Hyper-accountability, burnout and blame: A TFA corps member speaks out. *Education Week: Living in Dialogue.* Retrieved from http://blogs.edweek.org/teachers/living-in-dialogue/2012/02/hyper-accountability_burnout_a.html

Brewer, T. J. (2013). From the trenches: A Teach For America corps member's perspective. *Critical Education, 4*(12), 1–17.

Brewer, T. J. (2014). Accelerated burnout: How Teach For America's academic impact model and theoretical framework can foster disillusionment among its corps members. *Educational Studies, 50*(3), 246–263.

Brewer, T. J., & Wallis, M. (in press). #TFA: The intersection of social media and education reform. *Critical Education.*

Cersonsky, J. (2012, October 24). Teach For America's deep bench. *The American Prospect.* Retrieved from http://prospect.org/article/teach-america%E2%80%99s-deep-bench

deMarrais, K. (2012). Asking critical questions of philanthropy and its impact on U.S. educational policy: Tracking the money in school reform. In S. R. Steinberg & G. S. Cannella (Eds.), *Critical qualitative research reader* (vol. 2, pp. 276–294). New York: Peter Lang.

deMarrais, K., Lewis, J., & Wenner, J. (2011). *Bringing Teach For America into the forefront of teacher education: Philanthropy meets spin.* Paper presented at the American Educational Studies Association, St. Louis, MO.

Dillon, S. (2011, September 21). Global effort to recruit teachers expands. *The New York Times.* Retrieved from http://www.nytimes.com/2011/09/22/education/22teach.html?_r=0

Fernández, L. (2002). Telling stories about school: Using critical race and Latino critical theories to document Latina/Latino education and resistance. *Qualitative Inquiry, 8*(45), 45–65.

Goldstein, D. (2014). *The teacher wars: A history of America's most embattled profession.* New York: Doubleday.

Jacobsen, R., & Wilder Linkow, T. (2014). National affiliation or local representation: When TFA alumni run for school board. *Education Policy Analysis Archives, 22*(69), 1–28.

Joseph, G. (2014, October 29). This is what happens when you criticize Teach For America: An internal memo reveals how TFA's obsessive PR game covers up its lack of results in order to justify greater expansion. *The Nation.* Retrieved from http://www.thenation.com/article/186481/what-happens-when-you-criticize-teach-america

Kopp, W. (1989). *An argument and plan for the creation of the teacher corps* (B.A. dissertation). Princeton University, Princeton, NJ.

Kopp, W., & Farr, S. (2011). *A chance to make history: What works and what doesn't in providing an excellent education for all.* New York: PublicAffairs, Perseus Books Group.

Kovacs, P., & deMarrais, K. (Eds.). (2013). Teach For America and the future of education in the United States [Special issue]. *Critical Education, 4*(3).

Magan, C. (2014, November 9). Education issues drew millions in education spending. *Pioneer Press.* Retrieved from http://www.twincities.com/education/ci_26904363/education-issues-drew-millions-spending

Ness, M. (2004). *Lessons to learn: Voices from the front lines of Teach For America.* New York: Routledge.

Simon, S. (2013, October 21). Teach For America rises as political powerhouse. Politico. Retrieved from http://www.politico.com/story/2013/10/teach-for-america-rises-as-political-powerhouse-98586.html

Strauss, V. (2014a, February 20). #Resisttfa popular on Twitter. *The Washington Post*. Retrieved from http://www.washingtonpost.com/blogs/answer-sheet/wp/2014/02/20/resisttfa-popular-on -twitter/

Strauss, V. (2014b, October 25). Teach For America and protesting Harvard students open dialogue. *The Washington Post*. Retrieved from http://www.washingtonpost.com/blogs/answer-sheet/ wp/2014/10/25/teach-for-america-and-protesting-harvard-students-open-dialogue/

Teach For All. (n.d.). National organizations. Retrieved from http://www.teachforall.org/our-networ k-and-impact/national-organizations

Villanueva Beard, E. (2013, July 11). What we heard: Initial thoughts from the listening tour. Huffington Post. Retrieved from http://www.huffingtonpost.com/elisa-villanueva-beard/ teach-for-america_b_3576974.html

Section I:
TFA's Recruitment, Training, and Support Structure

The TFA Bait and Switch: From "You'll Be Making a Difference" to "You're Making Excuses"

JESSICA MILLEN
New Orleans, June 2013–October 2013

BIOSKETCH

Jessica Millen graduated from the University of Notre Dame in 2013, majoring in sociology with a minor in education, schooling, and society. As an undergraduate student, Millen was a founding officer of an education club on Notre Dame's campus that worked to expand student understanding of contemporary educational issues. She also completed an honors senior thesis on the Latino experience of school desegregation in South Bend, Indiana, and conducted research on parent engagement that has been published in the *School Community Journal*. In addition, Millen was a contributor to the book *College Student Voices on Educational Reform: Challenging and Changing Conversations* (Burke, Collier, & McKenna, 2013). She was a 2013 Teach For America (TFA) corps member in New Orleans, where she taught third grade. After realizing TFA was not what it purported to be, Millen resigned in October of her first year. She currently works as a preschool teacher in South Bend, Indiana.

NARRATIVE

This counter narrative explores the bait-and-switch phenomenon I experienced in my first 6 months of Teach For America (TFA). The story is likely to be similar for many other young college graduates, who are repeatedly and confidently told that they can improve students' lives but then are not taught the skills to make that difference a reality. This chapter highlights specific ways in which TFA preyed on my naïveté of the lived realities of urban schooling. By focusing incessantly, and solely, on the benefits of joining—the full salary, the educational bonus, the "prestige," the opportunities after 2 years, etc.—in the early stages of the program TFA knowingly and strategically baits young graduates into joining their organization. TFA recruiters and trainers exploited my desire to "make a difference," and I genuinely believed that joining was a win-win situation where I would certainly improve the quality of education for low-income and minority students in the American public school system.

The Bait

On the urging of a friend and campus recruiter, I applied to join TFA in October of my senior year at the University of Notre Dame. After a multipart interview process, I was accepted into the program's Greater New Orleans region. Soon afterwards, TFA began to effectively use social networks to bolster my desire to join. Former classmates and undergraduate campus recruiters reached out and stressed how wonderful it was that I had gotten into such a selective organization. My interviewer called to congratulate me on a job well done. After being bombarded with so many congratulations, I couldn't help but feel proud that I had passed through such a selective hiring process.

The official TFA recruiter on my campus held events for accepted corps members after each hiring deadline, offering free drinks and appetizers at an on-campus restaurant. I found it strange how much money TFA, a nonprofit organization, spent on us. We wore name tags, ate food, and discussed our excitement about the upcoming school year. Our recruiter, like the other TFA corps members and staff who had reached out to me, stressed the "prestige" of the program and how much TFA would help us in the future. He himself was a former TFA corps member who taught for 3 years before joining the recruiting arm of the organization. I found his enthusiasm for TFA contagious as he pointed out TFA's connections with graduate schools and the numerous opportunities that would be afforded to us post-TFA.

At the time, I was impressed by how many corps members were still involved in public education. According to TFA, more than 775 alumni were in school leadership positions at schools across the country (Teach For America, 2012a). I was glad to hear that TFA wasn't always just used as a stepping stone to more lucrative careers; information on the TFA website boasted that as of August 2013, 78% of alumni from the Greater New Orleans region were still in education (Teach For America, 2012b). I didn't bother to look up the evidence behind TFA's claims. I trusted that the information from this professional organization that seemed to care so much about children was ethically collected, compiled, and reported. I now know that the organization's assertion that "Teach For America corps members help their students achieve academic gains equal to or larger than teachers from other preparation programs, according to the most recent and rigorous studies on teacher effectiveness" (Teach For America, 2012c) is, at best, extremely misleading. Reviews of the research cited by TFA to back its claims of corps member effectiveness ultimately reveal a less favorable picture; the majority of studies listed by TFA are not peer-reviewed, are problematic, and/or produced mixed results (Kovacs & Slate-Young, 2013; Vasquez Heilig & Jez, 2014).

But taking TFA's claims of effectiveness at face value, I continued to be wooed by the organization. Besides the free events hosted by the campus recruiter, TFA offered additional financial incentives to make the bait even sweeter. I remember gushing to my parents that I would not only receive a full teacher's salary, but also get funding to cover the transitional costs of moving and living during the summer before I began teaching. As an indebted college student, it seemed that, on top of using my skills and education to serve in public education, I was making a solid financial decision in joining TFA. Such tantalizing benefits convinced me that not only was I making a strong move for my future, but I would also be "making a difference" in the lives of low-income and minority students. As a young, well-educated, idealistic student, I took the bait—hook, line and sinker.

The "Training"

After a 7-hour drive to TFA's summer training Institute in Atlanta, I was excited to begin. Although I had been warned that Institute could be an overwhelming experience, the intensity of our schedule was still surprising. Breakfast at 5:30 am, followed by a full day at our school sites, a quick dinner, additional training sessions in the evening, and then trying to complete the next day's lesson plans was the perfect recipe for sleep deprivation and left little time to process all this new information.

During this training, the organization's "you'll be making a difference" message became more insistent. Each morning, after being bused to our school site in the early morning, we were greeted by our school director. After signing in, we all gathered in our school site's library to begin our morning with an inspirational video. Over the course of those 5 weeks we watched what seemed to be every single well-known, inspirational education video on YouTube. We saw Kid President's "Pep Talk to Teachers and Students!", listened to Taylor Mali tell us "What Teachers Make," watched Sir Ken Robinson's animation video "Changing Education Paradigms," and many, many more.

Their model was working! At the time, I was inspired and eager to be in the classroom. Here I was, part of this great movement that was going to make a difference! So swept up in the staff members' fervor, I did not stop to think about why we were being shown all these inspirational and emotionally charged messages, or what they would ultimately contribute to my ability to be a competent, caring, and effective teacher.

It didn't end with just morning bursts of "let's change the world." Throughout our training sessions, we were often shown videos of real TFA teachers working in their classrooms. They were always uplifting clips, showing well-behaved students and enthusiastic teachers. We were told they had started just like us at one point in time, although the teachers' educational backgrounds were never divulged. We were never shown any videos of "bad" teachers or teachers who were struggling, nor did we see how teachers deal with students who are challenging behaviorally, or even defiant. And we were certainly never shown how to handle students' physical altercations or emotional breakdowns.

I had expected more hands-on training throughout the program. But with only a half hour to an hour and half in front of students each day, I found that we spent more time *talking* about how we were going to make a difference rather than *learning* how to be effective teachers who could ultimately "make a difference."

In addition to watching inspirational videos, we listened to many TFA staff members give talks about the rewarding nature of teaching. They showed us pictures of themselves and their students and told stories of how they had impacted their students' lives. These peppy speakers were extremely positive, only occasionally using vague phrasing to describe teaching as "the hardest thing you'll ever do." There was no delving into why it was the "hardest thing I would ever do," nor was there space to ask the speakers to elaborate. While I recognize that it might be difficult to convey the specific challenges that come with the first year of teaching, when such uplifting testimony is paired with only examples of successful TFA teachers, it was easy and safe for me to assume that I would soon begin "making a difference" once I entered the classroom on my own.

The "making a difference" message was not limited to our sessions in classroom management and pedagogy. During our training, we attended two huge pep rallies, one at the beginning and one at the end of Institute. As the Atlanta Institute hosted multiple TFA regions, the auditorium was packed. At the opening rally we were greeted by a huge PowerPoint slide declaring "One Day," highlighting TFA's mantra that "One day all children will have access to an excellent education." The title of the evening's program was "Your Role in the Movement for Educational Equity." After listening to speakers thank us for undertaking the journey we were about to begin, I felt excited. It seemed like TFA was an organization that was actually making a tangible difference in communities across the United States.

Before the closing pep rally, each school site's corps members created a chant to be shared with the full assembly. Most corps members had purchased t-shirts for their school sites, and as we filed in to our assigned school site spaces, the chanting began. Huge groups of matching corps members were on their feet, yelling at the top of their lungs the cheers they had written. Soon, the TFA staff running the rally began to moderate the cheering, shouting each school site's name and encouraging each group to be louder than the rest. After more peppy speakers, a student brass band played the corps members out, matching the same frenzied enthusiasm that the hundreds of young, soon-to-be teachers had displayed. In retrospect, the techniques used at these rallies made it feel more like a multilevel marketing convention than a gathering of thoughtful educators. It is strange that TFA felt the need to use such manipulative methods of drumming up enthusiasm on a group of well-educated individuals already committed to their organization.

The Switch

After those 5 weeks of training, I was alone in a classroom with 27 eight- and nine-year-olds. I had no idea what to do with the rigorous and inflexible curriculum modalities that dictated what I taught and when. There was nothing in our training that indicated our teaching lives would be so scripted and controlled. Moreover, I was confused by strict administrative policies that were completely developmentally inappropriate; for instance, my third graders were allowed only 20 minutes of recess, once a week. Again, there was no mention of what to do when school-wide policies were completely incongruent with what I knew at this point to be developmentally appropriate practices.

Trying to balance the demands and expectations of both my school and TFA was challenging, especially when both parties were extremely focused on data and standardized testing to the detriment of what my young students needed. This made it difficult for me to realize my vision of schooling. While I understood the necessity of assessment and its usefulness in gauging how much students know, and therefore in future lesson planning, both my school and TFA's focus on testing overshadowed my legitimate concerns for students' emotional and social well-being and academic growth beyond what could be measured in omnipresent assessments. I had to prepare my students for weekly and quarterly testing, on top of looming state-mandated tests that would also measure my success as a teacher. The pressure from both the state and district to raise student test scores manifested in my administration's extreme concern with test scores and maximizing instructional time not only in specific subjects but also to specific isolated skill sets, always to the detriment of exploring other important areas of elementary education, such as exposure to culture, creative and scientific thinking, music, and art.

Armed only with TFA's strictly behaviorist methods of classroom management, I was unprepared for many of the issues I faced, and my classroom quickly spiraled out of control. From my 5 weeks of training, I was knowledgeable only about behaviorist management methods that focused on giving clear directions, narrating student behavior when they were following directions, and then giving consequences to those students not complying. These management methods were presented as best practices during our training; no other alternatives were mentioned.

After attempting to use TFA's preferred classroom management system in my own classroom, I realized that the behaviorist theory of management was not working for my students or for me. When I expressed these feelings to TFA staff members, however, my concerns were ignored and brushed aside. In one meeting with my real-time coach from TFA, who had 4 years of teaching experience, I expressed how uncomfortable I was with forcing my students to remain seated all the time. My coach insisted that students learn best when they are seated. He then noticed that, according to the scripted conversation template from TFA, we had gone over the allotted time for this portion of our meeting. Rather than continuing a conversation that could have helped me understand TFA's position, he decided that following the prescribed conversation model was more important and ended the discussion. Looking back, it is easy to see why I felt that I was not being supported or listened to by TFA staff. Suddenly, I found myself hearing a different story than the one I was told during the application and training process. Now, instead of "making a difference," I was told I was "making excuses," by not believing in myself enough and not being the leader of my classroom.

I met with my TFA manager of teacher leadership development (MTLD) every so often for a check-in. It is interesting to note here that corps members are "managed" by TFA, as if they were commodities, rather than "guided" or "mentored." At one of these meetings, my MTLD told me she wanted me to have lunch with all my students, so that I could work on "building relationships." I had already begun to have lunch with small groups of students occasionally, but I was having trouble finding the time to eat with students every day, given the other demands on my time as a new educator. When I brought up what I thought were legitimate concerns—the fact that I had only 25 minutes for lunch, which included dropping off/picking up my students at the cafeteria, and that my administration had concerns about me "rewarding" students who often were not following school rules (eating with students was seen as a reward, not simply a good practice to develop relationships)—my TFA manager told me, "I'm hearing a lot of excuses from you."

In addition to telling me that I was making excuses, my manager also said that I did not believe in myself enough. As a confident young woman who had had a successful experience at Institute, where I was told, "Your students are going to be so lucky to have you" and "You're doing so well," I knew I could be an excellent teacher. I believed in my students and their potential, and had a wealth of knowledge about education, children, and learning, largely from my undergraduate studies. My end-of-Institute award was for "believing in your students." To be told I didn't believe in my students or myself was insulting, and not the type of support I expected to receive from TFA staff members.

TFA staff members repeatedly told me that I was not being the leader of my classroom, in the sense that I did not have strict control over my students' bodily movements. Within TFA's model of behavioral control, I was expected to have all of my students sitting in their seats at all times, and to accomplish this particular aspect of classroom management by consistently giving consequences. On an intellectual level, I recognized that giving consequences was a necessary part of their management system. It was not that I was incapable of giving my students consequences; the problem was that my vision of schooling did not include a classroom where the teacher is all-powerful, all-knowledgeable, and in strict control at all times. What I was beginning to understand was that there was no room in their model for my vision; in fact, my vision was completely contrary to their understanding of how schooling should be conducted and why. TFA's Teaching as Leadership model is based upon the idea that teachers are responsible for everything that happens inside of the classroom, regardless of whether or not you agree with the techniques and content you are being forced to adopt (Farr, 2010).

My frustration deepened when TFA staff ignored the fact that there were other factors at work in and out of my classroom that affected student behavior and achievement. I was unable to choose curriculum or what was taught when. TFA's model of behavioral control and TFA staff instructed me to use extremely scripted sets of phrases, limiting my freedom to develop my own style of classroom instruction that suited my unique context. In addition to this, TFA staff ignored the life circumstances of many of my students. I could not change the circumstances that led Jerome[1] to bring a roach-infested notebook to school, or the fact that Peter's mother told him to "get his lick back," meaning that if someone hits him, he should hit back. Whenever I tried to bring up the lived realities of my students' lives and the real challenges they faced, once again, I was told I was "making excuses." Despite my having personal knowledge of my students and their families, my voice and ultimately my potential to use alternative methods and ideas for creating a more learner-centered, productive environment was repeatedly pushed aside, as it contradicted TFA talking points.

In the end, I decided to leave. I could not, in good conscience, continue to work for an organization whose guiding educational philosophy varied so greatly from my own. It was not a decision I made lightly, leaving the very students I was trying to love and teach. But after I decided to leave, there came a small moment when I knew I had made the right choice. As I was waiting on duty for the last of the buses to arrive, Sarah caught my eye. She and her younger brother were role-playing the teacher-student relationship and the words coming out of Sarah's mouth broke my heart: "You're receiving a consequence! You have earned a lunch detention. You get a consequence!" These are the words and phrases she had heard me use repeatedly, again and again, over and over, as I strove to enact my MTLD's mandate to give lots of consequences. I had spent 3 months with this child and all I taught her about what it means to be a teacher is that a teacher gives conse-quences. This was devastating to me, and it was then that I realized that the bait and switch was complete.

The Displacement of Culturally Knowledgeable Teachers

Overall, this chapter showcases the harm that comes from such a shocking bait and switch, and the trauma it created for both my students and me. Ultimately, it is my hope that graduates currently being recruited by TFA will have the courage to look past the seemingly enticing benefits of joining and understand that the reality of teaching after 5 weeks of training is not always what TFA makes it out to be. There should be widespread concern regarding an organization that uses emotional manipulation as managerial practice, taking advantage of the bright, optimistic, and inexperienced young people they specifically and systemically recruit. In light of the growing number of counter narratives about TFA, we must pay attention to what happens in schools and districts where experienced and culturally knowl-edgeable teachers are being displaced by cadres of young, alternatively certified teachers (Delpit, 2012).

In my own experience, the vast majority of teachers at my school were familiar with the unique culture of New Orleans and had an intimate knowledge of my stu-dents that was not immediately accessible to me. Contrary to my MTLD's guilt-in-ducing claims that my students would be "worse off" without me, they finished the year under an experienced teacher who could offer them things I could not: years of experience, and knowledge of their neighborhood, of their families, and of their varied languages. Although not often focused on larger discussions of school reform, children do need to see and learn from teachers who know about their communities (Delpit, 2012; Ladson-Billings, 2009; Michie, 2014). My students needed to see teachers who look like them, teachers who know how to pronounce their names, and teachers who are not initially confused by the phrase "cuttin' up," meaning acting up. And I, as a new teacher, needed the freedom to develop and use practices that were child centered, and to not subject my students to a never ending barrage of standard-ized tests that did not fully capture all their abilities.

My initial knowledge about New Orleans before moving there came from the stark images following Hurricane Katrina shown on the news and the experience of eating a "King cake" in third grade. TFA's 3-day crash course called "Induction" did little to teach incoming corps members about the culture and people of New Orleans. Various lecture-style sessions, a van tour of assorted sites around the city, an afternoon spent at a local (empty) high school, and a community service project could hardly prepare us to truly understand our students, their families, and their communities. In the 3-hour session "Greater New Orleans: Education Yesterday & Today," I hardly felt that we had accomplished the session description provided in the TFA handbook, which stated that we would explore regional inequities and deepen our understanding of the complexities of race, class, and privilege that influence the opportunity gap. Even after 4 years of studying topics like race, class, and privilege as part of my undergraduate degree in sociology, I am constantly developing deeper understanding of both inequity and the social constructs that support inequity. With such cursory exploration of these deeply nuanced and personal topics, it should be no surprise that researchers such as Bybee (2013) have found "serious gaps in Teach For America's ability to develop the necessary cultural competence in its teacher recruits" (p. 36).

The students who need culturally competent teachers the most are instead left with a revolving door of inexperienced teachers unfamiliar with the students' culture and community. This is a particularly relevant issue in New Orleans, where the existing teaching force drastically changed when all employees in the Orleans Parish school system were terminated post-Katrina. The Fourth Circuit Court of Appeal in the State of Louisiana recently found in *Oliver v. Orleans Parish School Board* (2014) that the Orleans Parish School Board wrongly terminated its teaching staff. The board was legally required to create a "recall list" to rehire the teachers who had been teaching in New Orleans schools before Katrina. Even though the school board had the necessary information to identify approximately 7,000 displaced employees, it did not use this information in any rehiring processes.

This wrongdoing, accomplished by emboldened neoliberal school reformers who saw post-Katrina New Orleans as a "blank slate" for the reform agenda, opened the door wide for programs such as TFA to increase the flood of mostly young, mostly White teachers into the city—teachers unfamiliar with New Orleans, lacking in cultural competence, and without the freedom to teach as the children they serve deserve and need. As the New Orleans *Times-Picayune* reported, "though many schools have made a conscious effort to hire pre-Katrina teachers and New Orleans natives, eight years later, people still come to public meetings charging that outside teachers don't understand the local students' culture" (Dreillinger, 2014).

Although TFA baits young graduates with the dreamy promise that they will "make a difference," their current practices and model of support does not equip corps members with the skills or knowledge to become effective teachers. Despite TFA's claims of being receptive to feedback, pushing back on the TFA model will only lead to assertions that "you're making excuses," as I experienced repeatedly firsthand. We must critically examine whether TFA's system of teacher recruitment and training is really doing anything to benefit the students who need excellent teachers the most, and how it is impacting our educational system as a whole. Never mind the bait and switch played on me; the larger issue is the bait and switch TFA is currently playing on the American educational system. Our nation's children deserve better.

REFERENCES

Burke, K., Collier, B., & McKenna, M. (Eds.). (2013). *College student voices on educational reform: Challenging and changing conversations.* New York: Palgrave Pivot.

Bybee, E. R. (2013). An issue of equity: Assessing the cultural knowledge of preservice teachers in Teach For America. *Critical Education, 4*(13), 28–44. Retrieved from http://ojs.library.ubc.ca/index.php/criticaled/article/view/183949

Delpit, L. (2012). *"Multiplication is for White people": Raising expectations for other people's children.* New York: The New Press.

Dreillinger, D. (2014, January 16). 7,000 New Orleans teachers, laid off after Katrina, win court ruling. *The Times-Picayune.* Retrieved from http://www.nola.com/crime/index.ssf/2014/01/7000_new_orleans_teachers_laid.html

Farr, S. (2010). *Teaching as leadership: The highly effective teacher's guide to closing the achievement gap.* San Francisco: Jossey-Bass.

Kovacs, P., & Slate-Young, E. (2013). An analysis of Teach For America's research page. *Critical Education, 4*(11), 67–80. Retrieved from http://ojs.library.ubc.ca/index.php/criticaled/article/view/184138

Ladson-Billings, G. (2009). *The dreamkeepers: Successful teachers of African-American students.* San Francisco: Jossey-Bass.

Michie, G. (2014, July 22). On the importance of mirrors for students (and teachers). *Huffington Post.* Retrieved from http://www.huffingtonpost.com/gregory-michie/on-the-importance-of-mirr_b_5604494.html

Oliver v. Orleans Parish School Board. (2014). 2012-CA-1520. LA. Ct. App. 4th Cir. Retrieved from http://la4th.org/opinion/2012/349002.pdf

Teach For America. (2012a). Educational leadership initiative. Retrieved from http://www.teachforamerica.org/corps-member-and-alumni-resources/alumni-leadership-initiatives/educational-leadership-initiative

Teach For America. (2012b). Greater New Orleans-Louisiana Delta. Retrieved from http://www.teachforamerica.org/where-we-work/greater-new-orleans-louisiana-delta

Teach For America (2012c). What the research says. Retrieved from http://www.teachforamerica.org/our-organization/research

Vasquez Heilig, J., & Jez, S. J. (2014). Teach For America: A return to the evidence. *National Education Policy Center.* Retrieved from http://nepc.colorado.edu/publication/teach-for-america-return

NOTE

1. All student names have been changed.

CHAPTER TWO

The Blip on the Resume or the Seed of Social Justice?: The Eight-Year Impact of Eight Months with Teach For America

ERIN M. NOLAN
St. Louis, 2007–2008

BIOSKETCH

After earning a B.S. in physics from Michigan State University, Erin M. Nolan moved to St. Louis as a Teach For America corps member. Lasting less than a school year, she nevertheless loved teaching and her new city, and spent the next 4 years as an informal educator with the Saint Louis Science Center. Traveling to schools and community groups across the region exposed Erin to students of a wide variety of ages, abilities, races, and socioeconomic statuses, and she is now exploring the importance of such issues by pursuing a doctoral degree in education from Washington University in St. Louis, focusing on informal science education and the social context of education. A firm believer in the power of committed community involvement, she serves as a Sunday school teacher, a "Big Sister," an English as a second language tutor, and a public radio station volunteer.

NARRATIVE

In June 2007 I loaded up my hand-me-down 1998 Pontiac Grand Prix and left metro Detroit as my typical joyful, confident, emotionally healthy self. As strip malls, trees, and eventually cornfields passed by my window, thought-provoking experiments, dazzling demonstrations, and powerful pep talks flitted through my brain. The western sky was still aglow when I reached St. Louis, the Arch silhou etted in all its architectural elegance and symbolic optimism. I had reached m gateway to a lifetime of teaching.

The following February, I sat in the principal's office as a stressed, sleep-de prived shell of a person. The principal—a good, capable man—said he didn't thin it was healthy for me to keep teaching, and I agreed. I had expressed similar, i more cautious, concerns to him and my department chair the previous month He told me he knew a retired physics teacher who could fill in for the rest of th year, and we discussed how my resignation would proceed. As I left the office the weight of 173 high school students was lifted off my chest. I could breath again. My program director (now referred to as a manager of teacher leadershi development—or MTLD) from Teach For America (TFA) had been in the offic as well, and she took me to a coffee shop to debrief. She proposed finding me new placement, this time in an elementary school. With a self-assuredness I hac not felt in ages, I politely but firmly declined. I had actually never stopped lovin the act of teaching, but I also knew my problems with being a classroom teache would not be solved by a simple demographic shift. My formal relationship wit TFA ended within the week, and my stress dissipated almost as quickly. Today 8 years after first applying to TFA, my 8 months with the organization are distant enough to feel like a bad dream, but they have made an undeniable, profound, and ultimately (if circuitously) *good* impact on my life's course.

I suspect that, much like Tolstoy's infamous families, every unhappy TFA corps member is unhappy in his or her own way. The reasons for my failure are a complicated knot of organizational and personal shortcomings twisted around some unfortunate events, but generally speaking, I believe I was unsuccessful be cause TFA, while excellent at communicating their overall vision of high expec tations for students, spent very little time on the "nuts and bolts" of the teaching profession, and I, in turn, struggled more than most to pick up these skills along the way. My experience at "Summer Institute," the 5-week crash course in teach ing, was atypical because I was assigned to teach a group of six incoming seniors who *chose* to take physics (a nonrequired course) over the summer. These students were clearly on the path to success with or without us, and all we had to do was teach them physics. This was difficult enough—I had never planned a high school lesson, designed a lab, or written a test—but it was nevertheless a soft training ground for what was to come. The combination of student ambition and a seminar atmosphere left no room for classroom management problems. When classroom management was discussed in training sessions, it focused on general themes (re spect, high expectations, consistency, etc.) and it seemed the few specific examples we did get came from elementary school settings. When I got my own high school students, I never found a classroom management strategy that didn't feel horribly contrived and disingenuous. My discomfort with all attempted strategies hindered my efforts at consistency, which, in turn, hindered my students' ability (or motivation) to meet expectations.

Although TFA's prerequisite reading included valuable essays about race and culture, and the Summer Institute included diversity sessions, there was little practical training to help corps members turn theory into practice. An anecdote about a first grade classroom with an assortment of skin-colored crayons is the only example I can recall. TFA did not help us to develop the cultural competencies necessary for fostering positive relationships in our school environments—or to at least avoid social faux pas. As it was, many of us were destined for missteps. Before winter vacation one White corps member (an English teacher) passed out holiday cards to his African American coworkers that seemed appropriate because they had a storybook character on them: Curious George (the monkey). I, for my part, had to apologize for an off-the-cuff remark to a Black student suggesting she was thin (always a complimentary adjective amongst White women), and had to clarify that I meant she looked fit and healthy. Even universally accepted truths such as "Show respect to get respect" looked different in unfamiliar contexts. Early in the school year, I had passed out raffle tickets for good class participation, and on the day of the drawing, I left out a small basket of "prizes" (rulers, pens, etc.) in between classes, rather than hide them away. To me, this was a way to demonstrate trust and respect, but to some of my students, this was just a sign of carelessness or stupidity on my part, either of which justified pocketing a trinket—which a few of them did. My relationships with individual students were, on the whole, positive—but rare. I usually felt out of place in my own classroom; I was pretty sure it was my fault. I realize Summer Institute would never be able to bestow all the cultural competencies its corps members would need to be successful, but that only suggests a need for additional strategies, such as vetting TFA applicants more rigorously based more on their prior experience with underserved students, or creating follow-up practical training for corps members during the school year.

The Summer Institute's academic training focused on traits of a quality "Big Goal" (a year-long goal that was central to TFA's version of high expectations), and our follow-up training in St. Louis discussed breaking these goals down into measurable objectives. The importance of monitoring progress was emphasized, but—in part because so much of the training was for teachers of all grade levels and subjects—tips for how to achieve this progress were vague. TFA offered suggestions like, "80 percent achievement on all Missouri Course Level Expectations," and showed examples of Excel templates to help us track this progress, but I was just trying to write the first page of my syllabus, wondering what weight I should give homework and participation in the final grade, and how much time I should spend introducing the scientific method. Sympathetic to our desire for content-specific training, one woman brought her boyfriend, a science teacher, to one training session so that we future science teachers could talk to him during our break. We literally stood at his feet to soak up all the information we could from this "expert" with 2 years' teaching experience.

Indeed, although talent and hard work abounded, the general tone of TFA was that ambition negated the need for experience—and not just with corps members. I eventually realized that only one TFA–St. Louis staff member was not brand new to his or her job. The program directors (PDs), who each served as a TFA supervisor/support person for a set of corps members, were not only new to their current jobs, but had only 2 or 3 years of teaching experience themselves. According to friends who remained in the program, only one PD stayed on staff the following year. In hindsight, it seems as if staff members were used as interchangeable parts, each prestamped with TFA dogma and molded to generate good data—much like first year corps members, come to think of it—which is a pity, because not only did this limit their ability to support us in nuanced, context-specific situations, it also removed them from their roles as highly successful teachers.

Summer Institute ended on a Friday, I flew back to St. Louis on Saturday, got the keys to my new apartment Sunday, moved in Monday, and on Tuesday began my district's new teacher orientation during the daytime and TFA's follow-up training in the evening. The transition was a whirlwind, and when students walked into my classroom 2 weeks later, I still felt far from prepared. This initial disorganization caused more stress, which made even small challenges seem large, and in spite of depressingly long hours at school, I quickly fell behind in grading and lesson planning. Students became frustrated because they didn't know how they were doing in the class, and they expressed this frustration through disrespectful and destructive behavior. Challenges from beyond the classroom walls rattled my students and myself, further compounding these issues. Combined with my weak classroom management, this all resulted in more chaos and stress which, in spite of my best efforts and the earnest support of others, led to an unsalvageable situation and my eventual resignation.

I often wish I could blot TFA from my résumé and avoid the inherently complex conversations about its role in education or my role in TFA. Many people from my cohort quit before or after one school year, but leaving midsemester feels especially shameful. Sometimes, though, I have to "own up" to my time with TFA, not only because to do otherwise would create a gap in my employment history, but also because it is the only way to explain how I—a White, suburban physics major raised in a culture that subliminally promoted "colorblindness"—began to care about and make life choices centered around social justice and urban education. My preparation for TFA provided my first exposure to the term *White privilege*, as well as an explanation of why colorblindness could be dangerously shortsighted, in spite of good intentions. Not only did TFA introduce me to excerpts from Tatum's (2003) *Why Are All the Black Kids Sitting Together in the Cafeteria?*, TFA introduced me to the fact that books discussing such topics *existed*. This exposure from TFA led me to join a church that emphasized racial reconciliation and social justice, dramatically deepening, broadening, and strengthening my commitment to these issues. This commitment to social justice and awareness of educational inequality then motivated me to become an English tutor for a refugee family and a "Big Sister" to a girl with an unstable home life—relationships that I treasure to this day. To warp metaphors, TFA led me down the rabbit hole *out* of a suburban wonderland and into a more diverse, complex real world.

Sometimes I am reminded how much my worldview has changed since my Grand Prix and I first made the trek to St. Louis. Several years after leaving TFA, I sat at work with my fellow science center educators as we attempted to adjust our schedule because of a recent cancellation of an off-site outreach program. "I don't want to sound racist…" a coworker hesitantly began, "but it seems like most of the disorganized schools have mostly Black kids." Indeed they did: The affluent, mostly White district that booked programs with us would create schedules months in advance and send us rosters with the names of the students whose families had paid to register them for the after-school science classes, and we would then prepare and present such programs accordingly. Our comparable programming in a poor, mostly Black district involved a third-party nonprofit organization that went through a "hurry up and wait" grant process to fund the classes, which then would attempt to work with the schools to arrange (often changing) space, time, and transportation. After-school busing took longer to set up than anticipated, so programs started weeks after originally scheduled, always with an uncertain number of students who may or may not be the same as the previous week. The result was that, even with the exact same instructor, curriculum, and student desire to learn, the students in the low-income schools were less likely to receive a coherent program. Neighborhood effects mattered, even for children making silly putty. Although my colleague was clearly disturbed by the pattern he saw, he did not yet have the tools to frame it in terms of cycles of racial and economic oppression—tools I had sought out because of my experience with TFA.

When I left the science center to become a full-time doctoral student in education, my experience with TFA and my subsequent community involvement formed a real-world reference point for the theoretical frameworks, regional studies, and national statistics used to discuss urban education. Exposure to such work helped to frame my approach to research on access to informal science education. As a teaching assistant for a course about American schooling, graduate school put me in contact with current college students, who once again reminded me what internal biases my St. Louis experience had alleviated. In several of the students' required written reflections, they acknowledged how fortunate they were to have parents who had instilled in them the value of education, and who had worked hard to give them the best (often private, elite) education possible. In the midst of this I saw very little to suggest awareness that there could exist parents who cared about education, worked hard, and yet *still* had children in struggling schools.

During my own senior year of college, when I was absorbing all things TFA, I began to embrace what I saw as the organization's two-tier vision: At one level, the goal was to get enthusiastic, driven, quality teachers into traditionally underserved schools. Beyond that, there was a more far-reaching goal to use corps members' 2-year classroom experience to forever shape the way these alumni approached all future occupations, bending the trajectory of future doctors, lawyers, politicians, principals, and scientists towards actions that would expand educational equity. TFA clearly did not achieve its first goal with me, and yet it still managed to fulfill its second goal—even within my limited time in the program. Several of my friends and colleagues—some who left TFA early and some who completed their 2 years in the classroom—continued in their commitment to the education of marginalized groups. Still others continued teaching at their original TFA placement school long after their affiliation with TFA ended. Notably, neither group sings the praises of TFA; even the most successful alumni seem to sigh or roll their eyes at the mention of the organization that led them to their profession. To the people I see teaching, researching, mentoring, and advocating, TFA was, at best, a slippery stepping-stone to a more robust understanding of urban education and the historical, political, and economic reasons for its current state. But of course, my social network is not a randomized sample of TFA alumni, but rather a group I stayed with or became connected to largely because of some other institution—typically, my church or university—which offered its own interpretation of urban education.

When considering the long-term impact of all TFA corps members, two questions then arise: First, does the program provide a net benefit for underserved communities, even after accounting for the immediate detrimental effects of unsuccessful teachers? Second—and more fundamentally—even if these long-term impacts are positive, are they worth the potential education risks to the students placed in TFA corps members' classrooms? Scholars seem skeptical. In *The Flat World and Education* (2010) Linda Darling-Hammond summarizes much of what is known about the effects of alternative-route and underprepared teachers while they are in the classroom. Findings include that students of novice teachers can face difficulties in later years, and that high concentrations of underprepared teachers in a school have negative effects beyond individual classrooms, because there is less opportunity for staff to share knowledge and expertise. Alternative-route teachers do eventually "catch up" to their traditionally-qualified peers, but only if they continue to teach—which they are less likely to do.

I find the long-term effects of short-term teachers most compellingly articulated by the fictional young author of an editorial published by the satirical newspaper *The Onion*:

> I realize that as a fourth-grader I probably don't have the best handle on the financial situation of my school district, but dealing with a new fresh-faced college graduate who doesn't know what he or she is doing year after year is growing just a little bit tiresome... I can't afford to spend these vital few years of my cognitive development becoming a small thread in someone's inspirational narrative. (The Onion, 2012)

With this all in mind, I have mixed feelings about the avid college student interest—and, for that matter, public interest—in TFA. I want to explain why TFA isn't the solution to our schools' problems, but I don't want to dismiss the experience of the many successful long-term educators I know who entered the profession because of TFA. I want to warn college seniors to resist the "prestigious" siren call of TFA, yet I fear the alternative is that they will spend their lives chasing the "American dream" across suburbia, utterly unaware of the gross social injustices happening in their own metropolitan areas.

So perhaps we need a new emphasis on alternatives for creating both teachers and allies in the fight for educational equity: Could Congress support colleges and departments of education that create programs which feel as urgent and elite (yet financial accessible) as TFA, but which take the time to properly train would-be corps members to be truly successful teachers in underserved schools? Or could TFA itself recruit students earlier and require them to student teach before getting their own classrooms? To create allies in the fight without leaving students with ill-equipped teachers, a résumé-boosting Summer Institute alternative could facilitate an intense engagement with the educational crisis (perhaps through a combination of coursework and volunteer tutoring) but then send the graduates immediately on to their next vocational or academic pursuits. In short: Perhaps educational communities can find ways to replicate what TFA *is* doing well: getting top-notch young minds committed to the seemingly Sisyphean task of rectifying what is in fact two centuries of inequality in American public schools (see, for example, Ladson-Billings, 2006; Moss, 2009).

As I finish writing this, I have been regularly interrupted by calls from Moriya,[1] my "Little Sister," who has been bored and stuck at home alone. After months of staying at her grandmother's apartment, Moriya, her sisters, and their mother moved into a two-bedroom apartment (the deposit on which may or may not have been subsidized by illegally sold food stamps) a few weeks before the new school year started. The younger sisters missed the first day of school because their paperwork was not yet complete (their mother was not given access to their old house, where the family birth certificates were), but Moriya has missed her first week of school (and counting) because she doesn't feel safe going to the neighbor-hood middle school to which she was assigned (she tells me students have brought guns to school), and her mother has yet to find an alternative. Between ill-timed moves and, in one case, a charter school closing midyear, Moriya has not spent an entire academic year at one school since fourth grade, and wherever she ends up for eighth grade will be her seventh school in 5 years. Will a Teach For America teacher be up to the challenge of preparing her for high school and beyond? Could *any* teacher be up to the challenge? Is our *society* up to the challenge? Even as the education community debates how to get the best possible teachers into Moriya's school, it is clear that for her to have any chance at breaking the cycle of poverty, she will need more than just the best possible teachers: She will need an entire community fighting to improve her education and all the societal issues that play into it, from parental employment opportunities to inequitable school resources to the all-pervasive structural racism. My time with TFA was soul-killing for me and unproductive for my students, which affirms that TFA's approach to *solving* this nation's crisis of educational inequality deserves criticism, but TFA's ability to *increase exposure* to the crisis is what brought me and countless others into this fight, and that too must be acknowledged, even as we keep debating.

REFERENCES

Darling-Hammond, L. (2010). *The flat world and education: How America's commitment to equity will determine our future*. New York: Teachers College Press.

Ladson-Billings, G. (2006). From the achievement gap to the education debt: Understanding achievement in U.S. schools. *Educational Researcher*, 35(7), 3–12. doi:10.3102/0013189X035007003

Moss, H. J. (2009). *Schooling citizens: The struggle for African American education in antebellum America*. Chicago: University of Chicago Press.

The Onion, B. (2012, July 17). Counterpoint: Can we please, just once, have a real teacher? Retrieved from http://www.theonion.com/articles/my-year-volunteering-as-a-teacher-helped-educate-a,28803/

Tatum, B. D. (2003). *Why are all the Black kids sitting together in the cafeteria: And other conversations about race* (5th anniv., rev. ed.). New York: Basic Books.

NOTE

1. Pseudonym.

CHAPTER THREE

Productive Mistakes: Teacher Mentorship and Teach For America

BRENDON JOBS
Philadelphia, Summer 2005

BIOSKETCH

The son of Trinidadian immigrants, Brendon currently teaches world history, African American history, and sociology at the Girard Academic Music Program in Philadelphia. He earned a bachelor's degree in political science from Columbia University and a master's certificate in secondary education from the Penn Graduate School of Education as a Philadelphia Teaching Fellow. He returned to Penn as a James Madison Fellow to earn an M.S.Ed. in teaching, learning and curriculum with a focus on gender and education. Last year he completed the National Board Teaching Certification process. Beyond the classroom, he affiliates with Teacher Action Group (TAG), a group of like-minded teachers working to organize, innovate, and empower other educators throughout Philly in the midst of this politically orchestrated school funding crisis. His experience includes work as a Lehman Fellow, a National Constitution Center Annenberg Fellow, and an Education Pioneer Fellow with the SEED Foundation in Washington, D.C. He is an advocate for public education interested in developing structures that support diversity and student voice in school communities. He also currently participates in the Black Male Educator Roundtable out of Penn GSE's newly formed Center for the Study of Race and Equity.

NARRATIVE

I've never been a good test taker. Predetermined expectations tend to block my growth and development—they always have. But even in the test-heavy climate of twenty-first-century teaching and learning there exist spaces for teachers like me: a teacher who had to master finding my voice within group dynamics; a teacher who recognizes and accepts the flaws in test measures and the unquantifiable growth within students; a teacher who recognizes his role as mentor and advocate before his role as data manager. As a young teacher, much of this identity construction happened out in the open, with students not only bearing witness to, but also participating in, the negotiation. Experience taught me the importance of constructing my classroom environment as a safe space for intercultural exchange. My primary goal is that my students feel seen, heard, and impacted by their learning each day. As a gay Black man, born of immigrant parents in a capitalist, White, patriarchal society, my dismissal from Teach For America (TFA) taught me early on that I would have to claim space and voice within this profession if I really wanted to teach.

Kids keep you honest—they see through any mask or smokescreen adults present to one another because they haven't yet discovered the worth or utility of such vestiges. The longer I teach, the less I understand the protective screens with which we shroud ourselves. I suppose they project who we want to be, or mirror the "self" that others expect of us. Either way, they function to protect an ego that guards our hearts. I've never been good at wearing masks, and in my work with kids, I have found ego to be more of a block than a support for building the trusting relationships necessary for engaging young people in learning. The best teachers I know exhibit a disarming connection with their students, which heavily depends on the cultivation of a relational trust built on a simple mutual understanding: "I've got your back and I won't let you fall, if you take the opportunity to grow each day."

Such growth contains a complexity not so easily yardsticked by data points and proficiency scores. Nor is it so readily energized by the "Big Goals" that we as TFA corps members had been trained to set for "significant gains" in our classrooms.

In this chapter, I reflect on the core values and mindsets that TFA requires each corps member to exhibit in the space of Summer Institute, by critically reviewing the terms of my dismissal from TFA as a preservice teacher. This chapter looks at literature that discusses the proportion of TFA corps members who become career teachers—teachers who critically engage with classroom practice beyond the 5-year threshold. The National Commission on Teaching and America's Future estimates that one third of all new teachers leave after 3 years, and 46% are gone within 5 years (Kopkowski, 2008). The story of my dismissal highlights the emphasis that TFA places on creating new teachers that are compliant with TFA's core values and mindset rather than teachers equipped to engage with the range of social and cultural demands that indelibly influence how students connect to school-based learning.

I was summarily dismissed from the Philadelphia TFA corps in 2005, with others, near the end of Institute following a series of conflicting classroom observations that determined that I was unfit to manage a classroom and engage students in learning. What complicates the terms of this dismissal is the purposeful career I have since built as an 8-year veteran teacher, after claiming my space and voice as a teacher in 2007 with the Philadelphia Teaching Fellows. TFA trains teachers to measure the worth of their teaching "performance" in terms of significant gains on flawed standardized exams. It is vital that new teachers recognize teaching and learning as a practice that responds to students' academic and socio-emotional needs with care and compassion—no one has yet discovered how to practically measure such growth.

What makes this story matter? Since my dismissal from TFA, the organization has only continued to grow in influence and flourish despite the 2008 recession and the subsequent epidemic of fiscal crises in urban school districts across the nation. For as long as I've taught, our district has never had enough money to provide basic supplies to all classrooms (i.e., paper), let alone the tools necessary to cultivating twenty-first-century thinkers.

In the most recent years, junior teachers have grown accustomed to negotiating the real possibility of being laid off or shuffled around school districts, while TFA benefits from the political capital that the organization has to place new teachers in both public and charter schools as the charter market grows in capacity and influence. Good schools function as trusting communities of practice (Bryk, 2010). TFA's mission of expanding the number of corps members it places in classrooms across the country threatens to further limit the powerful impact of teacher-student relationships based on the limited classroom tenures of the reform-minded neophytes it tends to attract and promote. As a member of a school community, trust takes time to develop—cycles of 2- to 3-year tenures don't cut it and strain the training resources of an industry that struggles with funding talent development.

Teaching Is a Love Supreme

I never planned on becoming a teacher. In American society, the disincentives to becoming a working educator abound. Other fields and professions carry more intellectual, social, or financial prestige. Urban teachers are rewarded by engaging in work we love with like-minded, socially conscious peers. Entering my eighth year teaching, I have realized that this work requires a level of activism and advocacy not required in other professions. Relationships I've formed in Teacher Action Group (TAG), a grassroots network that seeks to strengthen the influence of educators within schools and over policy decisions, has broadened my purpose for teaching. Discussions with the newly formed Black Male Educator Roundtable at Penn GSE's Center for the Study of Race and Equity have deepened the knowledge of self that is needed to connect with kids.

The popular image of teachers and teachers unions as lazy, ineffectual, and driven by self-interest drives some of the best prospective teachers to use their skill sets elsewhere—as does the perception of teaching as "semiprofessional" that fosters a belief that anyone could do it with some training. Many Americans have opinions on teaching and education based on their own schooling experiences. I did not originally envision myself as a teacher. Aside from my father's part-time work as an adjunct instructor at a local community college, I lacked the role modeling that seeing Black men as K–12 educators would have offered. My first interactions with educators who looked like me didn't happen until my second year of college. My job, my profession, I thought, would be one that helped my family build wealth.

College challenged this notion and helped me focus more sharply on happiness. Working as a tutor with the Double Discovery Center and the Harlem Village Academy changed my mind about what my impact in the world could feel like. I drew inspiration by helping people in a way similar to how I had been helped in my growth and development by formal and informal educators. Teaching and learning is about both teachers and students recognizing one another as partners in learning. Despite this knowledge, the drive and responsibility to make money postgraduation prompted me to obsessively visualize my future within a corporate context. TFA introduced me to teaching and catered to my postadolescent ego that focused myopically on building myself.

I entered the program with an attitude similar to that of many of my peers, searching for a meaningful transition from university life to the real world. I was searching for *purpose* and *place*; why not try teaching? After making the cut for a program as elite as TFA, the "calling" was clear and safely nonbinding. I learned about TFA from an elaborate recruitment campaign on Columbia's campus during my junior year that mirrored the efforts of some elite consulting firms vying for our curiosity and attention. Most of my friends had been rejected by the program outright, but TFA staffers took notice of my work as a student leader and campus activist focused on interracial cooperation with the United Students of Color Council. Throughout the interview process, they projected the image that effective teachers must operate as leaders in school communities.

I saw TFA as an opportunity to do something different and cultivate real-world leadership experience before I fell back in line and followed my more deliberately planned path to corporate law. Two years would be a short commitment, not an eternity. Besides, I had no true passion for going to law school, other than the social prestige it offered me as a first-generation son of Trinidadian immigrants. Because of TFA's popularity, even my law school supported my decision to defer acceptance and agreed to hold my place until I completed my service. A number of top programs in law, public policy, business, and medicine place value on the TFA experience for their future employees and use it to market their programs. This entry to teaching felt much more like entrance into a program like the Peace Corps and less like an introduction to the teaching profession or the communities we would serve. Master teachers must engage as community partners. I had some idea of what the structure of the summer training would be like after talking to past and current corps members and TFA staffers, but nothing they told me could have prepared me for my socio-emotional experience as a queer corps member of color.

Today, I recognize that the longer I teach, the more often I'm asked about how I became a teacher. I like to say that I had a "false start" to teaching with TFA. I moved to Philadelphia in 2005 right after college to join TFA. That July, the Philadelphia and New York corps members lived on Temple University's campus and practice-taught in the School District of Philadelphia's (SDP) summer program under a three-tiered mentor relationship. I practice-taught in rotation with three other corps members, mentored by a retired SDP teacher and an assigned corps member advisor (CMA), Sarah, who drew on her own experience as a Baltimore corps member to support the metamorphosis that we were making from college graduate to "teacher leader." The third tier of support came from our school director, also a former corps member who had taught for 2 years before moving up TFA's chain of command to run a school site. A curriculum director, also an alumnus turned corporate attorney, led diversity sessions where we unpacked our teaching experience. These four women (three White, one mixed race) served as my models for cultivating an effective teaching practice that inspired students to learn.

In the telling and retelling of this story it's clear that my journey has been a process driven by growth and reflection. Growth means change; change naturally inspires human fear and anxiety. What should I do differently? How do students perceive the difference when I change? What are the limits of my sphere of control? Teaching takes the bravery and safety to make mistakes—mistakes that inspire growth and change. Teaching takes the freedom to embrace the revision of practice. Good teaching generates innovation within the practice. I like the idea that the road to becoming a master teacher is built upon a foundation of reflective practice. Great teachers are not born but cultivated in very personal, very human ways best supported by trusting mentor relationships. I've noticed that like any expert, master teachers build a schema that enables them to respond in natural ways to complex situations with multiple variables. The best teachers respond to complexity in authentic and effective ways that inspire growth in students and honor the personality of their practice.

Since my dismissal from TFA in 2005 and my return to the classroom with Philadelphia Teaching Fellows after a brief stint as a paralegal, I have grown more curious about mentorship practices that empower new teachers (0–2 years) to embrace growth mindsets. Master teachers are made, not born, and rarely do they focus on test scores as appropriate measures of their impact or effectiveness in the classroom. As corps members in 2005, with No Child Left Behind in full force, we trained under the collective assumption that high expectations for "disadvantaged" or "at-risk" students meant teaching them to embrace "Big Goals" connected to measurable data that inspire success. Master teachers do not deny the importance of data but view teaching with a holistic approach. Effective practice addresses the needs of the whole child, which in underserved communities with limited support from homes sometimes means parenting, mentoring, and counseling large cohorts of students. My short mentorship experience as a corps member and my abrupt dismissal from TFA in the final week of Institute couldn't equip me for this varied work. The memory of my experience has certainly impacted the development of my classroom community and the interactions that I have with teachers who train under my supervision.

Trust Building: Strategies for Teacher Mentorship

Mentorship is the heart of teacher development. Regardless of teaching context, the path to creating an accessible, authentic teaching persona is littered with the remains of messy experiences that leave in their wake systems to streamline classroom functions and ways of thinking about and speaking to students that support their "buy in" to formal academic learning as relevant for their futures. Ideally, teacher mentorship is a trusting collaboration regardless of the intervention strategy (direct, reflective, or collaborative) used to offer support. Direct mentoring offers safe guidance through predictable aspects of the teaching practice. Reflective mentoring builds a schema for dealing with the less predictable aspects of the teaching practice that take impromptu decision making or long-range planning. This model encourages teachers to engage with their classroom as a scientist would a lab. Collaborative mentorship combines the direct and reflective models where the interaction between mentor and mentee can be viewed as a partnership. The collaboration is driven by trust and the open exchange of ideas.

The most productive mentorship relationships I have had training teachers combine these strategies to meet the needs of developing teachers in ways that promote the cultivation of a growth mindset—where failure presents opportunities for learning, revision, and mastery. As a mentor teacher, I try to instill in my student teachers a sense of what core questions to ask about their practice. Schools of education and professional journals offer representations of best practices in teaching. The work of deconstructing those representations into actionable steps drives teacher mentorship. Once that work is done, individual educators must figure out personal approximations for how to integrate best practices into their education philosophies and teaching personas. Teaching is at once an art and a science because it is based so much on discrete interactions that cannot be mechanized or fully predicted. Good mentors help developing teachers build the capacity for productive curiosity about the classroom environment they construct and how they operate within in it. Data counts. But the definition of relevant data goes well beyond standardized test results or benchmark exams. Classroom artifacts and even reflective student conversations or interviews help construct effective learning environments. "Reflective" mentorship interventions support productive curiosity—a mindset that separates master teachers from teacher-bots.

My TFA mentorship experience missed the mark on development and felt more like an accelerated course in compliance and baseline thinking. The grounds for my dismissal from TFA rested on the observations of those charged with my mentorship and development. Subjectively, the observers painted the picture and created the paper trail of a new teacher floundering in the classroom and incapable of encouraging students to learn. And they weren't completely wrong: I had a tough time teaching that summer. As a Black, gay male educator sharing teaching responsibilities with three White female corps members, I had trouble connecting with my sixth grade summer school students. Two in particular hurled gay slurs at me when they knew it would hit best. And I also think that they had trouble identifying a Black man as an authority figure in the classroom. I myself had never had a Black male teacher until college. My middle-class, immigrant background only made the reality of me more dissonant for these students. But in a classroom focused so much on standardization and "Big Goals" shared among four new teachers, there was no room for mentorship that supported the notion of unpacking these clashes of identity with students. "Big Goals" had to be based on data that could be measured using standardized tests with the goal of "mastery" or "proficiency."

The CMAP Process: A Gross Failure to Master Objectives

After 3 weeks of training, TFA recommended that I find something else to do and demanded payback within 30 days of the loan they had extended to me to relocate from New York City to Philadelphia. I had 24 hours to leave the dorm that housed corps members. I was dismissed on the grounds that my mentors did not feel "100% confident" in my ability to achieve significant gains in my region as a first year teacher. They never explained how they measured 100% confidence, but the fear is understandable when the goal is constructing a teaching force based on 2-year commitments. In curriculum sessions, we talked about reflective practice and the importance of collaboration and partnership in the classroom; however, directives and data monitoring drove the mentor relationship I experienced as a corps member.

TFA offered minimal support for helping me as a developing educator to be productively curious about these identity-specific environmental factors that drove my classroom environment. In response to the slurs regularly hurled my way by two students in particular, my well-intentioned faculty advisor, a 35-year veteran, directed me to "be more of a man" with my students. So I tried. I yelled, deepened my voice, and pulled my neck-length, neatly manicured locs back in a more traditionally masculine style, but as a 21-year-old TFA corps member, following these orders only scratched the surface of broader societal currents that drove a wedge between me and my students. In a podcast I recently contributed to, with the Black Male Educators Roundtable out of Penn GSE's Center for the Study of Race and Equity in Education, one of my colleagues highlights the key role that context learning played in his first years as an educator. Broader social currents cannot simply be intuited by new teachers in ways that make for effective interaction with the daily realities that students face—realities that too often are much different than our own.

Currents of classism, White privilege, and cultural hegemony permeated the training sessions all corps members attended as a part of that summer's Institute. In these sessions, I remember both my CMA and school director assuring us that they wanted pushback during the sessions about how TFA training could be improved for future cohorts. The message was that we as corps members had a critical part in crafting how TFA supported new teachers. The sessions were led by a curriculum specialist and a former TFA corps member who, according to a LinkedIn profile, now works as a lawyer in a large corporate Philadelphia firm.

In sessions overwhelmingly populated by people of wealth, privilege, and disproportionately Midwestern origin (especially Wisconsin and Ohio), I asked questions to be expected from someone with a history, albeit short-lived at that time, of social activism. We learned that effective teachers know their students and worked to understand where they come from. We talked about "race." We talked about "privilege." We talked about TFA's mission and education as a "civil right." None of these ideas were new to me that summer, but I suspect that they were for many of my high-energy, scholastically accomplished, fellow corps members, based on the way they talked about "those kids" and "these communities."

As one of a handful of brown faces in the room, thinking of friends rejected from TFA, I asked, "Where are all of the folks from this region (Delaware Valley) who could do this work?" There was absolute silence around identity issues related to gender and sexuality, even amongst corps members. Although I forget the response to my question, I remember the issue being indirectly addressed with platitudes and positive uptones from TFA staffers. I also remember the feeling of being in awkward, clumsy conflict with the very program that, just months earlier, I had worked so hard to enter. But I wasn't alone in this dissonant thinking. At Institute, staffers encouraged us to construct affinity groups that would meet on a regular basis around common areas of interest or concern. I joined a group where students of color openly voiced concerns about the tone of TFA. We demanded our teacher training and mentorship address the realities of the challenging school and community environments that we would find ourselves in just weeks.

Collectively, we still had a minimal sense of what challenges we would face as teachers, but knew that TFA wasn't imbuing us with some of the key tools we would need to be productively curious in our schools. TFA instead focused on instilling key habits of mind believed to be practiced by highly effective educators. With only a month of training, we learned surface-level notions of what we would have to seriously explore as professional educators, or "teacher leaders," as they liked to remind us we would certainly become. I can understand the practicality of such thinking, but I would never call it teacher mentorship—perhaps, simply "crash course" teaching.

In retrospect, I recognize that these questions, born of my angst from the combination of a hostile, distrustful student teaching experience and stunted diversity training sessions, were actually the precursor to me developing a sense of how to be productively critical about my teaching practice. I needed to know how to connect my identity to my teaching practice in order to reach my students, and simply donning a mask of masculinity wouldn't do it. Kids intuitively see through facades and disconnect from the disingenuous educator unless they are collectively programmed to respond otherwise. I think this is where school-wide reward (i.e., carrot-stick) systems fight great utility.

The Corps Member Action Plan (CMAP) process—essentially a form of probation, highlighted in a formal grievance I wrote against my dismissal, highlights key deficits in relational trust (Bryk, 2010) that may have supported the reflective corrections of problems or mistakes in my classroom. The plan called for regular meetings with my mentorship team about my training progress. Specifically, it required me to visit the classrooms of fellow corps members as a way of building a toolkit of best practices for my classroom. The visits showed me just how much we all similarly fumbled in our teaching assignments, with emergent strengths in different areas. Once I was placed on CMAP, each and every word I spoke or action I took in the classroom was documented and scrutinized by the same people charged with my development and growth as an educator, which naturally deterred me from taking the necessary risks I would have to take to actually connect with my students. At that point I hadn't even a clue of what those risks would have to be, and the conversations did not generate ideas. They instead offered focus areas for correction.

CMAP also severely limited the collaborative mentorship critical in helping new educators discern the difference between productive and unproductive mistakes. Once the CMAP process had begun, my efforts seemed sufficient to meet "standard." Oddly, peer teachers not on CMAP whom my mentors directed me to observe for improvement didn't appear to be far better prepared than I to command the classroom as teacher leaders. These teachers, however, did a fantastic job of ensuring that their kids repeated "Big Goals" connected to standardized test improvement and parroting or showing evidence of the mindsets unpacked in our diversity and curriculum sessions about what good teaching looks and feels like.

What frustrated me most were the team's inconsistencies in feedback about my teaching practice. While my faculty advisor, a 35-year veteran teacher, observed, "There is definitely improvement in your lessons from last week. Your written objectives, delivering of lessons, and classroom management are much better," TFA staffers reviewed the same lessons with a negative slant, as if my dismissal was their goal. For context, it is important to note that not one of the TFA staffers evaluating my performance had more than 4 years of classroom teaching experience—by no means were they experts.

The actual dismissal included the final decision of the vice president of Institutes. A 2001 corps member, she taught through her 2-year commitment before leaving the classroom to become a TFA program director (now referred to as a manager of teacher leadership development, or MTLD). Not long after my TFA experience, she left the organization to earn a master's degree in business, completed a summer internship with the Boston Consulting Group, and worked briefly with Sears before returning to TFA as president of teacher preparation, support and development. In her observations she commented on a vocabulary list scaffold I created to support students during a read aloud, "You assume that the students understood the words on the list." It appeared nothing I attempted could meet the objectives TFA had set for my development. The dismissal conversation happened abruptly one night before bed.

On July 21, 2005, under the auspices of discussing my progress on the CMAP, I was called to a meeting with Susan Asiyanbi, vice president of Institutes, Cate Reed, school director, and Sarah Kenders, CMA. Minutes into the meeting, Ms. Asiyanbi informed me that the meeting would serve as my official dismissal from TFA, without prior warning, without egregious failure on my part to master objectives. Ms. Asiyanbi informed me that she, along with Cate Reed and Sarah Kenders, had made the decision for my dismissal on the grounds of not "feeling 100% confident" in my ability to achieve significant gains in my region as a first year teacher. It is important to note that this meeting with Ms. Asiyanbi was the first official meeting that she had attended concerning my progress in which my presence was requested. Ms. Asiyanbi was sure to let me know that "nothing [I] had to say against [their] justifications for [my] dismissal would alter the decision that had already been made." I pursued the grievance process because of the documented discrepancies between Ms. Asiyanbi's cumulative assessment of my teaching and my documented progress during Institute.

According to Susan Asiyanbi, my dismissal was based on an "inability to master key objectives of training, while also, transferring components of the corps member action plan to observable growth in my work with the students." After reviewing official documentation on my behavior in the classroom and my implementation of key objectives of training, I am troubled by the assertion that I was dismissed on the basis of a "gross failure" to master those objectives. My dismissal more accurately reflected a conflict between the natural trajectory of my development as a new teacher and the negative interpretation of that trajectory as noted by a single observation by Susan Asiyanbi and the subjective observations of officials Sarah Kenders and Cate Reed at Tanner Duckrey Elementary School, my summer school placement.

I protested my dismissal because somewhere in that summer training, I bonded with the teaching profession. I began to find a voice, and understood that it would be a voice I could have in no other profession. The last day that I was formally observed, my full day of teaching, I proved that I had grown over the course of TFA training and had the capacity to grow as a new teacher in the Philadelphia School District, if given the chance. The oral and written general feedback from my faculty advisor who knew my style best convinced me. My students began the morning showing some disrespect during the morning meeting in the cafeteria; however, before my students had entered our classroom, I made sure that I had them refocused. By the end of the first lesson, my students were responding to me with the respect I expected of them—and maybe even a little curiosity. My full day of teaching showed that I could manage a classroom for an extended period of time, exhibit high expectations for my students, and implement formal lesson plans. That same day, the vice president of Institutes observed my first period of instruction as a part of my CMAP and made largely negative comments on a lesson that both my faculty advisor and coteachers noted as well done—comments she would soon use to substantiate a gross failure to master key objectives and an egregious failure to demonstrate TFA core values. That observation seemed a cursory part of the dismissal process.

During one of the CMAP meetings with my CMA and school director, a story they shared highlighted the extent to which fear and anxiety drove the dismissal decision and my mentorship. It was the story of a young male corps member in my CMA's advisory group in a prior Summer Institute. The CMA expressed that she had felt uneasy about her decision to graduate him from Institute, and in. In fact, her worst fear came true upon hearing he had quit just months into his first year, leaving thirty students without a teacher. She shared with me that she felt guilty about his failure to complete his commitment because she could have redirected his decision to commit. From then on, each time we had a CMAP meeting, it felt as though they were extending an invitation to me to quit before it was too late. I felt pressure to leave from the very people charged with my growth and development, but it renewed my determination to become a successful corps member and I remained committed to teach for my students and for myself.

I made a commitment to TFA that I never broke; it was ultimately broken by TFA's leadership. The CMAP process became a vehicle for producing unfair judgments and projections about my potential as an effective teacher in my region. Based on the feedback I received during my last full day of teaching observations, my teaching ability had grown. The grounds upon which I was dismissed were overly subjective and influenced by factors other than just my personal growth as a teacher and corps member.

Best Practice: A Trusting Collaboration

Mentorship is undoubtedly subjective; however, it is also deliberate, buoying, and most crucially sustained. The CMAP process operated as a justifying vehicle for dismissing corps members whose values failed to align with TFA's corporate line. In 2005 the Philadelphia-based TFA Summer Institute suffered from a deficit of mentorship models that promote a growth mindset over "competency." The CMAP process, despite the improvements in my teaching noted by the 35-year veteran teacher left out of the final decision, empowered staffers to recommend that I find another line of work. I realized then that my dismissal had less to do with my teaching and more to do with the complications I presented as a developing educator and mentee.

TFA had no mentorship model for supporting my growth as a new teacher—a severe limitation that impacted me and has truncated the careers of too many pre-service educators with something unique to offer the profession. I found my voice after returning to teaching with the Philadelphia Teaching Fellows and training under the capable mentorship of Mrs. Obermeyer, a veteran teacher and former corps member of color all too familiar with the identity issues I would have to unpack as a new teacher. I'm forever grateful to her for uncovering the pathways to great, fearless teaching. She emphasized connecting with students before engaging them in learning content: "Nothing you say matters [to students] until you matter [to students]."

Good mentoring is about establishing a trusting, collaborative relationship where failure offers opportunity for growth. TFA did not provide opportunity for productive mistakes for all corps members, particularly ones who questioned the mission, goal, or method of the organization. The data-driven tone of my experience did not foster collaboration with peers. The paperwork and documented interaction did not engender trust between myself as a new teacher and those charged with facilitating my development. Mentorship is about making connections between people, ideas, and practices. I eventually found safe spaces to cultivate the unique practice I had within, but if it were up to my mentorship I would have skipped the classroom for something more manageable, like corporate law.

Beyond Teach For America: Why I Continue to Teach

For me, teaching has been a love supreme that has expanded my human growth and development. I have the capacity to connect and feel and laugh and cry in a public space with others. The longer that I teach, the stronger this love grows in depth and complexity. Feeling safe enough to make mistakes and learn from them has shaped the development of my practice. Nowhere in my preservice training or mentorship team had we explored the kind of connection I feel to the craft today—which is not shocking, given the average teaching careers of my TFA mentorship team and the career-driven mindsets popular within my cohort. It's funny to reflect on my TFA experience at this moment in my career. Now in my eighth year of teaching, I feel particularly empowered as a teacher activist and accomplished as a teacher leader.

In 2005 I felt lost, angry, and voiceless. Even if I had survived the mindset framework that Institute offered, I wonder whether I would have moved "past" teaching, like many who trained with me that summer. I thought that this TFA dismissal would bar me from entry to the education profession. Instead, it offered me a critical lens for considering new modes of teacher development and teacher retention. Despite the problematic nature of the way that TFA trains new legions of teachers to think about what it means to enter this profession, they maintain the political will to grow their brand. How does TFA's method of recruitment, training, and retention stymie the flood of teachers that exit the profession within the first 5 years? How does it support true diversity within the nation's teaching force?

It's important to note that TFA isn't to blame for the gaps that exist in the public education system, in the same way teachers' unions aren't to blame. Let's stop passing blame and figure out which set of pathways help retain teaching talent. Teachers shape the citizenry, and we need a stable and invested base to do that work in a way that engages thinkers and dreamers. As I composed this narrative, I questioned what it could mean for my career progression, since it is nearly impossible to engage in shaping the edusphere without TFA being somehow present. However, I find it far more important to offer this story to broaden the conversation that teacher-training entities—both traditional and alternative—have about engaging future teachers and training the millions of teachers who skillfully motivate and mentor students every day. Teacher mentorship matters, and it takes more than 5 weeks and a rubric to determine the potential impact an educator may have or the voice s/he will develop. Review of the dismissal paperwork has reminded me of just how little Institute prepared me for the heart and mind work teaching would take. Luckily, I have found some rad thought partners and mentors who have helped me build a pedagogy that reflects my values and vision for a better world, where students learn to think, feel, respond, and talk to each other in ways that promote the commonality of our human experience.

REFERENCES

Bryk, A. S. (2010). Organizing schools for improvement. *Phi Delta Kappan, 91*(7), 23–30.
Kopkowski, C. (2008, April 5). Why they leave: Lack of respect, NCLB, and underfunding—in a topsy-turvy profession, what can make today's teachers stay? *NEA Today.* Retrieved from http://www.nea.org/home/12630.htm

Ignoring the Ghost of Horace Mann: A Reflective Critique of Teach For America's Solipsistic Pedagogy

MICHAEL J. STEUDEMAN
Greater New Orleans, 2010–2012

BIOSKETCH

Michael J. Steudeman began Teach For America (TFA) after completing a master's degree in rhetorical studies. As a researcher of political language, he quickly realized he had entered an organization that contradicted his beliefs about the function and conduct of public education. Despite his misgivings, he sought, with little success, to proactively alter the organization from within its confines. As a corps member advisor (CMA), he trained new TFA members for two summers at the organization's Institute. There, he experienced firsthand the struggles of new teachers who often finished their training insufficiently prepared for the challenges of working with students in low-income schools. Now a Ph.D. student in rhetoric and political culture, Steudeman studies education policy rhetoric throughout American history to unearth the historical antecedents to the language of contemporary education reform.

NARRATIVE

My future principal reviewed my résumé. Noting my experience teaching an introductory speech class to college freshmen, he perked up. "Well, at least you've taught before," he said—a resounding vote of confidence. I had taught, in a sense, if two 75-minute periods a week of extemporaneous lecturing to a docile group of college students counts as "teaching." When I joined Teach For America (TFA), I naively rationalized that my background as a college instructor would help me avoid the fate of many unprepared corps members (CMs). Like so many others who have contributed to this volume, I quickly learned that the challenges of educating children mired in systemic poverty would require expertise that I did not possess prior to my commitment—expertise I certainly did not develop during TFA's Summer Institute.

Of the many ways that TFA leaves teachers unprepared for their commitments, I found the thinness of its pedagogy the most glaring. The organization's 5-week training model taps into a prevalent myth that teaching can only be learned "in the trenches." The entire trial-by-fire structure of Summer Institute assumes that teachers learn best when placed before actual students as quickly as possible. Preparatory work in pedagogy, child development, and theory is limited to a short collection of "pre-Institute readings," which CMs study independently and without guidance or sustained discussion before their training begins. Once they arrive at Institute, they are presented with a single perspective on teaching—a perspective that is shallow, narrow, ahistorical, and often presented as the "final word" on how to teach.

In this chapter, I argue that this narrow pedagogy does a tremendous disservice to CMs and their students. I advocate for more intensive, theoretically robust, and long-term training programs that respect the complexity of the teaching profession. I make this argument from three perspectives. First, I speak as a former CM who struggled—not from lack of work ethic, and not from lack of content knowledge, but from a severe absence of training regarding the pedagogical needs of high school students. Secondly, I speak from my experience of two summers as a corps member advisor (CMA), entrusted to help train new teachers in a matter of 5 weeks. And finally, I speak from my post-TFA position as a Ph.D. student of political rhetoric. As a researcher, I analyze the history of American educational movements to reveal rhetorical antecedents to TFA and other contemporary reform organizations. Sifting through the oratory of statesmen, presidents, scholars, and theorists across history, I have been frustrated by how often TFA ignores other voices in the conversation about how best to (re)vitalize public education.

To put matters another way: TFA ignores the ghost of Horace Mann. I do not reference the first Massachusetts secretary of education to suggest that TFA has departed from some idyllic past. Rather, I invoke Mann as a stand-in for the litany of ideas, strategies, and foibles that characterize the theoretical development of public education. In its solipsistic rejection of others' voices, TFA harms its CMs—and ultimately, their students—in three ways: by denying them theoretical expertise, insulating them from dialogue and criticism, and isolating them in a sphere of idealism. The rest of this chapter explores these forms of solipsism and the consequences of each for students.

An Absence of Theoretical Expertise

Upon becoming secretary of education, Mann began his tenure by promoting "normal schools" for teacher education. He lamented the prevalence of teachers "who never received one lesson of special instruction, to fit them for their momentous duties" (Mann, 1855, p. 110). Despite the obvious benefits of training in any endeavor, TFA eschewed preparation from the start. In the senior thesis that sprouted the organization, TFA founder Wendy Kopp stressed that inexperience could be supplanted by "the enthusiasm and knowledge that sharp, recent college graduates would provide" (Kopp, 1989, p. 50). With this assumption that "grit" and wit supersede pedagogical knowledge, the organization subjects teachers to only 5 weeks of training. The demands of short-term development translate into a one-size-fits-all pedagogy that leaves CMs underprepared for the unpredictable contingencies of the classroom.

As in any situation demanding efficiency, the pedagogy of Institute trends toward the formulaic. All materials are pre-prepared for staff and CMs alike. As a CMA, I received massive binders with time-stamped, scripted sessions to facilitate. My trainees were similarly provided massive spiral-bound books consisting largely of templates to complete. From these materials, TFA explicitly, linearly depicts every step of the teaching process. For example, during the first week of Institute, CMs attend "PLAN 2a" and "PLAN 2b"—full-school sessions dedicated to teaching the steps of setting a "daily vision" for classes. All of the steps—such as writing objectives, defining "key points" for students to follow, and creating aligned assessments—are explicitly detailed in *just 3 hours*. The majority of training sessions pertaining to classroom management, lesson planning, assessment, and other subjects are similarly rigid, and often tethered to standard PowerPoints shared by session coordinators at every Institute school site.

Though CMs discuss why these formulae matter, the conversations are largely deductive and staff-directed. CMs are driven toward key "takeaways" during each session, and, given the rapid pacing of Institute, little time is dedicated to sustained reflection on the deeper purposes of their pedagogical training. In the absence of deep, foundational knowledge, CMs persist in rote application of formulae without recognizing *why* they do so. During one Institute, I worked with a CM who was enlisted to teach high school English but lacked theoretical knowledge in literary analysis and interpretation. He could assemble lesson plans that went through the motions of posing guiding questions to help students toward themes, but only because those themes were announced in provided curriculum. He simply lacked the expertise to dissect a text, let alone teach students to do the same. I do not blame him, of course. English was not his major, and TFA had reassured him at every step of the application process that he had the "enthusiasm and knowledge" to learn analytical skills that take most English teachers many years to develop. Like a beginning guitar player with no understanding of music theory, this CM was following a piece of tablature without knowing what any of the notes meant. Without a theoretical underpinning—the sort that traditional colleges of education provide—he and his students were condemned to wander aimlessly through texts, no matter how many hours I spent trying to remediate him.

More problematically, TFA's narrow pedagogy often prevents teachers from identifying and cultivating their own styles. Institute molded my assumptions about behavior management and lesson planning in systematized ways that translated poorly for the students I taught in the fall. When students deviated from the expectations of my behavior management system, I was paralyzed. When I was enlisted to teach elective courses outside of my English language arts (ELA) training, I sacrificed hours of sleep each night. Over my breaks and weekends I studied countless books to discover alternative approaches that better complemented my style of delivery and pedagogic philosophy, as opposed to the myopic TFA approach. Only then did I truly learn to feel comfortable in my own skin—and still, I struggled.

Isolated from Dialogue: TFA Pedagogy as the Only Pedagogy

Mann approached his initial task with a strong reflexivity about his own limited experience in education. He long contemplated whether he had the necessary expertise for the role; upon taking up the task, he dedicated much of his first year to extensive reading of pedagogical literature (Messerli, 1971, pp. 242–253). CMs are trained to bypass this stage of humility and leap directly to complete certainty in their endeavor. At Institute, they are given a single way of seeing the task of teaching—but, as rhetorical theorist Kenneth Burke asserts, "A way of seeing is also a way of not seeing" (Burke, 1984, p. 49). TFA materials seldom recognize the evolution, complexity, or contentiousness of most learning theory. TFA presents its curriculum as the *only* way to teach, insulating CMs within a pedagogical vacuum.

While studying my pre-Institute readings in 2010, I immediately began to notice the stubbornness with which TFA treats competing approaches to educational practice. The mandatory reading *Teaching as Leadership*, for instance, barely recognizes the controversies surrounding learning standards and testing. "Whatever your view of learning standards," the book dismissively says, "all states and districts now use them to guide instruction, and it is important to think about your role as a teacher within that reality" (Farr, 2010, p. 22). This disregard for competing opinions is connected to a more general lack of engagement with theoretical disputes. In TFA's *Required Readings*, a brief section on theory remarks that "hundreds of books have been written on learning theory, each representing a different collection of approaches and angles." After this acknowledgement, the text selects a few basic theories that "are extraordinarily useful for new teachers" and provides a straightforward summary of each (Teach For America, 2010, p. 295). This trend continues throughout Institute, as CMs enter a world without nuance and unamenable to critique.

For some CMs, following TFA's prescribed curricular approaches *does* work—and TFA is quick to elevate those CMs to positions of leadership, either as CMAs or as year-long managers of teacher leadership development (MTLDs). In my experience working at two Summer Institutes, all of my fellow staff members were hired from TFA or like-minded organizations. Few of my colleagues had more than 3 or 4 years of teaching experience; fewer still were over the age of 30. About a week into each Institute, a small number of more experienced teachers from local schools were introduced to aid new CMs as "faculty advisors." Unfortunately, TFA significantly limited these teachers' participation and devalued their expertise when it departed from organizational orthodoxy. The problem of insularity, in turn, perpetuated itself: the blind led the blind.

Due to the inevitable groupthink that emerges from these conditions, TFA tends to develop CMs and staff who disregard legitimate criticism. For instance, during my first year, TFA often requested that I submit performance data from my elective classes. To me, this request sounded epistemologically dubious. My elective courses were not standardized and were taught by few others in the state. Unlike scores on a standardized test or a normed rubric, my data would be utterly meaningless to anyone other than me and my students. I did not want these scores aggregated alongside other statistics TFA would present to the public to tout progress toward their "growth goals." Though I repeatedly communicated these concerns, TFA staff members pressed me for my Excel spreadsheets until I finally acquiesced.

It turns out I was not alone in my apprehensions. Shortly after my commitment ended, TFA's former research director Heather Harding revealed that only 15% of CMs teach classes with state standardized tests. The majority of TFA teachers thus "rely on assessments they design themselves"—rendering much of organization's data inconsistent and unreliable (Simon, 2012). While this fact is troubling in its own right, it also underscores a deeper problem. I presented sound, reasonable arguments about the practicality of sharing my data, yet TFA continued to press, making me feel stigmatized for questioning an organizational motive. I was challenging a cornerstone of TFA's "data-driven" pedagogy, and the staff—seldom exposed to any other points of view on education—had no framework with which to consider my arguments.

TFA has its share of thoughtful internal critics, but their proposals and reforms are often hamstrung by the organization's structural rigidity. During my two summers as a CMA, I worked with a secondary ELA training program seeking to alleviate problems with the organization's "one-size-fits-all" approach. The program focused on cultivating teachers who could lead students to critical interpretations of literary texts through the analysis of literary devices. Despite its promise, the program was often compromised by the structures of Institute. Teachers heard contradictory messages across the arc of their 5 weeks. In week 1, session leaders stressed the deep, often unmeasurable influence of literature in students' lives. Yet, as Institute continued, TFA's data focus crept back into conversations with staff obsessing about students' results on daily assessments. At one point, the staff demanded that I intervene in a CM's classroom on her last day of Institute teaching because her students failed to show substantial progress in their exit ticket results. I protested, but fearing a poor evaluation and feeling responsibility for the CM's "poor" performance, I again acquiesced. The CM was demoralized; the students were confused; and I was incensed by the staff's shortsighted impulsivity dictated by data. Thoughtful reforms can happen in TFA, but only within the confines of an inadequately brief and rigid training program.

Solipsism as Idealism: The Teacher in a Vacuum

Mann's legacy lives on in another, more problematic way. According to Taylor (2010), Mann conceived of education as the cure for "the pathologies, failures, and dangers of democratic society" (p. 14). This mindset persists today when TFA touts the individual teacher's capacity to push children to transcend the social ills of poverty and prejudice (Kopp, 2011, p. 10). TFA calls this idealistic, and it is—it centers the locus of change within the individual. As Burke wrote, "idealistic philosophies think in terms of the 'ego,' the 'self'"—in other words, they stress the virtue of what has been ratiocinated by the individual mind over the cultivation of social development (Burke, 1969, p. 171). The consequence of this idealism is a sort of pedagogical loneliness. To imagine 2 years in TFA, do not picture just the challenges of the school day—but night after night spent alone at a computer, crafting worksheets and lesson plans while abandoning any semblance of work-life balance.

Early in its history, TFA made a choice to leave CMs to their own devices. Faced with budget shortfalls, Kopp opted not to reduce the size of the corps or to pursue more modest goals, but to slash funding for CM support. As she explains, "By guiding our corps members' professional development ourselves, we had prevented many of them from taking the initiative to find the support they needed within their schools and communities. When there was a problem, it was assumed that it was Teach For America's responsibility rather than that of the school or school system" (Kopp, 2001, p. 110). As this passage underscores, TFA elected to place the onus of responsibility on the individual CM. For me, this meant minimal professional support during my earliest travails in the classroom. In the first 6 months at my placement site I was observed by TFA only five times. I was hired at a school about 90 minutes away from the TFA office and most placement sites, and so fell on the periphery of TFA's concerns. My local staff manager, stretched between more than 30 CMs, simply did not have the capacity to trek out to my school on a regular basis. As Kopp would prefer, I sought other sources of help; but my resource-stretched school district was understandably reluctant to provide in-depth on-the-job training. Likewise, I was deeply anxious about conveying my challenges to my employer—I feared losing my first job.

In the absence of sufficient support, I was on my own. I had to reinvent the wheel more often than most educators. Where a traditional teaching college graduate would know where to look for resources, I built hundreds of lessons and curricular materials from scratch. Peculiarly, TFA tends to privilege this type of individualistic pursuit. Their model, as Kopp has asserted time and again, is Jaime Escalante (as depicted in the film *Stand and Deliver*)—the suffering servant struggling alone against a broken system (Farr, 2010, p. 234). The expectation is that effective pedagogy emerges as an epiphany from a vacuum—that the teacher should work relentlessly to become brilliant, rather than stand on the shoulders of giants.

Listening to the Ghost of Horace Mann

TFA has recently exerted a response to criticisms like mine. In March 2014 they announced the creation of a "pilot program to offer TFA recruits a year of classes in educational theory and pedagogy" (Layton, 2014). The effort is substantially limited, however—it offers this training while students are still completing busy senior years of college, and provides it to only 500 CMs of the thousands who will join next year's corps. Moreover, little is known about the details of what that training will look like and how it will be led. It is a somewhat promising sign for an extremely solipsistic organization, but I remain skeptical. I have witnessed too many indicators that TFA changes only reluctantly. TFA has cultivated an organizational structure prone to groupthink—one that, for a quarter century, has funneled unprepared and unsupported teachers into the classrooms of the most underprivileged students in the United States.

At its heart, TFA's resistance to change stems from the foundational myths that are, by now, fully interwoven into every aspect of the organization. TFA feeds upon a perverse misconception that every teacher's first year should be hell. From the start, TFA embraced a contention that teachers should be lonely heroes; that pedagogy can be learned only from practice; that dialogue does not matter; and that critics, internal and external, present a threat to be silenced, not a spur to organizational reflection. To this end, I implore principals to look elsewhere to fill their classrooms: to traditional colleges of education that provide years of foundational knowledge and reflection on the challenges of teaching; to certification programs that require several months of heavily guided in-service training. I urge school districts to cultivate their own support systems to retain their teachers and ensure their years in the classroom do not constitute a lonely struggle. And I urge policymakers to elevate teachers who question received wisdom, who critique misguided curricula, who challenge their colleagues, and who participate in an ongoing dialogue about American public education.

REFERENCES

Burke, K. (1969). *A grammar of motives* (3rd ed.). Berkeley: University of California Press.

Burke, K. (1984). *Permanence and change: An anatomy of purpose* (3rd ed.). Berkeley: University of California Press.

Farr, S. (2010). *Teaching as leadership: The highly effective teacher's guide to closing the achievement gap.* San Francisco: Jossey-Bass.

Kopp, W. (1989). *An argument and plan for the creation of the teacher corps* (Undergraduate thesis). Woodrow Wilson School of Public and International Affairs, Princeton University.

Kopp, W. (2001). *One day, all children… The unlikely triumph of Teach For America and what I learned along the way.* New York: PublicAffairs.

Kopp, W. (2011). *A chance to make history: What works and what doesn't in providing an excellent education for all.* New York: PublicAffairs.

Layton, L. (2014, March 10). Teach For America tests out more training. *Washington Post,* Retrieved from http://www.washingtonpost.com/local/education/teach-for-america-tests-out-more-training/2014/03/10/c4685558-a617-11e3-84d4-e59b1709222c_story.html

Mann, H. (1855). *Lectures on education.* Boston: Ide & Dutton.

Messerli, J. (1971). *Horace Mann: A biography.* New York: Alfred A. Knopf.

Simon, S. (2012, August 16). Has Teach For America betrayed its mission? *Reuters.* Retrieved from http://www.reuters.com/article/2012/08/16/us-usa-education-teachforamerica-idUSBRE87F05O20120816

Taylor, B. P. (2010). *Horace Mann's troubling legacy: The education of democratic citizens.* Lawrence: University of Kansas Press.

Teach For America (2010). *Required readings 2010.* North Billerica, MA: Curriculum Associates.

CHAPTER FIVE

What Is an Excellent Education? The Role of Theory in Teach For America

LAURA TAYLOR
Houston, 2007–2009

BIOSKETCH

Laura Taylor is currently a doctoral student in the College of Education at the University of Texas at Austin, where she studies language and literacy practices within the Department of Curriculum and Instruction. She first encountered Teach For America (TFA) as a sophomore at Cornell University. Laura served as a campus campaign manager for TFA for 2 years while a student at Cornell, working with full-time staff to recruit corps members at her university. After graduating, she joined the 2007 corps and taught in a second grade ESL classroom in Houston, Texas. Laura taught at her placement school for 5 years while earning her master's in education from the University of Saint Thomas, before moving to Austin to pursue her doctorate. While earning that degree, she works with preservice teachers as a teaching assistant and facilitator.

NARRATIVE

When people ask me how I became a teacher, I tend to answer in a cautious whisper: "Actually, I was in Teach For America." My admission is followed by a hurried explanation that I no longer support the program, an attempt to distance myself from those alumni who remain committed to the organization. Teach For America

(TFA) has become almost a guilty secret in my history, rather than a proud accomplishment. It wasn't always like this, though. When I was first introduced to TFA in college, I was one of the organization's most enthusiastic cheerleaders. Not only was I a corps member after graduation, but I also worked for TFA to recruit my classmates to the organization during my junior and senior years in college. This shift from champion to opponent of the organization came not from reading or listening to the many convincing critiques of the organization, but from my own experiences in the program. The simple answer to the question of what changed my opinion about Teach For America is this: my time in Teach For America.

In order to understand how this shift took place, I've reflected on my experiences with the organization: as a campus campaign manager (CCM) recruiting for the organization, as a corps member in my first 2 years of teaching in Houston and the 3 years that followed that, and now as a doctoral student and teacher educator who sometimes advises undergraduates considering the program. I have considered how my own teacher preparation compared to the experiences of my traditionally prepared peers, recognizing the inadequacy of the training I was provided. Certainly, my teaching would have been improved by many things: by more experiences working with students prior to entering the classroom, by more time spent learning about language and literacy acquisition, by more instruction in how to develop relationships with students, and by learning to build community in the classroom. What was most crucially missing from my preparation, however, was an attention to theory. In *Teaching to Transgress*, bell hooks (1994) reminds us that our theories—our understandings of how the world works—can serve to oppress or liberate. These theories, whether explicit or implicit, guide the daily decisions we make as teachers, yet it is precisely around the question of theory that corporate reformers attack traditional teacher preparation. They claim that schools of education require preservice teachers to spend too much time considering theories of teaching and learning. As the U.S. Secretary of Education Arne Duncan told Andrea Mitchell during an interview on her show, they believe that schools of education require "lots of history of education, philosophy of education, psychology of education, not enough teaching 28 or 30 diverse children in a classroom" (De, 2014). Analyzing my own experiences in education has led me to a very different conclusion on the role of theory in teacher education.

Meeting Teach For America

It wasn't long after I was hired as a CCM that I had memorized TFA's vision statement: "One day, all children in this nation will have the opportunity to attain an excellent education." It was this vision that spoke to me. As a young adult in her college years, I was beginning to understand that the world I inhabited was a grossly unequal place, and I was in search of a way to be part of changing that appalling status quo. When I first learned about TFA and their hopeful mission for change, I believed I had found the cause, and the organization, that I might dedicate my life to. Throughout my junior and senior years, I trekked all over campus repeating this vision of a better future to my classmates: in the practiced class announcements I gave, in the hundreds of flyers I hung up, in the e-mails I sent to prospective applicants, and in the brightly colored chalkings I made around campus when an application deadline was coming up. The vision statement expressed everything I wanted to say: that our educational system was unfair, that the status quo was unacceptable, and that we could all play a role in changing that.

As I spouted this vision statement across campus, I also had an arsenal of statistics that had been provided to me by the organization. I recited these statistics throughout my announcements and conversations with potential recruits: statistics about the racial segregation that existed in many of our nation's public schools, statistics about the drop-out rates for students living in low-income communities, statistics about the "achievement gap" between White and African American students. As with the vision statement, I viewed these statistics simply as an effective way to convince others to join the organization without considering the implicit messages that such statistics conveyed. By talking matter-of-factly about the need to raise African American students' test scores to equal those of White students' scores, I was asserting that the tests being used were valid measures of student achievement and free of cultural bias. Even the use of the term *achievement gap*, which I viewed simply as a way to name educational inequity, was at the same time perpetuating deficit thinking about the students served by TFA—assuming that students of color from low-income urban and rural communities were lacking in something that White students in suburban communities possessed. By reciting these statistics, I was unconsciously perpetuating a particular view of students of color in low-income communities.

Alongside this view of students of color in low-income communities was a particular view of the teachers those students were learning from. TFA's answer to this "achievement gap" is, in part, to send TFA corps members into the schools and classrooms of these students. This solution is rooted in the organization's implicit views of classroom teachers in urban and rural schools. In our recruitment materials, we were encouraged to share the results of a Mathematica Policy Research study commission by TFA (Decker, Mayer, & Glazerman, 2004). The study, which found that the students of TFA corps members made *slightly* larger gains in math test scores and equivalent gains in reading test scores than students of other teachers, has been widely publicized by the organization as "scientific proof" that TFA "works." Although the study's findings and implications have been thoroughly critiqued by a number of educational researchers, the study itself should cause us to ask questions. What is the agenda behind such a study, one that hopes to demonstrate that corps members with barely any training can outperform traditionally prepared teachers?

This question is rarely discussed by the organization explicitly, but TFA's beliefs about public school teachers can be found in its focus on recruiting at prestigious schools and in the praise lavished on TFA's recruitment model: TFA corps members are smarter than current teachers, and they work harder. The implicit lesson is twofold: that existing teachers are simply ineffective and that extensive teacher preparation, like that found in traditional 4- or 5-year programs, is unnecessary. The concern with this is that these views largely remain implicit for corps members. If I had been asked as a senior in college whether this was what I believed about teachers and teacher education, I would have vehemently denied it. Coming from a family of educators, I have great respect for the talents and dedications of our public school teachers, and even before becoming a teacher myself, I knew the profession to be a challenging one. So why was I so eager to share the results of this study with my peers, given that its conclusions conflicted with my own beliefs about education? Like so many questions about TFA, this was not one I was asked to consider. Despite what TFA might claim publicly, there is clearly an unstated belief that corps members are simply more effective educators than the veteran teachers they teach alongside. This was present in the recruitment materials and events I was surrounded by as a CCM, and it continued as I was accepted into the corps and attended Summer Institute in Houston.

I have few vivid memories from my experiences during Induction and Institute; this lack of recall likely stems from the sleep deprivation that seems to be a crucial part of the experience. Most of my memories are bleary: moving between our dorms at the University of Houston, to the buses that carried us to our schools, to the portables where we listened to lectures, to the classrooms where we taught. I can remember the names and faces of many of the TFA staff and fellow corps members. I can remember the faces of a few of the students I worked with, but none of their names. And I cannot even picture the veteran teacher whose classroom we taught in for a few hours each day. While these memories (and lack of memories) are disconcerting for me, I believe that my sleep-deprived brain made memories of the things that seemed important and ignored the things that didn't. TFA made it clear that their staff members were important, while those not affiliated with the organization were less so. Looking back, it's unfathomable to me that we didn't interact more with the veteran teacher in whose classroom we worked. This was a man who had years of experience teaching in that community and was spending the summer working with the same students we were. Without question, he had a plethora of resources that he could have shared with my fellow corps members and me—but TFA opted not to utilize those valuable resources. Instead, we only saw him in passing, leaving the classroom at the end of his teaching time, during which we were in seminars with TFA staff members. This is not to say, of course, that the talented TFA staff that we worked with didn't have anything to offer. Many of them had years of classroom experience themselves, and I learned important lessons about teaching and learning from them during my time at Institute. However, their perspectives were limited. Many of them had less than 5 years of teaching experience, and none had taught in the school or community in which we were working. So in choosing to prioritize the knowledge and experiences of these staff members over the experiences of this veteran teacher, TFA was also sending a message to corps members about whose knowledge was valued and whose experiences we were expected to learn from.

One aspect of my Institute experience that I can recall quite vividly is the Teaching as Leadership (TAL) framework by which our teaching was judged. More than remembering it as a framework, I remember TAL as a rubric that was used to evaluate my teaching, a rubric that could be used to put me on a growth plan if my teaching wasn't up to par. The TAL framework, and its accompanying rubric, was the subject of direct instruction during my Institute seminars. We were told that it was a framework that captured what educational research had *proven* were traits of a highly effective teacher. There was little to no room for interpretation in either the framework or the rubric. An "exemplary" teacher performed one set of actions, and a "prenovice" teacher performed another. Again, the use of the TAL framework and rubric carries both explicit and implicit messages about teaching, with the implicit only becoming apparent to me much later. It is rooted in a particular view of teaching: a view of teaching as a science and as a set of skills that can be perfected by correctly sequencing a series of "research-based" practices. This view of teaching aligns with the views behind No Child Left Behind and Race to the Top; it assumes teaching can be scientifically assessed through "value-added" measurements based on student test scores. This view is, of course, but one view of teaching. Many scholars view teaching not as a science but as a craft or practice that is unique to each individual. This alternative view of teaching recognizes the existence of certain practices that seem to work well in many contexts, but rejects the concept of a single set of "best practices" in which teachers can be trained in order to become highly effective teachers.

It is beyond the scope of this chapter to offer a debate about the nature of teaching and learning. However, students in teacher education should absolutely be exposed to and encouraged to consider these multiple perspectives on teaching. This was not, however, the case with my preparation with TFA. My theory of teaching was the one presented to me; a narrow view that *promised* results if I learned how to correctly implement research-based best practices. This view of teaching, as science, followed me into my classroom, where I spent years searching for the magical "best practices" that would raise my students' test scores. This relentless pursuit of the "right way" resulted in my focus being on developing the right structures and methods for teaching, rather than on building relationships my students and growing from their strengths. It was years before I recognized there were other ways I could approach my practice.

Even in the development of a learning community in my classroom, a practice that requires nuanced understandings of every human being in the room, I searched for scientific solutions. One of my major struggles as a first year teacher, common to many inexperienced teachers, was finding ways to organize my classroom and engage students in the work at hand—what is typically referred to as classroom management. As with all of my teaching struggles, I was constantly in search of the one perfect management "system" that would fix what I saw to be problems in the class. Over the years, I tried out many systems: a clip system in which students moved to different "colors" (and consequences) based on their behavior, a system of table groups working as teams to compete against one another for points and prizes, a system rooted in positive reinforcement that placed star stickers on the desks of students who were behaving well. My one criterion for evaluating these different systems and techniques was how well it worked—in other words, how well it made students comply with my strict expectations for their behavior.

A few years into my teaching, one of the techniques I tried was to create a class motto that I hoped would encourage my students in their academic achievements. The motto ended with the words "Work Hard, Get Smart," a phrase borrowed from one of the videos of exemplar teachers we had watched in Institute. I didn't give too much thought to the phrase when I created the class motto, beyond thinking it was a catchy phrase with a good message. Because it was presented to us in Institute, I viewed it as a TFA-approved "best practice" that I could adopt without concern. Soon after I had placed a large poster with those words on my wall, my campus instructional coach came in to visit, and I proudly showed her my sign. She looked at it for a minute before hesitantly turning to me. "I'm wondering about that phrase," she said. "You might want to change 'smart' to 'smarter.'" "Why?" I asked. Gently, she replied, "Well, doesn't the way it's written now—'get smart'—imply that students are not already smart? Just something to think about." Our conversation quickly moved on to other things, but I kept thinking about what she had said. I had never considered that such a phrase—a phrase approved by TFA—might position my students in such a way. I knew that my students were smart, but as I looked at the sign, I realized she was right. By claiming my students should "get smart," it implied that the students in my class were not already smart, and that smart was something they had to become.

Perhaps, from the outside, this seems like a small matter—a grammatical difference that students perhaps wouldn't even notice. But for me, it was one of many small moments that caused me to question my own understandings of teaching, of learning, and of schooling. It was one of the first times I was encouraged to consider the implications of my actions and to ponder all the questions that had gone unasked. When I put that sign up, I was simply looking for something that would "work" in my classroom, but in doing so, I never paused to ask myself some important questions: What message does that phrase really send to students? What does it tell my students about how I view them and how they should view themselves? Is that the message that I really want to send to my students?

Reflecting on my time with the organization, that vision statement that once made me so enthusiastic—"One day, all children will have the opportunity to attain an excellent education"—repeatedly appears. But it no longer holds the answers for me that it once did. I see it as a carefully crafted corporate motto: a series of meticulously selected words that appear to say so much, but in fact say almost nothing at all. Rather than answers, it raises a series of questions. Why does it aim for this goal to be achieved in the nebulous future—"one day"—rather than demand its realization today? Why does it only promise "the opportunity to attain"—a nasty phrase that implies that some children presented with the opportunity will not want it—rather than situate education as a right that all children deserve? Why is this vision one that is pursued through a private, nongovernmental entity, rather than through the public education system itself? Perhaps the most pertinent questions stem from those last two words: "excellent education." Just what constitutes an excellent education in the eyes of TFA, and how does this vision compare to my own vision? How does it compare to the visions of parents and students in the urban and rural communities the organization works in? Raising these questions about TFA's vision statement provokes important conversations about the purposes of public education and the role of TFA in our schools. Yet, as I was spreading this message across my university, these were not questions I considered.

It was these questions, and so many others, that were missing from my experiences with TFA. My training provided me with information about how to teach reading and writing and how to manage my classroom (though, of course, not enough), but what the organization didn't teach me was how to ask questions about my practice. It didn't ask me to consider the consequences of my teaching—beyond the impact of that teaching on student test scores—or to question whether the techniques I was using were aligned with my beliefs about teaching and learning. TFA didn't provide me the tools to do those things, and I believe this is exactly why the organization is so adored by neoliberal education reformers—the same reformers who seek to end teacher tenure and implement standardized curriculum. Teachers who consider these issues of theory don't fit into that plan. Instead, these reformers want an educational system filled with teachers who will follow scripted lessons and focus only on raising standardized test scores, teachers who are interchangeable and can be quickly replaced by others if they begin to ask critical questions. And, too often, these are exactly the types of teachers that TFA is supplying to our nation's schools.

Not all corps members and alumni are conforming to this plan, of course. In recent years, more and more corps members and alumni have begun speaking up against the organization (this book itself is one example of that emerging movement). Each day, more and more of us are finding our voices and speaking out against the organization, our critiques deeply rooted in our own experiences within the organization and the observed impact of TFA on the schools and communities in which we taught.

And with these voices, we must demand better for our students and our schools. We must demand that the teachers in our nation's classrooms have the tools to ask questions, to consider the theories behind their teaching practices, and to recognize the social structures that their actions either support or disrupt. We cannot expect that those individuals preparing to become teachers will spontaneously begin asking these questions. The conversations that pose these questions, and begin to grapple with possible answers, have to be built into any program that intends to prepare teachers for our nation's schools. These conversations are long and difficult, and require teacher candidates to question their beliefs about not only education, but also about the world as it is and as it should be. They must begin before teachers enter the classroom and continue across their teaching careers. There is not enough time to even begin these conversations in a 5-week Institute. We must demand better for teacher education.

REFERENCES

De, S. (Producer). (2014). Andrea Mitchell reports [Television]: MSNBC.
Decker, P. T., Mayer, D. P., & Glazerman, S. (2004). The effects of Teach For America on students: Findings from a national evaluation. Princeton, NJ: Mathematica Policy Research.
hooks, b. (1994). *Teaching to transgress: Education as the practice of freedom.* New York: Routledge.

CHAPTER SIX

Teach for Ambivalence, Or How I Learned to Stop Worrying and Love to Teach

MATTHEW LYNDE CHESNUT
San Antonio, 2011–2013

BIOSKETCH

Matthew Lynde Chesnut is a high school teacher and a former Teach For America corps member in San Antonio, Texas. A San Antonio native, he began teaching in 2010 in Edgewood Independent School District at John F. Kennedy High School a year prior to joining TFA, then completed 2 years at the same school with TFA. Now in his fifth year with Kennedy, he continues to teach math, debate, and journalism. He lives with his wife, Michelle, and their son, Benjamin. Matthew graduated in 2008 from the University of Texas at San Antonio with a B.A. in political science and economics.

NARRATIVE

This chapter uses memoir to explore the shift in ideology of a Teach For America (TFA) alum. This story begins with my first job in the alternative teaching certification industry, pivoting to my application to TFA. And despite starting my teaching career with a proreform viewpoint, over time I came to see TFA in a less benevolent light and became disillusioned with the meritocratic, charter-aligned aspects of the organization. I found others on social media who feel the same way.

The chapter concludes as I sign my contract to start my fifth year of teaching and I reflect on how few of my colleagues here are doing the same.

I came to TFA in search of many things: employment, purpose, and opportunity. But unlike the majority of TFA's corps members, I didn't join TFA right out of college. My first job was as a desk jockey for a for-profit alternative teaching certification program. I was fired from that job days before both my twenty-fourth birthday and the final application deadline for TFA. I felt the stars were aligning. As I started to collect unemployment, with TFA as a possibility, I had hope again that I could pursue my dream of becoming a teacher.

Back then, I was the classic TFA type: an aspiring policy wonk who visited KIPP schools, kept abreast of positive media coverage of reformers, and genuinely believed education alone could level the playing field in the United States. When I applied, I included this groaner in my letter of intent:

> I've been following Teach For America for several years. Alums like Michelle Rhee at DC Public Schools or KIPP founders Mike Feinberg and Dave Levin have used their experience at TFA to transform the educational landscape. While what they do is certainly not short on controversy, I do not question their motive: they see an imbalance, an inequality of opportunity that, if ignored or ineptly addressed, will handicap the futures of a generation. They are doing something to change that.

In the years since joining TFA, I've transformed. Being a teacher at a school with a history of high levels of poverty and segregation led me to question the TFA model that sends mostly out-of-town twenty-somethings to teach for 2 years before they do something else. I see how attrition has made my school a less stable environment, how quickie certification sends underprepared people to work in one of the most challenging professions. I see how TFA funnels its alumni out of the classrooms into charter school leadership, the private sector, or the policy world. I see how things not measured by test scores don't get half the scrutiny that things that can be measured do. All the while, I've seen many, many teachers leave. I didn't know where to find community until I started blogging. I soon discovered others who were similarly disillusioned with the thrust of TFA. It was there I found a voice that spoke to what I was seeing in my work as a teacher.

TFA is notorious for its 2-years-and-done teachers. I'm one of a relative few who have stayed and committed to a career of teaching. By the time this book is published, I'll be in the middle of year 5 at the same school. The same school I interviewed with as an alternative certification program candidate prior to joining TFA—the same school that took a chance on someone with little training and even less experience, because they had to. For better or worse, I'm still here.

I'm unlike many TFA corps members. I say that because I feel like most of the people I met in the program went to more competitive universities, were actively recruited by TFA, and joined right after graduation. I went to a decidedly less prestigious, non-flagship state university and joined after working for a few years. There was no recruiter, no imploring e-mails or meetings. I applied for one reason: I needed the work.

A couple of days before my twenty-fourth birthday, I was dismissed from my job at a for-profit alternative certification program. For a year and a half, I had worked as a program advisor for prospective teaching candidates. When I was dismissed I was terminated without cause, so I was able to collect unemployment benefits until I found another job. With my wife still in graduate school, this situation left us in a precarious financial bind.

I had a suit, a Visa card full of unemployment benefits, and a will to do work with purpose. On my twenty-fourth birthday, I completed my application to TFA. My letter of intent might as well have been cribbed from a Students for Education Reform bulletin: praise for Michelle Rhee and KIPP founders Dave Levin and Mike Feinberg, talk about how nothing is more important for a child's success in school than who their teachers are, and use of the phrase "achievement gap." It must have been what they were looking for, because it—along with my college transcripts—got me into the final interview stage.

This last phase of the interview process meant tracking down old college professors and supervisors to say nice things about me, and driving up to Austin for an all-day interview which included a group activity, a sample lesson, a written exam, and a face-to-face interview. I had never experienced anything quite like it. Everyone there seemed to be poised and accomplished, and they looked like interns at Merrill Lynch. I sublimated all my nervousness into maintaining a façade of cool. My poise was but mimicry. Whatever I did, it worked. Sort of.

"*Congratulations...*" Two and half months of tension and waiting, and I finally got the vindication I was looking for. "*...and Welcome to Dallas!*"

Hmm. When I applied, I listed San Antonio as a "highly preferred" region. I listed Dallas as a lower preference because my wife is from the DFW metroplex. I do not hold this against her; it's not her fault. But I had no intention of moving, especially with my wife still finishing graduate school with a job all but lined up in San Antonio. Not since Derek Fisher hit an impossible shot with four tenths of a second left in the 2004 Western Conference Finals had my hopes soared so high and fallen so low in such an instant. I scrambled to shoot off an e-mail to someone who could reverse course and keep me in San Antonio for the 2010–2011 school year. No dice. The train to San Antone was full. I requested a year-long deferral, taking a gamble that I could find a teaching job on my own the next school year, knowing the alternative certification process and knowing what content areas were in high need. Mercifully, TFA allowed me to defer a year until 2011–2012, but I needed a job in San Antonio sooner than that.

My Pre-TFA Year in the Classroom

It's morning in the middle of June at a teacher job fair, and I'm wearing a suit and carrying dozens of copies of my résumé and certification test results. I am "highly qualified" in two areas that I know are valuable—high school math and special education. But I'm nervous; I know that my unemployment benefits run out in August. If I don't get hired this summer, I won't be able to start teaching until the following year.

The two big suburban districts in San Antonio have lines that are as ungodly in their length as they are hopeless in their prospects. I shuffle towards the other booths, for the less glamorous districts considered either too far away or too dangerous by many applicants.

I snag coveted afternoon interviews with two schools. I try to convey that I know what I'm talking about despite my utter lack of experience. They both go well enough: One school wants to do a follow-up interview, and I'm feeling better about it.

But a couple of days later, I got a voicemail while I was in one of my certification classes. The principal from the other school, Kennedy High School, offered me a job to teach math.

I began my first year at Kennedy with some hesitation. I didn't know anything about the community I was about to serve. Anything I could tell you about Edgewood ISD was strictly academic. All I knew was that I would be teaching geometry in room 203. I had not looked at a high school geometry curriculum in 10 years. Except there was another call, this time from the vice principal, who asked if I would be interested in teaching the special education math classes. I agreed to the switch.

My first year as a teacher was like many first years. I taught resource math, provided only for students with Individualized Education Plans (IEPs) who receive modifications to the state standards. I had three classes: algebra I, geometry, and math models. I had small class sizes but struggled with classroom management, connecting with my students, and meeting their needs. I struggled the most with my freshmen. There were, at most, nine students, but a few students used my class as an opportunity to play the class clown or show their defiance. I was not well equipped to respond. I often let inappropriate behaviors slide, used whole-class punishments for the infractions of a few, and went home frustrated many evenings.

I leaned heavily on the experience my school had to offer, including that of my mentor teacher, who taught resource English and had been at the school for decades, my science counterpart, who loved to talk about the big picture, and the lead teacher and the school psychologist, whom I went to for a million and one questions about writing IEPs, running annual meetings, and how to do paperwork correctly. I could talk with anyone in our department about how they got specific students to work, how they responded if a student was being unruly, or how they prevented the unruliness.

But I could not have grown as a teacher without the support of my coach, Zenda. As part of being alternatively certified, I had a coach who was to make, at minimum, three visits during that first year. She must have doubled that number. She saw what was dysfunctional in my classroom, gave me concrete solutions, and kept coming back to make sure I had implemented them. I trusted her guidance. She had taught everything from elementary to high school and had been an instructional coach for another decade on top of that.

By year's end, I was starting to feel more comfortable, though by no means was I where I wanted to be. But I felt that this growth was my crowning achievement, and it was not possible without the support of the entire special education department and a determined coach.

By summer, I was looking forward to bringing these experiences with me as a new TFA corps member (CM). I took the last week of school off to attend TFA's Induction, an opening salvo for corps members in a region. I got to meet the other 2011 San Antonio corps members and get pumped for Institute at Rice University in Houston a week later. At last, I was finally a corps member. I came into Institute eager to learn new techniques to bring back to Kennedy the next year, ones that would be sure to work and catapult me into teaching superstardom.

There is a mythology surrounding TFA's Institute. The first part is true: It is a grind. There are long days with planned activities from dawn to dusk, and there are new corps members staying up until the wee hours of the morning finalizing lesson plans; the stress of teaching for the first time and the never-ending carousel of TFA staff observing you is real. The second part is not as true: Five weeks of training is nowhere close to adequate preparation for being a full-time teacher of record.

For my experience with the first part, I was lucky. I had already taught for a year, so going in front of a classroom full of students was not new to me. I also knew that working by yourself is a sucker's bet and quickly found that team teaching is an excellent working partnership. We divided up the work, and we never stayed up past midnight. When your first year has you balance three preps and a caseload of nearly 20 students, Institute feels like another day at the office.

I noticed something that gave me pause about how the organization staffs itself. I expected that the people working for TFA would be like the teachers and administrators I had in school, or like my mentor teacher. I expected decades of experience, the seen-it-all types. I expected people with kids, maybe grandkids. I was astonished to find that nearly everyone—from the regional director, to the regional staff, to the Institute staff—was younger than 30 years old. Few were married, and even fewer had kids. Most were 2-years-and-done TFA alumni, though a few were still practicing teachers. My corps member adviser (CMA)—the Institute position in charge of a group of about 10 to 12 teachers of the same content—had at least taught for 4 years, but as a chemistry teacher. We were to be teaching high school math for 1 month in Houston ISD during summer school.

This staffing practice was not limited to Institute. When corps members return to their regions, most members of regional staffs are called managers of teacher leadership development (MTLDs). This position, once known as program director (PD), serves more or less the same function, to coach corps members through their 2 years in TFA. The majority of these staffers are former TFA corps members, and they have typically put in their requisite 2 years of teaching before leaving the profession. I was open-minded, though. I didn't want to believe that after all this hype and all this ego-puffery, I would be led astray. I bought into the program.

The classroom management taught at Institute uses Lee Cantor's behavior management cycle. It's three steps in action: Give explicit directions, narrate the desired behaviors being done in the classroom, and issue consequences for students not complying. We were encouraged to come up with positive reinforcements for students who did comply.

I've never taught elementary school, so I can't say what the merits and limits of this system are in that setting. However, as a high school teacher, it felt too much like B. F. Skinner for my tastes. And while my students may like stickers and candy, it seemed to be a cheap way to enforce teacher compliance rather than help develop adult behaviors. Still, I bought a bag of Jolly Ranchers and concocted point systems, hoping that this would be the way to motivate more students.

Aside from the one-size-fits-all classroom management, Institute had a streamlined lesson planning template. At the beginning of the summer, we were given the final exam of the course we were teaching. In our case, a team of two pairs of teachers split up the test, and we set about making lessons corresponding to each question on the test. *In the most literal way possible, we were teaching to the test.*

The five-step lesson plan went as follows: Start with a hook to get students interested in the lesson and outline key points including vocabulary they will need for this lesson; introduce the new material ("I do"); follow with guided practice ("we do") in which the teacher leads examples done with the class; employ independent practice ("you do") in which students are to practice examples on their own while the teacher checks with individual students for understanding and compliance; and end with an exit ticket, in which all students demonstrate their understanding by completing a question identical in form if not content to the question they will see on the final.

All of this is to say that we were being groomed to be test-prep tutors. Everything from pedagogy to content had been broken down into formulaic steps to be repeated ad nauseum. The limitations of the 5 weeks were now laid bare, stripped of the gloss from the effervescent staffers. Everything rested on our ability to move the numbers up on standardized tests.

That leads me to the data trackers. We were all e-mailed an Excel spreadsheet created by TFA that we would input with data on our students and their day-to-day exit ticket progress and final exam performance. The data generated from these questions would allow us to be ranked and rated. There, in colorful numbers, would be the cold, hard truth of our successes and failures.

In retrospect, it's an obvious nod to the ideology of TFA. Always data-driven, TFA would seek out that which can be easily measured as the sole means of gauging teaching effectiveness. This was buttressed by TFA's incessant emphasis on setting "Big Goals," which were almost always based on state standardized test scores. The default was to aim for an 80% passing rate for all your students.

It was no wonder so many TFA staffers felt they had mastered teaching so quickly when they had mastered the game of test preparation. There was always a feedback loop supporting this notion. But perhaps I had been spoiled by my first year of teaching, because I began to question the default Big Goal. I knew what kind of passing rates were average in high school, especially for math, and they weren't anywhere near that 80% level for the Texas Assessment of Knowledge and Skills (TAKS) test. I also remember how my students did the previous year on the modified test.

I remember talking with my CMA about this concern, and she seemed to agree that this would be a stretch, not just in my particular case, but for many others as well. It seemed to me that TFA had a narrative that it asked its staffers to convey despite their better judgment. I drove home to San Antonio from Houston with a corps member who confessed that he was in it for the AmeriCorps stipend. I started to question the benevolence of the organization I had just joined.

For the next 2 years, I taught under the TFA banner. At first, I wore neckties regularly and spent hours poring over student data. I taught with a lot of intensity. I stressed the importance of tests a lot more. I started getting back humbling results on those tests and wondered why my TFA magic pixie dust wasn't working. That year, I was juggling three preps of coteaching, a special education caseload, an after-school debate team, and meetings for TFA and faculty. And I was getting off light! My TFA colleagues had the same burdens on top of all their certification courses.

What was all of this for? I better understood how to connect with students, but the intense focus on data drove a wedge between us. Students were disappointed by their results on high-rigor exams, which led to discouragement and disengagement. I felt the same way about the curriculum and how teacher-centered my whole approach was. I didn't feel like I was nurturing thinkers; I felt like I was drilling soldiers. And despite my sticking by my college-bound mantras, a lot of students tuned out that message.

I started to question everything. If my experience in TFA couldn't fix my problems as a teacher, couldn't fix schools, and couldn't keep teachers in those schools, what was the point of this? Is sending 80% of your students to college feasible or desirable if the job market isn't there to accommodate that many college graduates, to say nothing of the student loan debt? Had we been hoodwinked by the game of meritocracy, fooled into thinking that by fixing schools we could make the game of socioeconomic standing in the United States fair?

By my second year in TFA, my first in general education and third overall as a teacher, I was a touch jaded. I abandoned collecting student test data for TFA. I told my MTLD that I wanted to measure something else this year, something more qualitative. I wanted to develop empathy, curiosity; I wanted my students to feel successful and empowered outside the narrow band of multiple-choice tests. My MTLD, who is still a good friend to this day, rode with it. It was by no means a perfect school year, but even without the constant measurement, my students were still on par on end-of-the-year assessments.

By then, I had begun to see two sides of the organization. There was my region and the corps members I had taught alongside. I saw their talent and their heart and their dedication. But I saw a lot of them leave teaching, leave San Antonio, or leave both after their 2 years—and occasionally, before then.

And then I saw TFA, the organization. I saw a nonprofit raking in millions of dollars in donations to expand, from the likes of the Walton Family Foundation, a group committed to undermining the promise of public education through privatization. I saw an organization slow to make any significant changes to their training model that sends a revolving door of unprepared novices into communities that deserve the best. I saw teacher layoffs and school closings in Chicago and Philadelphia, and I saw no solidarity from TFA. The bloom fell off the rose.

By the time my 2 years in TFA were done, I was disillusioned. I distanced myself from the TFA narrative, criticizing them openly and directly. It felt righteous, perhaps sanctimonious at times. I sought out others online, first through blogging and then through Twitter. I found a voice and then a community of educators and activists who had different visions and priorities more in line with my own.

You might ask me, "After all this time foaming at the mouth, why aren't you calling for the end of TFA?" Maybe it's my tepid, wishy-washy, muddling nature, but this is where the ambivalence of this chapter comes in. Of all the things wrong with TFA, I'm not convinced that their swift obliteration would change anything.

TFA corps members don't teach in their placement schools for longer than a couple of years? Neither do most of their colleagues from outside TFA. Teach For America corps members are staffing cream-skimming charter schools while charter networks are bragging about doing more with less? Sure. But without TFA, charter schools would still find a way to churn out idealistic twenty-somethings. TFA corps members are encouraged to leave teaching quickly to pursue law school or political roles in order to further neoliberal reforms. This is happening. Go to Louisiana, Tennessee, New Jersey, and you'll see TFA alumni out there pushing test-based accountability and keeping a firm distance from teachers' unions. But if TFA fell off the map tomorrow, you don't think politicians could find a bevy of novice apparatchiks to be state superintendents in its wake? Not to mention the TFA alumni who are tried-and-true union supporters who don't get the same media time.

You levy any complaint that could possibly be thrown at TFA and there is a problem that has existed since the founding of our country (White racism) or a prevailing political ideology that was ascendant a decade prior to TFA's existence—neoliberalism, for example. Teach For America is neither the cause nor the cure for these issues, merely a symptom.

I'm ambivalent, caught between idealism and pragmatism, optimism and cynicism. In an ideal democracy, philanthropic billionaires like the Waltons, the Kochs, and Bill and Melinda Gates would not have undue influence to move policy. But they do, and they support TFA. Pragmatically, how do we make TFA a more just organization that builds real stability and makes teaching a viable career when the money supporting them doesn't care about that? I am optimistic that TFA can change, and I'm cynical enough to think they probably won't do more than public relations—proverbial paint jobs to rebrand the same lousy product.

The point I always come back to is: Can the nonprofit organization Teach For America help schools? Absolutely, but with some important caveats.

First, despite doggedly sticking to the formula of a few weeks training in the summer, the preservice requirement absolutely needs to be ramped up. TFA has a new pilot program in which applicants are accepted before their senior year of college, thus allowing them a full year of preparation before teaching. What that looks like in practice is unclear, but I think that's potentially a good start. Now they just need to make that year of preservice standard for all corps members.

Second, TFA needs to get out of the "leadership pipeline" business and into the grassroots education business. Elite college graduates don't need help becoming lawyers or doctors, and the world is not better served by having school and government leaders with a smidgen of teaching experience. I'd sooner have state superintendents with no teaching experience and the humility to listen to their constituents than 2-year novices who think they mastered teaching and are ready to tear the education world asunder. If TFA wants to foster authentic change in education, it needs to happen with people committed to serve their communities. It needs to be bottom-up, and it requires a stable teaching force to build the lasting connections with families and other community members. Our schools deserve better than the revolving door of twenty-somethings they are getting now from TFA.

Third, TFA needs to improve its organizational diversity. TFA is already making huge strides in this area, making the effort to recruit more corps members and staff members of color and more first-generation college students. In 2014, 50% of TFA's incoming corps members were teachers of color. I don't think this should be overlooked at all; TFA responded to criticism that its members were overwhelmingly White, teaching children overwhelmingly of color.

Now, in order to better serve schools and the corps members teaching them, TFA needs to go a step farther, hiring more pedagogically experienced staff members. Within TFA, corps members are being led almost exclusively by people whose only teaching experiences have been filtered through the TFA lens, and almost exclusively by people who have not taught very much. This cannot continue if TFA is going to encourage more teachers to stay and grow as educators.

Above all else, I want TFA to focus on the first word of its name. I want them to instill at every level of the organization what an honor and privilege it is to teach our students, and that 2-year commitments do not fulfill the obligation we have to them to deserve such an honor.

CHAPTER SEVEN

Teach For America, Neoliberalism, and the Effect on Special Education

IAN SCOTT
Los Angeles, 2011–2013

BIOSKETCH

Ian Scott is a Ph.D. student in the program on education policy and social outcomes at the University of Illinois at Urbana-Champaign. His research interests center on the impact of incentivist and market-based education reforms on special education programs and access to mental health services in schools. His work attempts to answer broader questions about how social perceptions of difference are legislated, problems of distributional politics, and the political economy of education. Ian also works with the Chicago Anti-Violence Education program of the Education Justice Project at the University of Illinois and Danville Correctional Center. Prior to beginning his doctoral studies, Ian worked as a resource specialist teacher in South Los Angeles, initially placed through Teach For America. He holds a M.A. in special education from Loyola Marymount University and a B.A. in political science from UC Berkeley.

NARRATIVE

The first Individualized Education Plan (IEP) deadlines of the school year were approaching rapidly—I had just 3 weeks to develop learning plans for multiple students with disabilities; these would highlight accommodations and strategies based on each child's individual needs that teachers could use to successfully include those students in their general education classrooms. There was just one problem: I had almost no training on how to do this. From the first day of teaching, it was uncomfortably clear I was in no way prepared for the job I was assigned to do. This realization was quickly accompanied by an overwhelming sense of guilt and anxiety. Children were dependent upon me to aid in making sure their educational needs were met; these were children who, to one degree or another, had been marginalized and excluded because of their disabilities, and I had no idea what I was doing. It felt like an absolute betrayal of the reason I joined Teach For America (TFA). I joined to improve an educational system I had dropped out of as a high school student. I joined to help build a system that focuses on the emotional well-being of children and treats them as more than just "outcomes." I joined to be the teacher I needed growing up. Instead, I found myself a cog in the machine of neoliberal education reform hell-bent on creating a system of marketized education that reduces students and their learning to notions of return-on-investment, market potential, and the elimination of education as a public good. In other words, I found myself propping up an even worse system than the one I had set out to combat.

The dominant narrative in American education is one of crisis. While recent research has shown this narrative to be context specific—most notably, that academic performance varies widely and is inextricably linked to poverty (Berliner, Glass, & Associates, 2014)—one area that is unequivocally in crisis is special education. According to the U.S. Department of Education's *Teacher Shortage Areas Nationwide Listing* (U.S. Department of Education Office of Postsecondary Education, 2014), 46 of 50 states face persistent shortages of special education teachers. Additionally, students with disabilities face some of the highest dropout rates, are more likely to face multiple suspensions and be removed from instructional time for behavior, have higher expulsion rates, are less likely to attend college or be fully employed following graduation, and are more likely to enter the criminal justice system at some point in their lives (Cortiella & Horowitz, 2014; Stetser & Stillwell, 2014; U.S. Department of Education, 2014). The students subjected to the systematic neglect that leads to such dismal outcomes are more often than not members of already marginalized communities in the United States. Research has demonstrated that students who are Black, Indigenous American, or English language learners are most likely to be singled out for special education placement, and these groups are overrepresented in special education programs across the country (Aud, Fox, & KewalRamani, 2010; Sullivan, 2011). Many in TFA refer to this situation euphemistically as the "gap within the [achievement] gap."

I quickly found myself in the middle of this crisis after joining TFA in 2011. Like many others, I joined TFA because of what I believed was an urgent need to defend the state of public education in the United States. As a high school dropout myself, I knew the barriers those without a high school diploma face, and since I was fortunate enough to defy the dismal odds of obtaining a college degree, I wanted to focus on improving the challenges I faced as a teenager. I quickly learned that my participation in TFA would not serve the purpose of bettering public education, but would instead help in further privatizing education in the United States. Nowhere is the detrimental impact of this ongoing privatization more apparent than in special education, where policies that reduce students to their potential economic utility naturally have disastrous effects on those society deems unable or unwilling to produce one's fair share of GDP growth—a status long laid at the feet of persons with disabilities, who are treated as economic burdens instead of people. The well-organized philanthropic and political support for charter schools, vouchers, and high-stakes testing has placed the most vulnerable population in the American educational landscape in an even more precarious position. While TFA seeks to improve training and ongoing support for corps members placed in special education settings (Kramer, 2014), any improvements made by the organization will continue to be negated by TFA's support for education reform policies that are antithetical to the goal of providing a just and equitable education for students with disabilities.

Teach for America and Neoliberal Education Reform

Many of TFA's supporters attempt to invalidate criticisms of the organization by pointing to instances where TFA has improved over the years. For the 2014–2015 academic year, nearly half of all new TFA teachers identify as persons of color, and another 47% will have received Pell Grants as undergraduates, an improvement from the prior year, when only 39% of new corps members were Pell Grant recipients or persons of color (Sawchuk, 2014). TFA has also begun piloting a program that will provide some incoming corps members with a full year of training prior to entering the classroom—though there is little information on what this training will look like or what the qualifications will be for those responsible for the training. Even if TFA were to fix these and other problems faced by special education and general education corps members, and overhaul their inadequate training program, it still would not remedy the fundamental harm caused by TFA. TFA's unfettered support for neoliberal education reform and charter schools[1] is so disadvantageous to students with disabilities as to make other factors, like the quality of the student's teacher, nearly irrelevant. As long as TFA is funneling corps members into charter schools, and, subsequently, into neoliberal policy centers, charter school administrations, schools of law, public policy, and education, and governmental offices, it doesn't matter how much training or support corps members are provided—they will serve the forces of privatization and marketization nonetheless, which is the truly devastating result of TFA for students with disabilities.

In its broadest terms, neoliberalism is a theory of political economy arguing the fundamental functions of democratic governance are improved when subjected to the free market, which allows private companies to compete to provide important social services. This competition, advocates of neoliberalism argue, improves service provision to citizens within a society (Harvey, 2005). Although founded in the 1960s Chicago school of economics, neoliberalism did not begin to fully appear in the policy debates around education until the 1990s. Lakes and Carter (2011) note that the apparent goal in integrating neoliberalism and education is to "convert educational systems into markets, and as much as possible privatize educational services" (p. 108). This ideology manifests itself in social policies creating voucher programs, charter schools, and an increased emphasis on individual accountability for teachers and students—irrespective of economics, race, disability, or any number of other relevant factors impacting a child's education—tracked through standardized testing regimes. Further, this opens schools to philanthro-capitalists, whom it is argued will use schools as laboratories of innovation that will, in turn, create new technologies, consumer products, and more productive workers.

Although TFA claims to be an apolitical organization that does not take an official stand on policies, if one looks at where teachers are being placed it is easy to infer where their support lies. For example, in my region of Los Angeles, over 90% of corps members are placed in charter schools in 2013, a number likely to be maintained as more corps members enter the region thanks to a large grant from the Walton Family Foundation (Blume, 2013). According to the *Washington Post*, the $20 million grant provided to TFA makes it the largest recipient in 2013 of funds from the Walton Family Foundation, which spent a total of $164 million pushing corporate education reforms and charter schools (deMarrais et al., 2013; Strauss, 2014). Further, according to a recent network analysis by Kretchmar, Sondel, and Ferrare (2014), "it is evident that TFA sits at the forefront of a powerful network of interdependent organizations, foundations, and individual leaders that play pivotal roles in the growth of charter school reform," and "It is increasingly clear that TFA's movement 'to end educational inequity' has become market-based and charter reform-driven" (p. 756). It is the policies advocated by organizations like the Walton Family Foundation and implemented by TFA that are further eroding the educational and human rights of persons with disabilities inside and outside the classroom.

The Impact of Teach for America's Neoliberalism on Students with Disabilities

Journalists and researchers in the United States have documented what happens to students with disabilities when education systems become saturated with charter schools and test scores determine whether a school is a success or failure. Dudley-Marling and Baker (2012) noted that students with disabilities often face multiple barriers to charter school enrollment, there is no guarantee students will receive the proper accommodations at charter schools, and students with more profound disabilities are "counseled out" to the local public schools that still maintain self-contained classes. The practice of counseling out violates the Individuals with Disabilities Education Improvement Act (IDEIA), which mandates that all public schools are responsible for providing the appropriate academic setting, accommodations, and supports as determined by the student's IEP. If a school does not have the proper resources to provide a needed service it cannot just send the student away, but is required to either obtain the service or fund the service through an outside agency or partnership with the local public school. Further, studies have indicated that parents of students with disabilities fare the worst in market-based systems because selection of special education programs is often based on a consideration of specialized factors that makes selecting the appropriate school for a student with disabilities incredibly difficult (Welner & Howe, 2005).

In major cities across the country, the de facto policy of "counseling out" students creates enrollment gaps in public schools and charters. The results are higher concentrations of students with disabilities in public schools when compared to charter schools serving the same communities, especially students with profound disabilities such as intellectual disabilities, Down Syndrome, or Autism Spectrum Disorders (Miron, Urschel, Mathis, & Torquist, 2010; Zollers & Ramanthan, 1998). Another tactic employed in neoliberal charter schools is the use of harsh disciplinary systems to send students away (Mock, 2010). In New Orleans' Recovery School District, made up almost exclusively of charter schools as of this writing, nearly one third of all students with disabilities received out of school suspensions or were placed in an alternative placement school. As detailed by the Southern Poverty Law Center (2012) in a complaint filed with the U.S. Department of Education Office of Civil Rights against the predominantly charter Jefferson Parish Public School System, "The average length of stay in JPPSS' alternative schools for students with disabilities is 223.9 days as compared to an average length of stay of 94.5 days for students without disabilities" (p. 2).

Another aspect of TFA's neoliberal education reform is an increased emphasis on standardized testing to measure student learning and increase teacher accountability. The first problem with this is there is evidence demonstrating the difficulty many students with disabilities have taking standardized tests when compared to their peers without disabilities. When students with disabilities do not score within the same range as their peers, the burden of failure is placed on the students, completely ignoring other systematic factors leading to the students' test performance. The second problem with the testing and accountability regime inherent to TFA's education reform is the resulting desirability of sending students with disabilities to other schools so their test scores will not impact teacher accountability measures. Specifically, schools will not want to enroll students who could potentially drag the school's averages down (Dudley-Marling & Baker, 2012).

The effects of TFA's free-market ideology on students with disabilities can also be seen outside of school. Inherent in the idea of neoliberal education reform is the assumption that the value of individuals is determined by their ultimate contribution to society, especially their economic contribution (Lakes & Carter, 2011). In this view, "school failure is firmly situated in the minds and bodies of individuals who are expected to 'overcome' their physical and mental disabilities with plenty of models provided of people who have done so" (Dudley-Marling & Baker, 2012, p. 14), and anyone who does not overcome their shortcomings has no one to blame but themselves. In the end, this logic leads to an educational system that reinforces existing social structures (Journell, 2011), which is harmful to marginalized populations. This, ultimately, denies the fundamental humanity of persons with disabilities.

Special Education Selection, Training, and Support: One Alumni's Experience

Leaving my undergraduate program in political science, I was better prepared to discuss the intricacies of electoral coalitions in sub-Saharan Africa than the appropriate academic interventions and accommodations for a teenager with autism. Yet, that did not stop TFA from charging me with such a responsibility. What made TFA decide to place me in special education was the simple act of checking a box on my TFA application stating I would be interested in learning more about special education placement options. I was not, nor was anyone else I talked to, contacted by TFA to discuss special education as a placement option; instead, TFA staff took our interest in working in special education as consent to place us in this setting. At no point were the requirements, requisite knowledge, challenges, or settings discussed prior to being presented with a "take it or leave it" offer. This practice pressures corps members to accept the placement offer regardless of what their comfort would have been had TFA offered information and a genuine choice. This TFA policy creates cohorts of incoming special education teachers who have no background in abnormal development, learning differences, or special education case management. This is a result of TFA's focus on leadership development over content knowledge or pedagogy, feeding the mindset that classrooms need "leaders" instead of teachers skilled in their subjects.

Regardless of one's subject placement, all corps members receive the same training during Summer Institute. At no point at no point during the Summer Institute was instruction provided on how to collect evidence and write IEP goals. While the Los Angeles region provided supplemental training immediately following Institute to cover some of these topics—as do some other regions—a few extra special education–specific sessions are not enough to compensate for the overall inadequacy of TFA's summer training program. Further, the lack of adequate training on educational best practices for students with disabilities is not limited to those corps members placed in special education given that most corps members teach in inclusive classrooms. The result for students with and without disabilities is a network of inadequately trained teachers unprepared to include and accommodate their learning needs.

Ongoing support for corps members is inconsistent in quantity and quality between and within placement regions. In addition to information on special education law and policy, special education teachers also require a wealth of specialized knowledge in the areas of developmental psychology, abnormal psychology, and pedagogical best practices for children with a vast array of disabilities. The development of this knowledge requires consistent, high quality support and training. While some people received close mentoring and support, others, like myself, rarely had any interaction with the persons supposed to be aiding our development as teachers. The TFA staff member assigned to develop my skills and knowledge as a special education teacher visited my school and classroom only a couple times over my 2 years as a corps member. The overwhelming majority of support I received came from the university where I completed my teaching credentials and master's degree; this was the type of support I could have received in the college's regular teacher education program regardless of my affiliation with TFA. Professional development with TFA focused more on developing "leaders" instead of teachers. Staff led development sessions were spent telling personal stories and relaying anecdotal evidence used to justify our positions in schools and console our consciences for the shortcomings that resulted from nothing more than a lack of adequate preparation. Much of this is because many TFA staff members themselves had spent no more than 2 to 3 years in the classroom before being placed in authoritative positions of teacher development. Despite being well aware of the organizational shortcomings that created these skills and knowledge deficits, I and many other corps members still felt personally guilty for how this lack of preparedness manifested in our classrooms.

The consistent lack of preparation, beginning from the moment one is offered a position in special education with TFA, creates overpowering levels of anxiety. The pathologies of inadequacy and guilt that develop from constantly feeling like a failure who is not doing the right thing for the students one signed on to help leads to teachers leaving the classroom, regardless of their initial intentions. This is a shame, because special education is a field in desperate need of radical reform. What is needed is a system that develops and supports new teachers in difficult fields like special education. Not only is TFA failing to do this, but their structures, procedures, and ideologies make them incapable of fulfilling this role.

CONCLUSION

The reality of special education in TFA is one of increasing segregation, isolation, and punishment. The charter schools being filled with new TFA recruits are doing no better at educating students, and in many cases are doing worse, than the public schools they were designed to replace (Center for Research on Education Outcomes, 2013). In spring 2014, TFA announced a new "Special Education and Ability Initiative" geared towards bettering educational outcomes for students with disabilities. While this sounds good, the rhetoric used to roll out the initiative belies its stated intentions. According to TFA (Brody, 2014), the reason students with disabilities are not succeeding is because these students do not "have teachers who believe in them, and who help them achieve at the highest levels." In this view, the problem is simply that no one has ever had high expectations for students with disabilities. This is just another example of how TFA lays the blame on individual teachers in underresourced schools, not on the systematic oppression faced by people with disabilities—the same system that did not even guarantee the right to an education in public schools for a child with a disability until the passage of the Education for All Handicapped Children Act of 1975, more than 2 decades after schools were ordered to desegregate on the basis of race.

The rights of persons with disabilities have not improved dramatically since then, particularly in public education, and disability rights advocates are correct to continue pushing for greater reforms in education for students with disabilities. However, supporting an organization that reduces people to numbers and judges their worth based on work output is not the way to alleviate the systematic oppression of students with disabilities. TFA apologists attempt to deflect the type of criticism presented here with charges that critiques of TFA are rooted in one's individual dissatisfaction with their time as a corps member. The problematic aspects of TFA I discovered as a corps member are due to the organization's advancement of a neoliberal ideology that undermines the idea of education as a public good, and this would be true regardless of my personal experience. This isn't an issue of one's individual experiences within TFA—the cumulative detrimental effect of TFA's ideological platform far outweighs any individual's positive or negative experience. As long as TFA advances a reform agenda based foundationally on neoliberalism, the rights of students with disabilities will continue to be in jeopardy.

REFERENCES

Aud, S., Fox, M., & KewalRamani, A. (2010). *Status and trends in the education of racial and ethnic groups* (NCES 2010–015). U.S. Department of Education, National Center for Education Statistics. Washington, DC: U.S. Government Printing Office.

Berliner, D. C., Glass, G. V., & Associates. (2014). *50 myths and lies that threaten America's public schools: The real crisis in education.* New York: Teachers College Press.

Blume, H. (2013, July 31). Grant to put 700 teachers in L.A. *Los Angeles Times.* Retrieved from http://articles.latimes.com/2013/jul/31/local/la-me-0731-teachers-grant-20130731

Brody, R. (2014, March 21). Holding high expectations for all students [Web log comment]. Retrieved from http://www.teachforamerica.org/blog/holding-high-expectations-all-students

Center for Research on Education Outcomes. (2013). *National charter school study 2013.* Stanford, CA. Retrieved from http://credo.stanford.edu/documents/NCSS%202013% 20Final%20Draft. pdf

Cortiella, C., & Horowitz, S. H. (2014). *The state of learning disabilities: Facts, trends and emerging issues.* New York: National Center for Learning Disabilities.

deMarrais, K., Wenner, J., & Lewis, J. B. (2013). Bringing Teach for America into the forefront of teacher education: Philanthropy meets spin. *Critical Education, 4(11),* 1–27.

Dudley-Marling, C., & Baker, D. (2012). The effects of market-based school reforms on students with disabilities. *Disability Studies Quarterly, 32.*

Harvey, D. (2005). *A brief history of neoliberalism.* New York: Oxford University Press.

Journell, W. (2011). Teaching the 2008 presidential election at three demographically diverse schools: An exercise in neoliberal governmentality. *Educational Studies, 47,* 133–159.

Kramer, M. (2014, March 28). Teach For America launches special education and ability initiative [Editorial]. *The Huffington Post.* Retrieved from http://www.huffingtonpost.com/matt-kramer/teach-for-america-launche_b_ 5042388.html

Kretchmar, K., Sondel, B., & Ferrare, J. J. (2014). Mapping the terrain: Teach For America, charter school reform, and corporate sponsorship. *Journal of Education Policy, 29,* 742–759.

Lakes, R. D., & Carter, P. A. (2011). Neoliberalism and education: An introduction. *Educational Studies, 47(2),* 107–110.

Miron, G., Urschel, J. L., Mathis, W. J., & Torquist, E. (2010). *Schools without diversity: Education management organizations, charter schools and the demographic stratification of the American school system.* Boulder, CO and Tempe, AZ: Education and the Public Interest Center & Educational Policy Research Unit. Retrieved from http://epicpolicy.org/publication/schools-without-diversity

Mock, B. (2010, October 6). New Orleans accused of failing disabled students. *Newsweek.* Retrieved from http://www.newsweek.com/2010/10/06/new-orleans-accused-of-failing-disabled-students. html

Sawchuk, S. (2014, August 14). Diversity on the rise among TFA recruits. *Education Week*. Retrieved from http://blogs.edweek.org/edweek/teacherbeat/2014/08/diversity_on_the_rise_among_tf.html

Southern Poverty Law Center. (2012). W. P. on behalf of J. P., E. B. on behalf of C. B., Q. B. on behalf of D. S., and J. W. on behalf of G. A., and all, similarly situated students v. Jefferson Parish Public School system and the Jefferson Parish School Board. Complaint under Title VI of the Civil Rights Act of 1964, § 504 of the Rehabilitation Act of 1973, and Title II of the Americans with Disabilities Act Before the United States Department of Education Office for Civil Rights. Retrieved from http://www.splcenter.org/sites/default/files/downloads/case/complaint_0.pdf

Stetser, M., & Stillwell, R. (2014). *Public high school four-year on-time graduation rates and event drop-out rates: School years 2010–11 and 2011–12*. First Look (NCES 2014–391). U.S. Department of Education. Washington, DC: National Center for Education Statistics.

Strauss, V. (2014, April 2). Walton Foundation pours $164 million in 2013 education grants. Who won? *The Washington Post*. Retrieved from http://www.washingtonpost.com/blogs/answer-sheet/wp/2014/04/02/walton-foundations-pours-164-million-in-2013-education-grants-who-won/

Sullivan, A. L. (2011). Disproportionality in special education identification and placement of English language learners. *Exceptional Children*, 77, 317–334.

U.S. Department of Education. (2014, January). *Guiding principles: A resource guide for improving school climate and discipline*. Washington, DC. Retrieved from www2.ed.gov/policy/gen/guid/school-discipline/guiding-principles.pdf

U.S. Department of Education Office of Postsecondary Education. (2014, March). *Teacher shortage areas: Nationwide listing, 1990–1991 through 2014–2015*. Washington, DC. Retrieved from http://www2.ed.gov/about/offices/list/ope/pol/tsa.doc

Welner, K. G., & Howe, K. R. (2005). Steering towards separation: The policy and legal implications of "counseling" special education students away from charter schools. In J. T. Scott (Ed.), *School choice and diversity: What the evidence says* (pp. 93–111). New York: Teachers College Press.

Zollers, N., & Ramanthan, K. (1998). For-profit charter schools and students with disabilities: The sordid side of the business of schooling. *Phi Delta Kappan*, 80, 297–304.

NOTE

1. I differentiate between "public schools" and "charter schools" for the clarity of argument. It should be noted that "charter schools" refers to public charter schools that receive state and federal funding and are responsible for enrolling all eligible students regardless of need.

Section II:
TFA's Approach to Diversity

CHAPTER EIGHT

Dysconscious Racism, Class Privilege, and TFA

SARAH ISHMAEL
Baton Rouge, 2010–2013

BIOSKETCH

Sarah Ishmael is an Afro-Caribbean woman and first-generation American. She is the proud daughter of a retired U.S. Army colonel and an entrepreneur, both of whom moved to the States and worked to give their daughter an exceptionally bright future. Sarah is a second-year M.Ed. student in the Education Planning and Policy program at the University of Texas at Austin. Prior to her graduate studies, she earned a B.A. from the Fairhaven College of Interdisciplinary Studies at Western Washington University. She then completed the Teach For America program in Baton Rouge, Louisiana. She taught elementary and middle school for 3 years. Her research interests include policy implementation in minority communities, critical race theory, critical multiculturalism, and relationships between political bodies, schools, and community stakeholders.

NARRATIVE

"Stories by people of color," Gloria Ladson-Billings writes, "can catalyze the necessary cognitive conflict to jar dysconscious racism"[1] (Ladson-Billings & Tate, 2006, p. 21). The purpose of my narrative is to create such cognitive conflict. I am an Afro-Caribbean woman, a first-generation American whose grandparents moved her mother and father from Trinidad and Tobago for better life opportunities. I have lived in six states but grew up in a majority White town in Washington State. The daughter of an Army colonel and an entrepreneur, I grew up in the borderlands[2] of socioeconomic privilege, racial exclusion, and tokenism.

My resilient parents and supportive mentors have loved me through my stumbling and navigating these borderlands. They still do. Despite their support, I still trip and fall. As a first-year Teach For America (TFA) alumni in Baton Rouge, Louisiana, I woke up one morning exhausted after a sleepless night worrying about the problems I had connecting with my students. I thought about my own frustrations in school. Growing up, I resented people who rejected me because I did not fit into White middle-class norms. I had sworn that I would never make anyone else feel that way. As I got ready for work that morning I reflected on a conversation I had with a student the previous day. I realized that our discussion about his grades probably made him feel exactly like I did when I was younger, like no matter how much I tried, I would never measure up. But this time, it was not a White person telling me what I needed to do to be considered appropriate. It was an Afro-Caribbean TFA teacher who, despite her good intentions, made him feel that way.

Writing helps me reflect on and learn from my experiences in TFA. "Living in a state of psychic unrest," I follow Anzaldúa's (2012) lead, and through my writing, dig at the cactus needle embedded in my own heart. I write to "get deep down into the place where it is rooted in my flesh and pluck away at it" (Anzaldúa, 2012, p. 95). The cognitive dissonance I experienced as a corps member in TFA allowed me to see that cactus needle. This narrative is one of the many ways in which I try to get down to the root of that needle and find out how it got lodged there in the first place.

Systems of inequality graft themselves onto our lives every day. They touch us at the most personal levels (Alexander, 2006, p. 275). In other words, "It means that we are all defined in some relationship to them, in some relationship to hierarchy" (Alexander, 2006, p. 275). We are *all* responsible for accepting our roles as cultural actors, especially in a world with sociopolitical roots historically cut and carved by European colonial governments. We are all responsible for understanding how we exist in and perpetuate the social hierarchies we try to fight. Writing is one of the ways I take responsibility. Though my writing *is* critical it is *not* a blanket condemnation of TFA or those affiliated with the program. I share my story because it is instructive. As advocates for social justice, we must be accountable *to* those we affect for the *way* we affect them. This is my way of holding the organization and myself accountable for the impact we have on students in the classroom.

Critical scholars and social justice advocates criticize TFA for many things. They criticize the organization for failing to adequately equip corps members with the cultural competence to work in low-income minority communities (Bybee,

2013; Darling-Hammond, 1994; Lapayese, Aldana, & Lara, 2014). Anderson (2013) states that TFA operates from a deficit perspective. TFA, critics claim, creates a "savior" complex in their corps members (Popkewitz, 1998). Indeed, many compare TFA's philosophy to the "White Man's Burden" theory of change (see, for example, Césaire, 2000) in which the colonizer (upper-middle-class, mainly White corps members) takes pity on the colonized (minority students in low-income communities) and offers "help" by providing them with a "transformational education" (Stern & Johnston, 2013, p. 8).

My narrative illuminates and adds context to these criticisms. My story makes visible the ways in which TFA ignores underlying racial and class dynamics and perpetuates institutional racism in classrooms. It challenges the organization's dedication to racial equity and its ability to break down class barriers between corps members and their students. I weave research and parts of my personal history and experience in TFA together to illustrate how TFA's philosophy, based on achievement ideology (MacLeod, 2009), works in tandem with class privilege and insufficient training to perpetuate deficit thinking and structural racism in classrooms. My racial identity, experience as a cultural outsider, and socialization in upper-middle-class White society allows me to provide a story with enough cognitive conflict to offer a valuable perspective on how TFA and its corps members perpetuate dysconscious racism.

I remember writing my letter of interest to Teach For America:

> My objective as a teacher will be to help students take responsibility for their own learning. Success as a corps member looks like a student who is able to consciously analyze her circumstances, take ownership of her academic experience and find the support to rise above the deeply internalized lessons borne from inequity and hardship.

It is very difficult for me to read that letter today. TFA claims they try to change social class dynamics that largely determine one's access to education, resources, and social mobility. However, they do not acknowledge how they themselves reinforce class divisions. They need to. Most corps members have benefitted from being members of the upper-middle class or having access to upper-middle-class resources and opportunities (Labaree, 2010, p. 54). This is exceptionally important to understand; this privilege not only gave us access to elite programs like TFA but also buffers the effects of structural racism and classism in this country. It certainly mitigated the role institutional racism played in my life as a child and young adult. The uncritical lens I developed as a young adult became a problem for my students in the classroom; in fact, it became a problem that many students had with corps members in my region. It is a problem that I know affects students taught by TFA corps members across the nation. TFA specifically places corps members in low-income, majority minority schools (Anderson, 2013), but they have not effectively taken responsibility for *ensuring* that corps members have a truly critical understanding of race, class, White privilege, and the historically racist roots of educational inequity.

I took many classes about diversity and race in college and had many mentors who tried to help me build a critical understanding of race and privilege in this country. Yet, it was still an abstract concept. My own socioeconomic privilege distorted the effects of structural racism I experienced. The interactions I had with corps members during my experience led me to believe that very few of us had internalized a conscious, critical understanding of the history behind poverty, racism, and class in this country. Our cultural conditioning blinded us.

A critical understanding of race and racism in this country creates a consciousness that does not implicitly accept dominant White norms and privileges (King, 1991). Despite multiple classes on race, racism, and equality, I got the impression that very few corps members, including myself, had direct experience with structural racism, or had the language to name it when we experienced it. This type of dysconscious racism (King, 1991) perpetuates uncritical ways of thinking about racial inequity. This means we accept culturally sanctioned assumptions, myths, and beliefs that justify the status quo resulting from a history of colonization and economic exploitation. We are not aware of the deeply internalized assumptions, myths, and beliefs about minorities' communities we bring into the classroom.

I believed in the culture of poverty myth (Payne, 2003). I believed in meritocracy and achievement ideology because I was never deeply challenged to succeed without the opportunities social class and proximity to Whiteness gave me. I told our students they too could "succeed" if they just *"took responsibility for their own learning, rose above deeply internalized lessons borne from inequity and hardship and worked hard."* I was not alone.

Born in a post–civil rights era (but certainly not a postracial era) of intellectual conservatism and free-market solutions to social problems, it is hard for many of us to accept our role in perpetuating dysconscious racism. It is not fun, pleasant, or easy. As an Afro-Caribbean woman caught between constantly battling structural racism and benefitting from socioeconomic privilege, it is something I struggle with every day. I fight it and find ways to minimize the way I perpetuate it at the same time. "Both complicity and vigilance," M. Jacqui Alexander writes, "are learned in the process of figuring out who we are…the far more difficult thing has to do with the political positions that we come to practice" (Alexander, 2006, p. 272). Writing this narrative and encouraging others to reflect and write on this subject is not easy. It will never be easy, but for our students' sake, it is important that we do.

I start with my own personal history. My father and mother immigrated with their families to the United States from Trinidad and Tobago. They met and married in New York City. My father lived in Brooklyn; my mother lived in Queens. My father's family moved in shifts; at the ages of 12 and 13 my father and uncle lived in a boardinghouse until my grandmother and aunt could join them in New York. My mother's family moved to the States when she was 22 years old. My grandparents on both sides of the family moved them from the islands to the United States for a better life. What I bet they did not know was that they also moved to a country where institutionalized racism is normative and socioeconomic mobility depends on one's ability to assimilate. Indeed, one's access to economic resources in this country depends on one's proximity to White skin and ability to assimilate into White epistemology.

You could say that my family is one of the ones that "made it." Instead of waiting for the government to call his draft number, my father joined ROTC and became an officer in the Army—one of the first societal structures forced to integrate. He eventually worked his way up to full colonel, earning a Ph.D. in the process. My mother, after dropping out of high school to work, finished her associate's degree and opened her own business. My parents worked hard not because they are "highly motivated," but because non-Whites in America must work twice as hard to obtain half the stability that Whites in this country have access to. People of color are not the only ones who struggle with economic stability in the United States, but there are differences in how we experience and deal with these issues. My family's success is an example of the rare case in which non-White people navigated a racialized society in ways our White counterparts deem "successful."

Institutional racism was and still is ever present. It's in our courts, our tax system, and our political subdivisions. My parents learned firsthand that it was in our schools. "The unconscious but automatic assumption your teachers were making," my father told me, "was that Black people were inferior. They were lowering their expectations for you, they did not see the need to challenge you." Dissatisfied with my teachers and school, my parents chose to move to a majority White community in the Northwest with an excellent school system. My father, reminiscing on his experience with school counselors in inner-city New York, told me that they tried to dissuade him from attending an elite engineering school, claiming that "other schools" had the type of education he needed. "I never wanted that to happen to you. I wanted you to have opportunity to succeed. I wanted you to go to a school where your intelligence would be recognized and where the teachers would not unconsciously lower their expectations of you." We were lucky enough to have the financial resources to move to a school district with teachers who had high expectations of me.

As TFA corps members, we learned the dangers of lowering our expectations of our students at Institute. We learned the dangers of deficit thinking. The "diversity sessions," however, discussed deficit thinking at a surface level, and always within the context of achievement ideology and meritocracy. They had us read articles that linked the "achievement gap" to race and class. We read articles that warned us against lowering our expectations of students because of their "personal situations." Most of the sessions, though, failed to explain White privilege and the roots of deficit thinking in supremacist ideology. In her research on the cultural competency of preservice corps members, Bybee (2013) found that not only had TFA failed to distinguish between critical scholarly and lay definitions of privilege, but also the materials they used in diversity sessions created misunderstandings about the nature of privilege and what communities of color were like. They allowed corps members to treat the cultural differences between their students as deficits by emphasizing the importance of teaching students to rise above their communities' "low expectations of them" (Bybee, 2013, p. 13). Her evaluation of TFA's training materials and process resonated with my experience as a corps member. Many of us thought we could encourage students and criticize their communities; we did not identify that as deficit thinking.

We live in a society in which media, propaganda, and reports unconsciously shape the way we as people of color think about ourselves. TFA fails to interrupt this mainstream cultural mythology. The organization claims that it cannot fix society's problems with race or class, but they can stop contributing to them. They can train their corps members to develop this critical consciousness so that they question what they think about non-White people, racism, poverty, and access to education. They can make sure that frustrated corps members do not place the blame on families that "don't prepare their children for school." They can make sure that they do not place blame on non-TFA teachers (mostly of color) who "don't care," or worse, on the students themselves when they refuse to buy into achievement ideology. They can do this, so students in corps members' classrooms do not have to.

TFA and Social Class

We also live in a society in which class divisions warp our relationships with each other and disproportionally stratify opportunities in this country. Social class largely determines success or failure in school (MacLeod, 2009, p. 149). Schools serve as the trading post where socially valued cultural capital is translated into superior academic performance. I accrued socially valued cultural capital because I had access to opportunities that my students did not. I was in honors classes at my high school. I was captain of the debate team at one point and involved with Model United Nations. I also enrolled in advanced placement classes, and I took courses at the local community college for dual credit.

I had great teachers, but none so *transformational* as living in a privileged, safe, and secure community with money to support myself. My family's economic stability and access to these opportunities helped me accrue the cultural capital and habitus (MacLeod, 2009) that the exclusive and prestigious TFA (Labaree, 2010;

Stern & Johnson, 2013) seeks in their applicants. As TFA handily demonstrates, my cultural capital was then turned into economic capital by the acquisition of a job and access to TFA's professional network that leads to even more jobs (MacLeod, 2009).

TFA encourages corps members and alumni to pursue careers opening up these types of opportunities to students. They acknowledge that lack of opportunity hinders student success. The problem is that TFA does not acknowledge or explain to students and their families that corps members' brief time in the classroom is another one of those "opportunities" that becomes capital to advance careers. Corps members need to take responsibility for benefitting from a system that allows them *the opportunity* to teach these students; an opportunity that the students themselves might never have. We cannot ethically work to provide students opportunities for academic and social advancement and simultaneously refuse to acknowledge that coming into their lives for 2 years helps corps members build their own careers.

My First Day as a Teacher

I remember preparing for my first day as a teacher. I was ready to show my students that they too could *achieve*. My students were hilarious. Intelligent. Brighter than I ever was in school, and more motivated. They were not impressed with me. Neither were their parents. Students whose families have tenuous connections to forms of cultural capital highly valued by the school tend to blame themselves for their failures (MacLeod, 2009), but my students never saw themselves as failures. They did not see themselves as victims of the system. I did. And their parents knew that. Can you imagine what it must feel like to know that the person teaching your child thinks of them and of you as victims? That a young, privileged, and on top of that, *Black* woman saw you and your child as products of "unfortunate" circumstances? Yet, there I was: ready to Teach For America.

I am Black. But I am also someone who grew up in upper-middle-class White society. I was consistently rewarded for my ability to assimilate into White culture. TFA saw my success as a minority as a model for other minority students. Like many of my fellow corps members, however, I did not know how to handle students who resisted attempts to "save them" by instilling a no excuses, "big goals" culture. My acculturation into White upper-middle-class society led me to interpret my students' actions as misbehavior instead of a difference of experience and worldview. I did not learn how to create a classroom where my students' personalities and culture were valued and seen until my third year of teaching. My Blackness, and the presumption that it would allow me to automatically connect with my students, did not make me a "natural" in the classroom.

Ultimately, our differences did not completely obstruct my ability to teach or bond with my students, but we did struggle. My students saw every day what I could not see without guidance—that meritocracy is a constructed myth, and that test scores were not going to suddenly enfranchise my students in a world where only half the graduating seniors were accepted into state colleges. I needed effective instruction in interrogating our differences and similarities and how to build meaningful, authentic relationships—and my students gave it to me.

My students gave a lot. They dealt with many different changes in campus administration; they dealt with novice teachers who did not know what they were teaching; they dealt (and still deal) with so much more than I can fathom. My students and their parents were tired, angry, and burnt out from dealing with the instability—and after my third year, so was I. Sheer exhaustion and unquantifiable anger forced me to finally admit that you couldn't "backwards plan" students out of poverty or the incredible burdens put upon them. Eventually I left for graduate school. I was burnt out. Many of us who do leave the classroom cannot ignore how we contributed to the destabilization of our students' school by leaving.

My students interrupted everything I thought I knew about who I was, why I was there, and what TFA was doing in their community. They should not have had to. Too often, those with privilege come away "inspired" by what kids who face incredible barriers in their lives teach us. Too often, we view it as a "blessing," an "epiphany," and "the reason we fight so hard for them today." But the thing is, people of color, people who have been legally and economically disenfranchised, should never have to educate their more privileged counterparts about what it's like to be oppressed. Children should never have to show their teachers why and how their "no excuses" culture is harmful and based on deficit thinking.

My narrative is not indicative of every corps member's experience. It is, however, very important. Discussing my own class privilege, the privilege I gain from my proximity to Whiteness, and how it affected my relationships with students opens the door for others to do the same. This is not a blanket condemnation of TFA or those who work for the organization. I know many corps members who see TFA for what it is and use it, like any other organization in this racialized hierarchical society, to do some good. That does not excuse the *organization* for allowing deficit thinking and institutionalized racism and classism to bleed into the classroom.

TFA needs to prepare its corps members to interrogate what they believe about non-White people and our children. They need to use definitions of privilege that do not obscure the racist roots of educational inequity. To combat challenges students face with corps members in their classroom, TFA needs to guide corps members through understanding their privilege based on their Whiteness or proximity to Whiteness. Diversity sessions need to discuss how that, coupled with class privilege, perpetuates deficit thinking and harms the very students they claim to help. National leadership needs to reassess the program and question whether they are implicitly supporting the "White Man's Burden" theory of change (Stern & Johnston, 2013), and how that affects the communities that TFA specifically targets.

Digging deep into our own dysconscious racism and class privilege is challenging. It is a process that requires self-compassion, accountability, and honesty. I cannot stress this enough. It is a *process*; and it is necessary. There is a cost that comes with putting into classrooms people who do not have a critical understanding of race and racism in this country. There is a cost when you fail to carefully interrogate your own privilege and the benefits you receive from it, and the expectations you have for others based upon your own class advantage and proximity to Whiteness—and at the same time remain in the classroom. Too many students know that cost. I still trip over borderlands of privilege and institutional racism, but I remain vigilant. I keep digging at that cactus needle in my heart, uncomfortable with the knowledge that it may never fully dislodge, but grateful for the cognitive dissonance that ensures that I will never make another student feel the way I made my student feel that day in Louisiana. I have dedicated myself to practicing vigilance. To make sure that I do not perpetuate dysconscious racism, that I do my best to interrupt social hierarchies and stay honest about the privilege that benefits me and disadvantages others. I need Teach For America to do the same.

REFERENCES

Alexander, J. M. (2006). *Pedagogies of crossing: Meditations on feminism, sexual politics, memory, and the sacred.* Durham, NC: Duke University Press.

Anderson, A. (2013). Teach For America and the dangers of deficit thinking. *Critical Education, 4*(11), 28–47.

Anzaldúa, G. (2012). *Borderlands/La Frontera: The new mestiza* (4th ed.). San Francisco: Aunt Lute.

Bybee, E. R. (2013). An issue of equity: Assessing the cultural knowledge of pre-service teachers in Teach For America. *Critical Education, 4*(13), 28–44.

Césaire, A. (2000). *Discourse on colonialism.* New York: Monthly Review Press.

Darling-Hammond, L. (1994). Who will speak for the children? How "Teach For America" hurts urban schools and students. *Phi Delta Kappan 76*(1), 21–34.

Gordon, J. A. (2000). *The color of teaching.* London: Routledge-Falmer.

Grant, G. (1973). Shaping social policy: The politics of the Coleman report. *Teachers College Record, 75*(1), 17–54.

Kantor, H. (1991). Education, social reform, and the state: ESEA and federal education policy in the 1960s. *American Journal of Education, 100*(1), 47–83.

King, J. (1991). Dysconscious racism: Ideology, identity and the miseducation of teachers. *Journal of Negro Education, 60*(2), 133–146.

Labaree, D. (2010). Teach For America and teacher ed: Heads they win, tails we lose. *Journal of Teacher Education, 61*(1–2), 48–55.

Ladson-Billings, G., & Tate, W. F. (2006). Towards a critical race theory of education. In A. Dixson & C. Rousseau (Eds.), *Critical race theory in education: All god's children got a song* (pp. 11–31). New York: Routledge.

Lahann, R., & Reagan, E. M. (2011). Teach For America and the politics of progressive neoliberalism. *Teacher Education Quarterly, 38*(1), 7–27.

Lapayese, Y., Aldana, U., & Lara, E. (2014). A racio-economic analysis of Teach For America: Counterstories of TFA teachers of color. *Perspectives on Urban Education, 11*(1), 11–25.

Leonardo, Z. (2004). The color of supremacy: Beyond the discourse of "White privilege." *Educational Philosophy and Theory, 36*(2), 137–152.

MacLeod, J. (2009). *Ain't no makin it: Aspirations and attainment in a low-income neighborhood* (3rd ed.). Philadelphia: Westview Press.

Maier, A. (2012). Doing good and doing well: Credentialism and Teach For America. *Journal of Teacher Education, 63*(1), 10–22.

Payne, R. K. (2003). *A framework for understanding poverty.* Highlands, TX: aha! Process.

Popkewitz, T. S. (1998). *Struggling for the soul: The politics of schooling and the construction of the teacher.* New York: Teachers College Press.

Schneider, M. (2013, March 27). Former-TFAers-gone-LDOE-leaders: Incompetence at a premium. Retrieved from http://deutsch29.wordpress.com/2013/03/27/former-tfaers-gone-ldoe-leaders-incompetence-at-a-premium/

Skerrett, A. (2008). Biography, identity and inquiry: The making of teacher, teacher educator and researcher. *Studying Teacher Education, 4*(2), 143–156.

Smith, L. (2012). *Decolonizing methodologies.* New York: Zed Books.

Stern, M., & Johnston, D. K. (2013). I want to do Teach For America, not become a teacher. *Critical Education, 4*(13), 1–27.

NOTES

1. Dysconscious racism refers to tacitly accepting dominant White norms and privileges without calling racial privilege into question (King, 1991).
2. *Borderlands* is a term developed by Gloria Anzaldúa. To live in the borderlands means to live in multiple spaces and no space at the same time—between different cultures.

CHAPTER NINE

Perpetuating, Committing, and Cultivating Racism: The Real Movement Behind TFA

AMBER KIM
Metro Atlanta, 2001–2003

BIOSKETCH

Amber K. Kim earned her Ph.D. in curriculum and instruction from the University of Denver in June 2012. Her mixed methods research evaluated Colorado Teach For America (TFA) corps members' cultural competencies and beliefs about culturally responsive pedagogy. Amber is currently an education consultant who is passionate about promoting critical and culturally responsive pedagogy, helping educators reflect on and redress inequity in education environments, curricula, practices, and policies. She consults on innovative school/program designs that are student-driven, democratic, restorative, and project-based. She has worked with Tulsa Public Schools and San Francisco Unified School District, as well as Denver School of Science and Technology. Amber taught for 10 years in three cities—Chicago, Atlanta (corps member, 2001), and Denver. Most recently, Amber became a lecturer for the Universities of Colorado Boulder and Denver, where she teaches differentiated instruction and curriculum theory, respectively. She is a mother of three, a fat-cat lover, and a competitive kick-kickboxer.

NARRATIVE

> People know about the Klan and the overt racism, but the killing of one's soul little by
> little, day after day, is a lot worse than someone coming in your house and lynching you.
> — Samuel L. Jackson

I joined Teach For America (TFA) to be part of "the Movement" to end education inequity. Growing up in low-income schools in the south suburbs of Chicago, I sincerely, albeit naively, believed education was the great equalizer. TFA's
mission statement resonated in my mind and heart: "One day all children in this
nation will have the opportunity to obtain an excellent education." I accepted as
true—and TFA was quick to confirm—the myth that all that poor students (of
color) need is what affluent (White) students have: access to *great* schools with
the *best* teachers that hold students to *high* expectations. I believed that by joining
TFA, and teaching in an "underprivileged" school, I could provide students the
"excellent education" needed to end inequity. In the years since my TFA experience, though, I have come to know that the problem of education inequity is not
that simply defined or solved. I have come to acknowledge and recognize color-
blind racism and to see how it undergirds educational inequity. TFA, in my view,
perpetuates, commits, and cultivates this kind of covert racism. TFA *is* a movement. It recruited, used, and grew my racism, leading me to uphold the dominant
culture's notion of who is "educated" and to force the assimilation of my students
into such beliefs—no excuses. So I wonder, if TFA moved me and my students
backwards (in terms of equity and liberation), has it also moved other students,
corps members, schools, and, most importantly, education reform in this nation in
the wrong direction?

Teach for Leveling the Playing Field—TFA Recruitment Poster

TFA's method made perfect sense to me when I joined: (1) Recruit hardworking, high-expectation-holding, Ivy League–educated future leaders (usually not
education majors) to teach in low-income schools; (2) provide underprivileged
students an excellent education through corps members' sheer "grit," intelligence,
and the drive to never fail; (3) raise underprivileged students' test scores and close
the achievement gap; and, (4) utilize TFA alumni as leaders to create policies to
ensure that *all* children have access to an "excellent education." Simple. Movement
in the right direction.

Yes, TFA recruits leaders, and, yes, some of these leaders facilitate "significant academic gains." These gains seemingly close the achievement gap for the
students they serve, but this is a flawed standard for success. While it is true
that students of color and low socioeconomic status have been denied rigorous,

test-score-producing educations for generations (Ladson-Billings, 2006), the problem cannot be found in the achievement gap or the "unleveled field." It is more pervasive, insidious, and complex than test scores, and so is the solution. We must go beyond the creation of teachers and policies that ensure a level field. Instead, we must recognize the rigged, racist game—and then commit to being game changers in classrooms and society. Anything less recruits others to perpetuate racism.

Racism without Racists Is Still Racism

Just because the racism is not overt does not mean that racism is not there. The racism in my counter narrative is a new racism, one that has replaced the overt racism of slavery and Jim Crow. It is a racism that Bonilla-Silva (2006) described in his book *Racism without Racists: Color-Blind Racism and the Persistence of Racial Inequality in the United States.* Bonilla-Silva expressed that we live in a society where few people claim to be racist or even admit that they see color; yet, African American people still experience segregation and oppression, and constantly receive the message that they are "lesser." This daily oppression of people of color (and the privileging of Whiteness) is ignored, unrecognized, or accepted by the dominant culture. Furthermore, Whites have developed flexible frames or ways of thinking, saying, and doing that allow them to accept this White supremacy while still feeling "not racist" (Bonilla-Silva, 2006).

TFA is no exception. The organization is a product of the dominant culture, and, therefore, one that would most likely say it is not racist. In fact, at one point early on, TFA defined the problem of educational inequity only in terms of socioeconomic status, not race—in essence, that was TFA's way of claiming colorblindness. TFA, by not seeing color, by not owning its own inherent racism, was and is racist. Taking a position of silence that ignores structural racism and employing the façade of working towards social justice while actually reinforcing structural racism is nothing short of racist.

Additionally, TFA's very mission of an "excellent education for all" is an act of racism. Although TFA does not state it directly, it implies that an excellent education is the education that White affluent students get: an education that teaches about, affirms, and promotes the dominant culture. To be deemed "educated" often means to have read the classics (primarily the Western canon); to know White, male, heterosexual history; to command "proper" English; to know the scientific and mathematical theories of White men; and to apply those theories to the problems of the Western world. In other words, an excellent education is, at its core and in practice, a racist education. By joining the corps, TFA enabled and encouraged me—a White woman—to enter a segregated (all Black) school and indoctrinate students with dominant White cultural knowledge, skills, and values, all in the name of social justice. Participating in TFA had a profound effect on me…it cultivated my racism. And this is exactly what is so dangerous about TFA: TFA not only brought out my racist perspectives…it did so while making me believe I was *not* racist. My students had no excuses for failure to assimilate.

My TFA Experience: Colorblind Racism in Action

When I joined TFA, I was not the typical corps member. As noted earlier, most corps members do not enter TFA knowing how to teach. I, however, was already certified, with 3 initial years of teaching. I also had just earned my M.A. in instructional strategies when I joined the organization. Why did I join TFA? I thought that I could change the world by teaching in "tough" schools where underprivileged students (mostly of color) did not have access to excellent teachers. At my core, I was attracted to being part of a movement to improve education for low-income students since I myself came from a low-income community. Consequently, buying into the TFA recruitment rhetoric, I began my corps experience believing I would be their savior as I was eager to level the field. To be clear, TFA didn't make me a racist; I was unknowingly a racist when I entered the corps. TFA, though, unintentionally accepted, utilized, and cultivated my racism for its own purposes. TFA provided me the opportunity to perpetuate the status quo under the guise of social justice.

In July 2001 I officially began "Teaching for America" at its Summer Institute. From the beginning, this training developed a culture of compliance, not a culture of critique. TFA explicitly demanded that corps members should create a similar culture of compliance in their classrooms. Classroom management was about controlling student behavior to allow for rigorous learning (of the White dominant culture). TFA also remained silent regarding district Band-Aids of a "teacher-proof" curricula and standardized instruction; it did not advocate or prepare corps members for critical and culturally responsive pedagogy. Although we had diversity sessions that made White corps members superficially unpack their White privilege (only to pack it back up and carry it with them for constant use), and sessions that forced us to define asset-based thinking, there was still a palpable deficit-based culture where corps members complained about how parents "don't value education" and where we relayed our Hollywood-style horror stories of our inner-city teaching. There was no intentional processing of experiences using a critical race theory lens; instead, there was silence—silence punctuated with poorly planned and executed diversity sessions.

Thanks to weeks at TFA Institute, I knew how to control and assimilate students. I was armed with content knowledge, grit, and—as TFA likes to tout—"humility." Unknowingly, a lot of colorblind racism from my own life and from TFA hid in my back pocket. I walked into a middle school in a very segregated Black community near the Georgia Dome in Atlanta, excited to teach science and geography. That excitement didn't last long; instead, I remember quickly feeling frustrated and angered by systemic low expectations, a lack of structure and safety, and grossly limited resources. I remember being forced to utilize packaged quick fixes and scripted, "teacher-proof" programs that I have always felt were insulting and ineffective. I remember dreading that every part of my instructional day felt mandated and top-down. But because I was a TFA-er, I persevered; I worked hard, held high expectations, and made learning both engaging and rigorous (I hope). In short, I gave my students the opportunity to obtain an "excellent education," and many of my students learned. But what did they learn?

Moving Backwards: The Unspoken Impact of TFA

My students could recite facts, discuss texts, and define science and geography terms. Most could pass tests. But my students learned something else, too, something much more powerful—something hidden in my colorblind curriculum. That message was that something must be wrong with them and their community. So much so that White teachers would cycle into their community, do their time, and then be gone. Who they were and where they were from was not "good enough," and the goal was to "get out and go to college." Not a single lesson focused on their rich history, the necessity and beauty of their dialect, or the strengths in their community. They were not taught about the systems of oppression in place, or about a colorblind racism that cuts deep, is internalized but is hard to see and to describe, especially for adolescents. They did not learn how to redress inequity in transformative ways. Yes, they learned, and yes, I closed the standardized achievement gap for some, but at what cost? In effect, I killed their souls little by little, day by day, for 2 years.

And during those 2 years, my rhetoric changed. Unknowingly, I began to speak racial grammar in self-talk that, as Bonilla-Silva (2006) illustrated, normalizes the standards of White supremacy. I began to think: "If only I could take my students out of their homes and communities…then I could save them." I wondered, "Are they behind because they do not have the opportunity to obtain an excellent education? I am giving them an excellent education and some of them don't want it!" I witnessed Black-on-Black violence (physical and emotional) and thought, "They are doing this to themselves!" All of this self-talk, even though unspoken to others, worked to absolve me of my responsibility to work against institutional racism—it allowed me to "give up" on those who rejected their "opportunity to escape." It was their fault, I convinced myself. Upon reflection on my 2 years with TFA, I realize that I entered TFA thinking, "All they need is the opportunity" and, in stark contrast, I left thinking, "I tried to teach them, but they didn't want to learn."

Moving Forward: Unlearning What I Taught

TFA is powerful. TFA is important. TFA *is a movement.* However, TFA moved me—and perhaps thousands like me—backwards. Unfortunately, I have spent much of the past decade "unlearning" and redressing the covert racism I adopted as a TFA corps member. I have also critically evaluated my TFA experience, and I am certain that TFA as an organization, and its proponents, can also reflect, know better, and do better. Their actions, while harmful, are not intentional. Through this counter narrative I want TFA and others to see the need for a change in direction—a need to "stop leveling the field" and, instead, to start partnering with teachers, students, and families to change the game. I sincerely hope that in 10 years I will not look back on TFA and think, "I tried to teach them [TFA], but they didn't want to learn."

REFERENCES

Bonilla-Silva, E. (2006). *Racism without racists: Color-blind racism and the persistence of racial inequality in the United States* (2nd ed.). Lanham, MD: Rowman & Littlefield Publishers.

Ladson-Billings, G. (2006). From the achievement gap to the education debt: Understanding achievement in U.S. schools. *Educational Researcher, 35*(7), 3–12.

CHAPTER TEN

Teach For (Whose?) America

JAY SAPER
Philadelphia, Summer 2013

BIOSKETCH

Jay Saper was dismissed from Teach For America for standing in solidarity with the Philadelphia community demanding support for their public schools. He received an education from the Philadelphia Student Union, Youth United for Change, Teacher Action Group, Caucus of Working Educators, Alliance for Philadelphia Public Schools, Parents United for Public Education, and Philadelphia Coalition Advocating for Public Schools. A Phi Beta Kappa graduate of Middlebury College, Jay is currently studying to become a social justice educator of young children at Bank Street College. Jay is intrigued by play and other joyful, creative, and cooperative endeavors. He is an activist and organizer involved at the intersection of various struggles to challenge oppression and build a just world.

NARRATIVE

"I have a $100. Do we have $150? There is a $150. What about a $200?"
"Oh yeah, easy!" a confident man shouted as he leaned forward to raise his hand.
"Thank you in the back. And $250?"
Hands flew up across the room.

"Anyone with $300? All right. Do we have a $350?"

One hand remained. The announcer ran over, "Congratulations on winning the How Much Did You Spend At Staples Subsidizing Political Abandonment Game!"

At this Back-To-School Story Slam organized by the Teacher Action Group, a sense of community was prioritized. Educator voices were listened to and validated. The event carved a space of hope during trying times.

Retiring the auctioneer hat, the middle school teacher and community organizer wrapped up the evening by saying, "I know you did not join the teaching force to fight global capital and neoliberalism. But this is just the truth. Our stories are of structural abandonment. We need to tell them and fight back. Thank you all for sharing and coming out tonight."

The passion of these educators made me feel at home. Yet, I knew our stories were not the same. While structural abandonment was the recurring theme of the evening, I arrived as an educator in Philadelphia upon structures of support. I arrived as a Teach For America (TFA) corps member.

"Isn't it a little odd that we begin teaching today, the day the teachers get laid off?" my roommate asked while turning off the alarm. "Indeed," I replied.

Blasting music greeted us at the dorm as we returned on buses from the charter schools where we had just begun teaching summer sessions. Balloons waved in the wind. TFA unfurled a red carpet for us on the precise day the layoffs of 3,783 educators went into effect. Cameras flashed and staff cheered.

Nestled in the corner of my room, I read *Faces of the Layoff* (Teacher Action Group, 2013) obsessively. The Teacher Action Group launched this website to humanize those educators who had cared for the children of Philadelphia and were now without a job. I kept scrolling, somewhat expecting to find my own image; I felt as though we were faces responsible for the layoffs. A corps member who grew up in Philadelphia resigned. "I feel like a scab," he told me. These educators had shaped his conscience. He could not be complicit in harming them.

The week before Institute was Induction, our introduction to the local TFA office. Before we wrote our first lesson plans, we received lessons on our pathway to leadership. We were coached by the director of PennCAN, an organization regarded by Philadelphia community members as having played a role in the dismantling of their public education system, and a representative from Leadership for Educational Equity (LEE), the branch of TFA that puts corps members in elected office.

While being lectured on how we knew more about the problems in communities than the members of the communities themselves, we were also taught TFA's core values, one of which was humility. I looked forward to seeing this value in action during the time marked off on our schedule for community service. This desire proved naïve. Onto the bus and over the river we went. Hunched over in the sweltering summer heat, we performed our community service, pulling weeds at a new high-discipline charter school. There are few things in life I love more than gardening. Yet, I did not feel rejuvenated by getting my hands dirty that day.

Institute began the following week. In the morning we taught for around an hour. The rest of the day we attended lectures and were shown videos of "exemplary" classrooms to emulate. I looked for something inspiring and lively in them, but could never find either. Apparently, I was supposed to be taking note of how silent the students were, what a straight line they could form, and how willingly they obeyed their teacher.

We never critically explored the history of White people (which most of us corps members were) controlling the bodies of people of color. History was only appropriated to serve interests already decided upon. The motto the staff chose for our school was, "By any means necessary." We were spoon-fed Black revolutionary rhetoric to help make its antithesis palatable.

The person leading curriculum sessions taught us "Compliance leads to freedom." That night, my roommate pointed out that a sign with those words would look good hanging on the walls of a sweatshop. I told him it was too close to the German motto that sickened me when I walked through Dachau's gates to honor the millions of my ancestors who were brutally murdered by those merely following orders.

Despite our discomfort with a conception of education nearer to the opposite of what several of us believed in, we nonetheless were held accountable for enacting TFA's method of instruction. I was given an earpiece to wear during class. Someone in the back of the room would speak into a microphone and tell me exactly who to punish, when to punish them, and how to punish them. This felt enormously uncomfortable to me. I dreamed of becoming an educator, not a dog trainer or prison guard.

I met briefly with the White woman who would be coaching me. "What does discipline look like in your class?" she asked.

"We have been working to build community and resp—"

"No, like, what do you do to punish your students when they disobey you?"

"Well," I said, "I am not so interested in having students rigidly obey me. I would much rather have them disobey me and anyone else if they believe something they are told to do is wrong."

Her jaw dropped, "Teaching disobedience to *these kids* would cultivate murders," she said.

Before I arrived in Philadelphia, I was deeply inspired by the thousands of students who took to the streets demanding support for their education. Were these students, who organized the largest walkout in Philadelphia since 1967, supposed to be in class following the orders of their teachers? Sometimes taking a stand in life and refusing to tolerate injustice, even when it means breaking a rule or two, is the right thing to do. To me, these students with the critical conscience to subject themselves to harm and demand what they deserved are our greatest hope.

Our literacy instruction focused exclusively on phonics. Instead of being embedded in and responsive to students' own interests, we were taught to reduce language to its most disembodied parts. Fortunately, we were less supervised during our morning small group reading time, so I was able to sneak in some learning that might have been worthwhile.

With the students, we read about a parent who worked a night shift. We discussed how even though the people we love may work hours that make it difficult for us to see them often, the small moments we do share together remind us how special our relationships are. We shared with one another about when the people we love work and what they do. One student had a father who was gone for a few days at a time since he was a truck driver. A couple other students had loved ones who were janitors. Not janitors who helped keep our school clean so we would have a beautiful environment in which to learn—no, janitors who had to clean up after those "big kids at the high school who are really messy."

We also read about migrant workers. "Please, please, can you bring in more books with Spanish?" asked an excited third grader who spoke the language. As I learned more about my students, I adjusted lessons to create meaningful connections with and engage them. While we were encouraged to print off bland stories from a leveled online reading program, I trotted from library to library and bookstore to bookstore looking for texts I thought my students would love.

They eagerly read about the janitor strike in Los Angeles. Each page was in Spanish and English. Each page affirmed the agency of students' loved ones. We explored many questions. What did the people who owned the big buildings downtown think of the janitors? How did they treat them? What did the janitors do? Why did they do that? What did the owners discover after this action? Do janitors do important work? Should they be treated fairly?

Our discussion was lively. Students were eager to share their thoughts and referenced places in the book to support their perspectives. Something one student said still echoes in my mind just as vividly as when she told me that day: "Yes, janitors are important. My daddy matters. My daddy matters." Her daddy does matter. She matters, too.

The last 10 minutes of Friday afternoons were allotted for completing a feedback survey. "We were waiting for you," frustrated corps members on the bus said to me while wiping sweat off their faces. If anyone else decided to share thorough thoughts in the following weeks, I would wait until they were done and we would walk to the bus together. I did not want anyone to have to confront alone the intense shame I was forced to feel for providing honest feedback.

Back at the dorm, one corps member told me the surveys were never anonymous. "I am confronted whenever I mention anything critical. I will never fill out another survey honestly until I complete my 2 years." Another corps member, who ended up quitting a few months later, explained, "I had more of a voice in the military, whose mission is war, than I do in TFA, whose mission is to help kids."

I opened my room on Sundays, welcoming corps members to bring questions, concerns, or thoughts they had. We did readings together to help prepare us to become educators for social justice. We were frustrated by the way our diversity sessions were saturated with racism and came up with a proposal to change them. A reading we suggested spread across Institute. All was not perfect, but it was powerful for corps members to be exposed to an asset-based way of thinking about the students and caregivers we would be working with, as opposed to one that fixated on deficits.

A regular at our meetings wrote a petition to get TFA to seriously address the frequent fire alarms. Well aware of a tragedy at Seton Hall University a few years prior, he was adamant that fire safety in dorms should not be taken lightly. Staff repeatedly downplayed the concerns of this man of color, encouraging corps members to unscrew the detectors in their rooms, put in earplugs, and go back to sleep. He quit only a few weeks later, eloquently summing up his distasteful experience: "This is all a bunch of bullshit."

A few weeks into Institute, one of my college friends died. I was heartbroken. I decided we would read a book on loss during my student reading group that next morning. We discussed losing people and animals we loved and what we do to try to remember and honor their lives. One student shared that his little brother died and they made T-shirts for him. Another shared that her dog died and they kept his bowl. There was an intense level of engagement that morning. The empathy and care made me recognize the power of being vulnerable in the classroom, the power of welcoming in our common humanity.

I shared that my friend passed away and I would be going to his funeral that weekend. "Oh, your friend died. That is sad," one student said. "You should write to remember him." I took out a pen and wrote. During his outdoor memorial service, which started in rain and transformed to sunshine, I promised myself I would try to practice the values he lived. I promised myself that for the remainder of my brief existence I would not sit silenced, but rather stand up and try to act as courageously as he had.

I eagerly noted the session on our calendar that indicated we were going to learn about the community where our students come from and the teachers who work with them during the school year. My hopes were usurped. TFA never actually planned anything of the sort. All along, the session was a placeholder for a surprise afternoon free of sessions. There seemed to always be enough time to teach us how to pass out papers more efficiently, but never for anything of substance.

As my urge to get involved in the community would not be fulfilled through work with the organization, I began attending neighborhood discussions and activist demonstrations. With less than 24 hours's notice, the unelected School Reform Commission called a meeting to make substantive changes to the school code. I put on a red shirt and headed down Broad Street to join the gathering crowds.

Hundreds of teachers, students, nurses, counselors, parents, and other community members were present. Most were shut out of the meeting and forced to watch a simulcast in the lobby of 440, the district's headquarters. Young activists with the Philadelphia Student Union and Youth United for Change stood up and shouted, "It's our meeting, let us in!"

The cops were frantic. What is a city to do when its students come to demand an education and the plan was to lock them out and sell it away?

"It's our meeting, let us in!" they kept demanding.

After skillful maneuvering, the students made it past the cops and charged into the meeting room. The audience cheered at their arrival. Community members gave fiery testimony. Ultimately, they were ignored by the School Reform Commission, which voted unanimously against each one of the community's demands.

In the sea of thousands of educators who took to the streets and attended meetings over the summer, never once did I see a staff member from TFA. During these meetings, people were eager to share with me their perspectives on the role of the organization in facilitating and exacerbating the public education crisis. I promised I would try to relay their concerns to staff. I scheduled a meeting to do so. The date kept getting pushed back.

Months prior, I told TFA I did not want to take the job of another educator. I was promised that the office had a contract that would not allow any corps member to be hired at schools where any teachers had been laid off. Confusion turned to clarity: While TFA could not place any corps members in public schools in the district, if teachers were fired and their former schools opened up as charters, hiring was free range. TFA provided the teachers to enact these controversial policies that the broad Philadelphia Coalition Advocating for Public Schools came together to oppose.

During interviews at these schools, I asked why I was in a chair across from the interviewer and not one of the thousands of educators irrefutably more qualified. A separate system of charters thrives off disinvestment from and disregard for traditional public schools. When a family is given an option between a school receiving extra foundation funding and one without counselors and nurses, a family does not exercise choice but is trapped in a bribe. Fortunately, students have repeatedly stepped up to pierce the silence TFA maintains on the matter. From the steps of 440, the district's headquarters, a young activist boldly shared,

"You are leaving us with just principals, security guards, and empty classrooms. This is like a warden, guard, and cell."

I thought we would have passionate professors in our university certification courses who would push us to think and practice beyond the narrow conception of education advanced during TFA's Institute. I quickly learned that my expectations were foolish. The previous director of the University of Pennsylvania Graduate School of Education program for TFA had deliberately supported corps members in exploring questions suppressed by the organization but was promptly ousted from the position. Corps members organized to express discontent, but their concerns were not addressed.

With criticisms of TFA from passionate students, dedicated community members, and respected educators rising across the country, I was surprised that the University of Pennsylvania was eager to maintain an uncritical relationship with the organization. The dean's remarks at our orientation helped everything make sense. To him, the laid-off veteran educators were every bit as disposable as TFA had encouraged us to believe. We were Whiter and more privileged than these teachers. We represented greater hope.

"If you go to rural Wisconsin, you can get a teaching job very easily," he said. "There is a shortage of teachers there. Now, there may not be a shortage of teachers everywhere, but know that while there may not be a shortage of teachers in Philadelphia, there most certainly is a shortage of good teachers, so that is why you are in such high need. There is no better time than 2013 to join Teach For America and become a teacher in Philadelphia while learning at an outstanding institution like the University of Pennsylvania."

While lunch was catered during orientation, several educators out in front of 440 refused food to draw attention to the crisis. The demonstration helped restore some positions, but schools were still set to open without adequate resources. The night before the first day for students, hundreds gathered outside the governor's office for a vigil and solemnly marched to City Hall. Dozens fewer schools would open in the morning than the year before, despite adequate funding for ongoing prison construction nearby. Thousands fewer educators, counselors, nurses, librarians, and other support staff would be there to provide critical services for students.

The next month we came together for another vigil. In the dark cool rain, we crouched under umbrellas. Nurses shared a few words and then we lit candles in silence. A brilliant and beautiful sixth grade student had an asthma attack. Budget cuts had left no nurse at her school to address it promptly. By the time she was taken to the hospital after school, it was too late; Laporshia Massey died (Denvir, 2013).

As I took action in solidarity with Philadelphia community members demanding support for their public schools, I became a liability to TFA. A staff member called me as I rode the 36 trolley out to West Philadelphia for what

I would later learn to be my final interview. She warned, "Jay, your opinions need to remain silent."

Only once in history have Philadelphia firefighters turned away from a blaze. It was Mother's Day 1985. Philadelphia dropped a bomb on its own people. The man who approved the act of terror that burned 11 people alive, including 5 children, went uncharged. He founded a school to promote amnesia about his role in the atrocity. I refused to bite my tongue. Subsequently, I was not hired by the school. A few days later, during the afternoon break between services on Yom Kippur, I strolled to a demonstration taking place down the street from the *schul*. I shared with Ramona Africa, the only living survivor of that horrific bombing, how deeply inspired I was by her tremendous courage and compassion. She thanked me for disobeying my instruction to remain silent.

The meeting I scheduled to share community concerns with TFA staff finally took place. Instead of listening to what I had learned in spaces the organization had been glaringly absent from, the meeting was coopted to aggressively force me to resign. I refused.

A man sat on steps overlooking a cemetery as I returned to the TFA office for a follow-up meeting. In passing, we greeted one another. I stumbled back as he confided that he woke up that morning and thought it should be his last. "They are no longer here," he said, while gesturing across the street toward the cemetery. "I feel so miserable. I want to join them. I could hang myself and it would all be over."

While my brain was cognizant that the clock ticked on, the entirety of my heart did not allow me to budge. I tried to listen and honor the pain. I tried to hear the tremendous love he had for his children. I tried to communicate back to him what I heard as tremendous love they had for him. I tried to thank him for kindly entering my life. I tried. We began walking toward the TFA office. I invited him in so we could find a support number and call. As we entered, the executive director, who has two degrees in marketing and none in education, welcomed me with an urgent "Jay, I have a two o'clock."

I nodded in understanding. I continued to dial because I wanted my new friend to have a tomorrow. The hotline recommended the hospital a few blocks away. I offered to go with him, but the frantic energy in the office led him to insist I stay. "I will go to the church, then the park, then the hospital," he promised. "Thank you. Pray for me."

As I entered the conference room, I broke down in tears. They told me I was being emotional. I was raised as a man in a world that tells us we do not have any emotions, or at least any worthy of revealing. Fortunately, I have learned this is a lie. I was emotional in that moment and forever will be. I am a human. I care. That is nothing to hide.

It was not a day for a meeting. As I was excused, I walked to the church. The door was locked. I strolled up the street and found my friend on a park bench. We lost ourselves in conversation. Finally, we walked over to the hospital. School buses passed by and children ran about. He jotted down my number and we exchanged gratitude. "Pray for me," he said.

When I got home I tried to learn how I could have better acted in that situation. My search revealed to me that it was World Suicide Prevention Day. The meeting with TFA was rescheduled. Perhaps worried my compassion might again interfere with my punctuality, they downgraded it to a conference call. I helped the person sitting on the steps overlooking the cemetery because I did not want him to die yet. I do not want to die yet. And when I refuse to speak up, I abandon any dignity attached to life. The conference call was quick to reach its conclusion: "Jay, we are recommending you for dismissal from Teach For America."

I knew dissent could not be quelled by dismissing me, for I only echoed concerns of a community who remain restless for justice. I started to share a quote from Dr. King that moved me during my turbulent time with the organization: "Our lives begin to end the day we become silent about things that matter." Before I could make it to the final word, my phone speaker began to play cool jazz. I was the only person left on the line. Teach For America hung up. Teach For America became silent.

REFERENCES

Denvir, D. (2013). He says his daughter might be alive if not for school-nurse cuts. Retrieved from http://citypaper.net/News/He-says-his-daughter-might-be-alive-if-not-for-school-nurse-cuts/
Teacher Action Group. (2013). Faces of the layoffs. Retrieved from http://facesofthelayoffs.org

Elite by Association, but at What Expense? Teach For America, Colonizing Perspectives, and a Personal Evolution

ANNE MARTIN
Metro Atlanta, 2008–2010

BIOSKETCH

Anne Martin is a Ph.D. student in educational policy studies at Georgia State University with a concentration in research, measurement, and statistics. Originally from Kansas, she attended Kansas State University, majoring in psychology and French. After graduation, she joined the 2008 Teach For America Atlanta Corps. She works as a third grade teacher and has taught first through fourth grades over the past 6 years. During that time she completed coursework to earn her renewable teaching certificate as well as a master's of education in elementary education with a mathematics endorsement from Georgia State University.

NARRATIVE

I first learned about Teach For America (TFA) during my junior year of college at Kansas State University when a friend I met through a mutual interest in campus involvement applied. She was the hardest working and most involved person I knew, heading up several campus-wide programs. When she was rejected by TFA, any initial interest I had in applying dissolved, as I perceived her to be a much stronger candidate than I would have been. With thoughts of TFA long gone, I was surprised, and a bit flattered, to be contacted by a TFA recruiter early in my senior year. She was persistent in scheduling a meeting with me, and although I told her I was already applying to law schools, I agreed to meet with her for an on-campus lunch. During our one-on-one meeting she intently reviewed my résumé, stating that I was a great fit for TFA. She said they were looking for people like me. Towards the end of the meeting she made a persuasive argument that I should apply to join TFA, considering so many of my experiences centered on equity and education. She pointed out that TFA was a great bridge to law school and they had numerous partnerships with said programs. During this conversation I began to agree that TFA was a good fit for me, then thought back to my friend who was not chosen, and remembered that TFA was selective. I felt validated by the recruiter's enthusiasm, especially considering I had not attended a prestigious undergraduate institution. After this meeting, I consulted TFA's website and felt increasingly satisfied with myself as I read about their rigorous admissions criteria.

Although I had numerous experiences in education throughout college, I had never considered teaching. After meeting with the TFA recruiter, that changed overnight. Within days I had completed my application for the first deadline and spent numerous hours researching the program and the cities I could potentially be moving to as a corps member. While I had quickly revamped my postgraduation plans around TFA, I still didn't think of it as wanting to become a teacher or wanting to teach. What TFA presented to me was a glamorous 2-year experience in which I would help some children in desperate need of a good education while better preparing myself for my future endeavors. After being accepted into the corps, I felt a sense of accomplishment. I thought this experience would be the first stepping-stone in my quest toward achieving prestige. Essentially, I joined TFA because they made me feel elite, special, and powerful.

My TFA experience is best understood as a series of tensions between personally benefitting from the privilege bestowed to me, by default of association, and simultaneously critiquing the colonizing perspectives that facilitate the organization's presence as a legitimate educational endeavor. I identified this colonizing perspective when I realized I was one of many outsiders who would benefit from entering a community they knew nothing about in an attempt to take over local education. In this chapter, I intend to explore these tensions by sharing my TFA story and my personal evolution of thought while situating my experiences within my wider critique.

Status of a Corps Member

After being selected by TFA I instantly began to enjoy a period of increased credibility and sophistication that came with being associated with the organization. Many of my family and friends were impressed by my postcollegiate plans to join the corps. The fact that I had been accepted by TFA was typically equated with being high achieving and altruistic. Others noted the opportunities I would have to network and the potential partnerships with businesses and graduate schools.

After arriving in Atlanta for Institute, the period of networking began. I was impressed with the credentials of many of my peers. I had never before met anyone who had attended Harvard, and there were several corps members who had, in fact, attended Harvard, among other elite institutions. I felt more sophisticated just by my proximity to them and anticipated that this networking would continue. Additionally, I enjoyed the social and organizational aspects of TFA. It had a very corporate-world feel. There were catered dinners with influential speakers, parties with open bars, holiday events, and perks like executive bank accounts waiving the standard fees.

This sophisticated culture is ironic, considering the juxtaposition between it and the impoverished communities TFA professes to help. This networking and culture of TFA is made possible because of the reality of inadequate education for many children of color in our country. TFA has used this reality to build an influential organization on a platform of ending the achievement gap. In this sense, using this space for networking and growth is treating education as a kind of capital that can be owned and leveraged to increase the organization's value. The education of low-income students of color becomes a phenomenon from which affluent outsiders can benefit. While improved education can increase capital for students in terms of opportunities that are accessible, this outcome seems to be secondary for TFA.

Perhaps the biggest example of increased capital that I received through affiliation with TFA was access to a special master's program at a local university. TFA created a partnership with the university to facilitate corps members earning their renewable teaching certifications and subsequent master's of education degrees. The program was restricted to TFA corps members and offered substantial benefits over other M.Ed. programs. It was accelerated (certification and master's in 2 years), counted TFA trainings for coursework credits, delayed payment with agreement to use AmeriCorps funds distributed at the end of TFA service, and was flexible around our schedule. This elite partnership existed because of the achievement gap, and it created an opportunity for corps members to personally benefit through joining the organization. A master's degree certainly benefited the corps members who participated, increasing their salaries and opening up future job opportunities. While it is impossible to measure the quantifiable and quantitative benefits corps members enjoy compared to any increased educational opportunities (capital) for the students they teach, the benefits appear to be strongly weighted towards the former.

Through treating urban education as a type of capital, corps members are able to profit from the experience. TFA corps members, in turn, achieve sophistication by teaching low-income students of color and subsequently through affiliation as alumni of the organization. This perceived sophistication facilitates upward social and professional mobility. Additionally, this sophistication can be understood through what Miranda Fricker (2007) calls credibility excess, which happens when the identity of the speaker positively influences the credibility of their testimony, even when it is not justified. Due to their status as a group of mostly White people educated at elite institutions, TFA corps members enjoy credibility excess, particularly in the realm of educational policy, despite their limited experience in classrooms.

Celebrated Yet Unprepared

While TFA corps members enjoy many advantages through their association with the organization, this is not because of an increased skill set as educators—despite the perception. TFA operates with its philosophy of "Teaching as Leadership," claiming that strong leadership skills can be leveraged in the classroom to enact effective teaching. The pedagogical strategies taught to corps members are limited to procedural steps for teachers to take in order to achieve the desired actions in students. Corps members are taught to script lessons using an "I do, we do, you do" model, which generally limits instruction to teacher-centered and whole-group lectures while privileging behaviorist approaches to classroom management and learning.

After beginning work at my placement school, I quickly experienced dissonance with the image TFA had constructed about the status of urban schools. I expected to see a declining facility, burnt out and instructionally ineffective teachers, and students in desperate need of saving. In contrast, I was greeted with a colorful, well-kept school, and experienced staff and faculty who knew well the children and community where the school was located. The staff was willing to take me, an unprepared corps member, under their wing to fill in the numerous pedagogical gaps I had.

I realized before I even entered my placement site that I had no idea what I was doing and that TFA was not going to prepare me in the ways I needed to be prepared. During Institute, the corps members in the Atlanta region were informed that we would interview with principals. Naturally, the principals at the TFA-run job fair were there to interview teachers and came into the interviews with a set of assumptions about what potential candidates should know. Considering I had no experience in K–12 education outside of TFA trainings, I realized I was vastly unprepared. Principals asked me questions about my teaching philosophy, classroom management, how to teach literacy, and about approaches to providing research-based interventions to struggling students. Many terms the principals used I had never heard before. I felt embarrassed and instantly became aware that I was not prepared for what I was about to do. Despite my performance during these interviews, I knew they were a formality. I got a teaching job regardless of my ill-informed responses during the interviews. All the corps members did.

During Institute and the subsequent trainings TFA facilitated, I still believed a moment would come when TFA would give me the information necessary to prepare me to be the classroom teacher of record for my first grade class. While TFA did guide us through a week-long workshop of preplanning, none of it applied to my actual teaching. During my first days of work I knew little. Luckily, veteran teachers and staff at my school helped. They gave me what I did not know I needed, showed me where to find materials and resources I did not know existed, and gave me the words to say when I had none. When the first day of school arrived, I honestly felt shocked that I was left alone and trusted to educate a class of 6-year-olds. I knew I was responsible for teaching them to read (and now I know I should have been equally concerned with developing their number sense), but I lacked even a basic familiarity of the developmental stage of my students. I was surprised when confronted with children who needed help tying shoes and confused when my students did not seem to know what to do when I gave multistep directions and abstract examples.

Fortunately, my school and district had many resources in place for all teachers. There were two reading coaches and a math coach at my school who spent hours teaching me the pedagogical knowledge I would have likely received in a traditional teacher education program. One of the reading coaches spent the entire 90-minute reading block in my classroom, supporting me for 2 full weeks. The other planned with me individually, giving me resources, showing me how to conduct and interpret multiple literacy assessments, and modeling how to conduct small-group guided literacy instruction. The district also provided monthly professional development that continued to build my competence as a teacher.

The support I received in my school and district was supplemented and complemented by the coursework I engaged in while working towards my renewable teaching certificate and master's degree. In these classes I learned the theoretical and philosophical underpinnings of various pedagogies. My program had a strong focus on constructivism and culturally relevant pedagogy, which had a positive influence on my classroom. Through these courses I gained both a broad understanding of what education is and specific methods to teach the content areas I was responsible for.

What I learned about teaching from my colleagues at my school and in my coursework was in sharp contrast to most of what TFA provided me with, in both increased quantity and quality. While TFA offered some support to me and other corps members, I found their perspectives to be ill-informed about the community where I was working, and often superficial. From what I learned in my school and classes, TFA's suggested lesson cycle was inadequate and inappropriate to educate my students beyond rote memorization and procedural skills.

In addition to the 5-week Institute experience, corps members participated in monthly "Power" sessions as a form of continued professional development. I was frequently perplexed with TFA's approach during these training sessions. The assumption, either explicit or implicit, was that the faculty at the local schools were ineffective, or at best uninformed, because it was perceived that they did not use data-based decision making and TFA's Teaching as Leadership rubric. I was confused as to why TFA seemed so detached from the local schools and districts where we worked. From my experiences, I saw multiple strengths to draw from the local district and community. Why was that disregarded by TFA staffers?

Legitimating the Mission

Despite my initial excitement after being chosen by TFA and moving to Atlanta, I felt a disconnect with TFA early on. I wondered how the organization justified continuing its mission when, in many regions, there was no longer a teacher shortage. Why did TFA seem to operate from the assumption that corps members deserved those spaces more than career teachers did? I did not understand why TFA had their own pedagogical strategies that were so different from those used by local districts and supported by traditional colleges of education. Interestingly, I think the phrase "the mission," as TFA refers to it, indicates why these discrepancies exist. Paralleling a missionary mindset of entering a space that needs saving, TFA operates from the perspective that some communities need them to physically come in and bring their own tools and strategies to replace what already exists.

The notion that education is something that can be taken over by outsiders illustrates TFA's colonizing perspective. This perspective is reflective of epistemologies of Whiteness outlined by Leonardo (2002), where Whites colonize myopically—lacking knowledge of the spaces they seek to colonize. I became aware of this during TFA training sessions when my fellow corps members desperately sought help on how to teach the children they were prematurely charged with educating. Most of our TFA support came from alumni with 2 years of teaching experience and little or no formal education training. They were limited to sharing what they had learned through trial and error and any tricks they had picked up along the way. I quickly realized that TFA distanced itself from the local knowledge of the communities they infiltrated, claiming their methods of Teaching as Leadership were the most rigorous and valid pedagogical tool for corps members. I recognized this approach as a form of colonization and instead turned to veteran practitioners at my school for mentorship.

Claiming ownership of and capitalizing on the education of low-income students of color is legitimated through an epistemology of ignorance, as characterized by a systematic refusal to seek out or accept truth in order to achieve domination (Sullivan & Tuana, 2007). The lack of teacher shortages illustrates this ignorance. TFA continues to expand and enact its mission despite significant changes in the realm of urban education. The organization was founded in 1990 to address teaching shortages; however, since the Great Recession of 2008, these shortages have ceased to exist in most of the regions where TFA sends its teachers. In my placement site we experienced yearly leveling, in which teachers were moved to different schools or even released from their contracts if there were no available spaces for them.

In my first year with TFA I was assigned to teach first grade. I had 11 students in my class. Overall enrollment at my school was low, and the district mandated one teacher be moved from my school to another that needed an additional teacher. The district policy dictated that the last hired should be the first to move. The other TFA teacher and myself, however, were not moved. In a faculty meeting our principal explained that we could not be leveled because we were TFA teachers. She later told me in private that this was not true; rather, she decided to keep us over some other teachers already in the building because she had had success with TFA teachers in the past. At this point she had only known me for a month. Once again, I was privileged due to my TFA status and was simultaneously aware of the effects on the existing community. TFA corps members seemed to be valued over traditional career teachers. As my school district went into a hiring freeze, I wondered why TFA was in this region. Where was the teacher shortage I was supposed to be filling? Meanwhile, the organization did not heed these concerns. Instead, they tripled the number of corps members in my region during my second year, which led to a frenzy of panic when TFA staff frantically tried to find placement sites for worried corps members who outnumbered the teaching vacancies.

By the end of my TFA experience, my attitude had shifted dramatically from the superficial reasons why I originally joined. The networking and increased opportunities and sophistication were not the important outcomes of my experience. While I met many interesting and talented people whom I care about, most of our paths went in different directions. Many of my TFA friends went to law school or took jobs in the corporate sector. Those who stayed in education moved to charter schools, where several now serve in leadership roles. As I continued to teach at my placement site, I became more distanced from TFA. Although much of this has to do with my personal feelings towards the organization that discourage me from participating in alumni events, I do not think the distance is completely one-sided. At the alumni induction dinner TFA staff members asked us what our plans were after the corps. Staffers seemed most excited about corps members who were going on to law or medical schools. There is also an affiliate organization that supports alumni to be elected to public office. These avenues of impacting education differ from mine due to the tensions I experienced as a corps member.

The dissonance I experienced with TFA did not lead me to leave the classroom. I just completed my sixth year teaching at my TFA placement site. I love my job and I love teaching, which I attribute to my early rejection of TFA's methods in favor of those methods shared by my district mentors and coaches. My firsthand experiences of enjoying prestige and credibility through my affiliation with TFA, at the expense of the students they claim to serve, led to my decision to pursue a graduate degree in educational policy. This work is motivated by my commitment to further examine the philosophical, ideological, and political perspectives that fuel TFA and other colonizing educational policies, as I contend they do not fully consider the best interests of the students they serve.

In reflecting on my TFA experience, I deliberately did not include stories about the students I taught. A typical marketing device TFA employs is to have corps members share deeply personal narratives describing the dramatic impact a corps member had on a specific child's life. While stories are important, I reject this method, as it constructs a single narrative of what TFA does for children while ignoring the broader effect on all of the children and communities impacted by TFA. I certainly had several students from when I was a corps member who are special to me and I still remember, but it is more poignant for me to focus on what I could have done if I had been prepared to teach the entire group of students, before entering the classroom. Ultimately, I think it is essential to acknowledge and fully explore the negative consequences enacted on the community due to my privileged position as a TFA teacher.

REFERENCES

Fricker, M. (2007). *Epistemic injustice: Power and the ethics of knowing*. Oxford, UK: Oxford University Press.
Leonardo, Z. (2002). The souls of White folk: Critical pedagogy, Whiteness studies, and globalization discourse. *Race, Ethnicity and Education, 5*(1), 40–41.
Sullivan, S., & Tuana, N. (2007). *Race and epistemologies of ignorance*. Albany: State University of New York Press.

CHAPTER TWELVE

"I Always Finish Everything": The Challenge of Living Up to My TFA Commitment

MONICA CHEN
New Mexico, 2012–2014

BIOSKETCH

Monica Chen graduated from UC Berkeley, where she created her own major in environmental education and public policy. Her primary schooling included Waldorf, single-sex, and public schools. As a high school senior, she homeschooled herself, took community college classes, and began working as a docent at the Hidden Villa wilderness preserve in Los Altos, California. In 2011 she worked at Outward Bound in Costa Rica and later helped cofound Wild Child Freeschool—an outdoor nature program for homeschoolers in Silicon Valley. Her main interests include humane/environmental education, animal rights, equitable admissions policies, the anti-commercialization of childhood, and challenging corporate personhood. Upon joining the TFA New Mexico corps in 2012, she was placed as a third grade teacher at a Bureau of Indian Education school on the Navajo reservation approximately 45 minutes northeast of Gallup, New Mexico. She received her master's in elementary education from the University of New Mexico.

NARRATIVE

Looking back, I know the exact moment the decision was made to accept me into Teach For America (TFA). During my final interview in 2011, I was sweetly asked, "Can you think of any reason you wouldn't fulfill your 2-year commitment?" My swift response was, "Oh no, I always finish everything I commit to." My interviewer smiled as she jotted down my answer. What followed were 2 years that were more overwhelming than I could have ever anticipated. I found myself questioning that earlier naive commitment every single day. This chapter details my journey as a corps member, my struggle with evaluations and tracking, and finally, my reflections on testing as it relates to TFA and the larger standards-based reform movement in education.

Placement

I was assigned to the New Mexico (NM) corps, a TFA region that had dwindled to half its size in the 3 years prior to my arrival. Unbeknownst to most who think of TFA as a single national organization, regional TFA offices are responsible for much of their own funding. The lack of big donors in rural native education, combined with TFA's seemingly constant need to expand—in this case, expansion into a southern New Mexico corps—had negatively impacted the size of each incoming corps.

Unlike many big U.S. cities where TFA operates, rural New Mexico's Gallup-McKinley County School District—which covers over 5,000 square miles—and the Bureau of Indian Education have always had teacher shortages. On the reservation, it is not uncommon to appoint long-term substitutes, many of whom only have an undergraduate or high school degree, due to a severe lack of applicants. As a result, principals continue to call TFA looking to fill some of their vacancies even months into the school year.

Yet despite all of these openings—many with close proximity to town—TFA NM required all of its 2012 corps members to accept their very first job offer rather than choose a school from several options. Some corps members were hired in extremely isolated parts of Native American reservations—over an hour away from their evening university graduate classes. I was placed at Mariano Lake Community School (MLCS), a "turnaround" (or failing) school with little trust in teachers—near the southeast corner of the expansive Navajo reservation.

Reservation schools often have housing on their property called "teacherages." Based on everything I'd heard about the first year of teaching, I moved into a trailer for about $450 per month, expecting that I wouldn't have much of a life beyond school anyway. Unsurprisingly, within a few days, I started to face challenges that I wasn't prepared for.

The first challenge was mostly bureaucratic—completing the lengthy U.S. government paperwork process for the Bureau of Indian Education. The whole week prior to the start of school was considered "on my own time," even though veteran faculty members received a salary during mandatory staff training. I never was compensated for this time, and because the paperwork didn't come through by the first day of school, I still wasn't legally allowed to be on campus.

Safety and lack of support were other challenges I experienced, surrounding an incident of sexual assault on me by the school janitor while I was working after hours in my classroom a month into the school year. Though I reported this incident to TFA and my administration, I didn't receive any help apart from a notice in my mailbox that a different janitor would be responsible for my classroom. My principal later informed me that the janitor could not be fired since his previous offense had happened more than 2 years ago.

Another challenge during the first few months was the underwhelming scripted curriculum called Reading Mastery that I taught to second, third, fourth, and fifth graders during reading block. We followed the prescribed second grade texts with me reciting questions from a book while robotically snapping my fingers—or using a dog clicker—to signify choral responses. My inexperience with behavioral issues coupled with the uninspiring curriculum led to significant problems with classroom management.

Then, there were issues with the administration and my school instructional coach—a veteran teacher and second year TFA corps member—who would stop me in the middle of a lesson to rearrange desks and openly criticize my teaching in front of my students. Subsequent debriefing sessions with this person—who was also my next-door neighbor—were overtly harsh and personal.

Evaluations

Above all, I found that the biggest challenge I faced as an inexperienced teacher was the constant pressure to be held to standards that were not my own. I was observed by my professor for my master's class, by consultants, by instructional coaches, by the principal, by the Bureau of Indian Education (BIE) administration, and, of course, by TFA. There were days when multiple people observed me teaching my class, coming and going as they pleased. I was critiqued. I was filmed. Every word I said could be and was noted. Did I refer to my objectives throughout the lesson? Did I use enough technology? Was a child gazing off into space? It was as though I was always being judged for a performance that I hadn't adequately rehearsed for. As a new teacher I tried to do what I was told to do and learn the intricacies of "Bloom's taxonomy" and "culturally responsive teaching." I was willing to believe all my observers had something important to share that would improve my teaching. I went to every all-corps region-wide professional development and TFA professional learning community (PLC) sessions—no matter how banal.

In 2012, TFA New Mexico was using the Teaching as Leadership (TAL) comprehensive rubric that our manager of teacher leadership development (MTLD)—a TFA supervisor who usually had only 2 years of teaching experience—could use to evaluate us. We were evaluated in areas titled "Set Big Goals," "Invest Students and Those Who Influence Them in Working Hard To Achieve Big Goals," "Plan Purposefully," "Execute Effectively," "Continuously Increase Effectiveness," and "Work Relentlessly." In each of these areas, there were multiple subcategories where we were labeled as pre-novice, novice, beginning proficiency, advanced proficiency, and exemplary—all of us "worked relentlessly" to try and move up the proficiency ladder. This is why we were picked—our strong sense of commitment to seeing things through. Like most corps members, I put up a poster stating my Big Goal of 80% mastery with corresponding color-coded trackers on the walls. Per the request of my MTLD, I authored a vision for my classroom that incorporated my far-reaching dreams of social justice.

Every lesson I "executed" had a hook and followed the standard gradual release of responsibility—"I do, we do, you do," emphasizing teacher modeling, then an activity done together, then independent work by the student. It was formulaic and time-consuming paperwork to fill out. Still, there was always more to do each night. During an all-corps meeting, an MTLD held up a 10+ page lesson plan for reading and announced, "If you're not doing this, then you're not doing justice for your children." "Justice for your children" or "doing right by your kids" was introduced from day one of Induction as "drinking the TFA Kool-Aid." Staff and corps members would make fun of themselves for drinking the Kool-Aid, but in the end it was the reason for everything. We believed teachers could change their students' lives if they only worked hard enough. Thus, nobody ever said at an all-corps meeting that your best is good enough. It was implied that you should do whatever it takes to help your students, school, and community. At TFA events, we watched videos of the Sue Lehmann corps members—the nominees for the best TFA teachers in each region—"doing" justice for their children. While the aim of these videos was to highlight teaching, they also encouraged competition and a divisive sense of inadequacy among many corps members.

Tracking and Support

TFA's grandiose mission reads, "One day, all children will attain an excellent education." An excellent elementary education, according to TFA, means that students "grow 2 years of reading" in just 1 academic year. How such growth is measured can vary, but a common test at the elementary level is the Developmental Reading Assessment (DRA), which is highly subject to interpretation. The DRA—introduced to corps members in a whirlwind session at Institute—requires a lot of one-on-one time with individual students to go through books at different reading levels and copy their corresponding tests. I was never able to find time to administer this assessment thoroughly. Nevertheless, I checked out the big DRA boxes three times per year, a TFA requirement, and submitted their scores to my MTLD.

TFA also monitored my progress via the computerized Northwest Evaluation Association (NWEA) assessment three times per year. The administration of this assessment was difficult, given that the school only had one computer lab with a faulty Internet connection. All students (K–6) took the NWEA, which was limited in its depiction of student knowledge and growth—particularly for my beginning readers. I was required to input beginning, midyear, and end-of-year NWEA test scores into the TFA trackers despite the fact that I already had my own trackers (both personal and those required by my school).

I never received any specific help from TFA regarding my data, but I do know that it was used to track us as teachers. On the wall of the TFA office where many coaching sessions were held was a magnetic board with each corps member's name along with their class achievement percentages. Our names were color-coded just like those of our students—green for proficient, yellow for needs work, and red for intensive.

In general, what I hoped for in terms of mentorship and support from TFA was never fully realized. My MTLD said part of his job was to "help me help myself hold myself accountable"—an additional pressure that I really didn't need. He wasn't familiar with the nuances of lower elementary curriculum and could not help me develop my pedagogy to help my lowest performing readers. He performed Google searches and provided me links, but in general, the problem of MTLDs' lack of teaching experience, coupled with their not being familiar with the content areas of the corps members they supervise, is a common issue. My MTLD was a really good person, but his attempts to provide a vision or execute a great lesson on fractions didn't help my most pressing needs. With nearly all of my students reading below grade level, I learned that the teaching of reading is difficult and requires knowledge of vocabulary like *diphthongs, digraphs, breves,* and *macrons*— none of which I learned at Institute. For the most part, I remember Institute as a time of pep rallies, sitting, acronym memorization, and getting-to-know-you games—with about an hour of daily supervised teaching. Unsurprisingly, when I entered my own classroom, I did not know how to teach reading to English Language Learners—many of whom had learning disabilities. Furthermore, due to the remoteness of my teaching assignment, both of my required graduate courses on the foundations of reading were online and did not sufficiently prepare me for teaching reading in my classroom.

Standards and More Testing

Prior to entering the classroom, I was well aware of the effects of No Child Left Behind that had led to the current state of education. I knew that the states were compelled to administer standardized tests on an annual basis, and that the emphasis placed on these tests resulted in anxiety and the kind of "teaching to the test" that all stakeholders find abhorrent. Yet, even with this level of awareness, I was caught off guard by how higher test scores are automatically associated with better teaching and more student learning. The emphasis placed on test scores is immense and can validate corps members or make them feel inferior. Every teacher knows that there is more to this profession than growth percentages, but the threat of test scores and associated evaluations are always relevant and on one's mind.

As a third grade teacher, I was required to implement regular progress monitoring exams that simulated end-of-year tests, even though students hadn't yet been taught a majority of the subject matter. Although this district mandate may have been helpful in introducing the children to new words and categories, the need to incrementally improve scores generated an excessive amount of week-to-week anxiety in both test takers and test givers alike. I was required to digitally graph and chart my students' Storytown reading tests (MLCS transitioned from Reading Mastery to Storytown midyear); their Harcourt reading tests; their Aimsweb MCOMP and MCAP scores; and their DAZE scores and their DIBELS scores. We underwent extensive test preparation for the New Mexico Standards Based Assessment (NMSBA) utilizing the New York Regents examinations as a guide. We even took the World Class Instructional Design and Assessment (WIDA) to measure their English language development despite the fact that we never saw their scores to offer NMSBA testing accommodations—which was the intended purpose. During very lengthy professional development sessions on Fridays, teachers had to learn everything about each of these assessments, and their corresponding computer programs, when applicable.

As was expected of me, I met with individual students to discuss their growth goals. Some students cried and revolted by throwing objects or putting their heads on their desks. Other students became used to the asinine testing drill and mechanically filled in their multiple-choice bubbles. All were expected to sit in silence for hours on end as we waited for the rest of the school to finish their tests. These students were 8- and 9-year-old kids living in homes that might not have running water or electricity. These were kids who despite the snow, the wind, the stray dogs, and the dark, walked on muddy roads to their bus stops every single morning, whether they wanted to or not. Each day, they rode the bus for an hour to get to a school that discouraged free play and considered eliminating recess.

It was in this school that I taught to the tests and standards. The school and district were concerned about the "huge shift" in public education to the adoption of the Common Core State Standards. This was the push for the hiring of new consulting companies with names like the Common Core Institute and the Common Core Writing Academy. I participated in daylong professional development sessions with these new companies and was forced to obtain my "black belt" and "green belt" certification on the Common Core online. My school paid for the deconstructed standards that I was required to post on my back wall, and all of my observers checked that my students chanted these standards at the beginning of each lesson using the sentence frame "Students will be able to..." Then during the lesson, I was required to refer to the objective and revisit it at the end to ascertain whether or not we had met said objective. I quickly concluded that not only was assimilating to the scripted curriculum and method of teaching unpleasant, but absolute compliance to the standards carried incredible weight in my school community. Teachers were encouraged to deliver Common Core math and reading lessons to the exclusion of all other subjects. Whether or not something was Common Core–aligned or would help my students pass their Common Core–aligned tests became the barometer for what I could or could not teach. It was clear that school-wide best-practice curriculum theory had shifted from what-to-teach to how-to-evaluate.

In May 2014 the New Mexico Public Education Department signed a contract with Pearson to write and administer new Common Core–aligned tests for the Partnership for Assessment of Readiness for College and Careers (PARCC). PARCC is expected to net Pearson over $1 billion and affect 6 to 10 million schoolchildren (Peters, 2014). The threat of the PARCC tests started to loom over our heads a year before the contract. At a TFA professional development (PD) session, we analyzed the third and sixth grade released test questions that seemed overtly challenging—even for adults. We were told that helping our students become "college and career ready" was related to "high expectations"—something that we had been told from the beginning of Institute was the key to student achievement. It took me a while to realize that while terms such as *high expectations* and *big goals* make great sound bites, they have their limits. Choosing to believe in your students learning doesn't mean that they need to meet the arbitrary passing grade for PARCC.

In these PD sessions, I was led to believe that the more experienced educators and creators of these tests and standards knew my students better than I and could help them be "college and career ready." It took me a long time to trust that I knew each of my students; how each of them learned; what intrigued them; and what would really be meaningful and useful to them later in life. This is what longtime educators mean when they say that teaching is an art.

The Art of Teaching

Since Mariano Lake Community School was a turnaround school, the focus was solely on implementing a standards-aligned curriculum and accompanying testing regime. Teachers are evaluated on the teaching of those standards and the performance of their students on the standards-aligned tests. The ideal educator at a turnaround school fits neatly into a rubric that includes usage of technology, objectives, formative assessments and the like. In general, TFA and BIE policy seem to complement each other in their support of this regimented teaching style.

During my 2 years as a corps member, I felt like a hardworking pawn in a much larger bureaucracy. I was constantly torn between my commitment to what I thought was good and useful for my kids and my commitment to larger systems. My mental and physical health unraveled to the point that I spent a week in the hospital.

Most days, I wanted to quit, but I did what I could to make teaching bearable. First and foremost, I moved into town and commuted—often carpooling with other TFA corps members. My fellow corps members became my best friends, roommates, and support team. We formed our own informal "learning team," which was really just our house sharing lesson plans, ideas, and resources on how children learn. Given my background in environmental education, I happily taught science after lunch using my own curriculum that incorporated lively experiments, connections to other subjects, and time outdoors. Interestingly, in my second year, I was appointed to be the third and fourth grade representative to the MLCS Leadership Committee. This position gave me greater insight into our school's operations, accreditation process, and connection to the BIE—all of which helped me understand how all these policies sifted down to my classroom.

At Mariano Lake, there was such high turnover of TFA and non-TFA teachers alike that in the 2013–2014 school year, I was the sole credentialed (albeit provisionally credentialed) third grade teacher. For most of that year, I supported the other third grade classroom taught by an assistant, until finally the entire class was brought into my room full-time. With too many students in half of a portable, I was ready to quit again despite being so close to finishing my 2 years as a corps member. Yet, contrary to what cynics might say about TFA corps members, I really did love every one of my students, and I know my colleagues loved theirs, too. This is why, in my mind, that there has always been such a huge categorical difference between the TFA national organization and the individual corps members themselves. TFA National is a set of corporate offices located far away from the Navajo reservation. They are entrusted with the preparation of thousands of teachers nationwide in a short period of time, and unfortunately they resort to mechanical pedagogy and rubric observations. They haven't met my students and therefore cannot know how their challenges are unique. My students and I spent every single school day together from 8:00 a.m. to 3:30 p.m. I knew when they needed to hear a joke, when lessons were perceived as unimportant, when a song would help with memorization, when an intervention was necessary, when they were sleepy, when somebody was embarrassed, when an objective was too hard, when somebody's mom wasn't home, and a million other things that a teacher always has to be aware of. I admired my students' resilience as they persevered through academic problems and the very real issues associated with poverty, domestic violence, sexual abuse, gambling, neglect, and alcoholism. In addition to being my students' teacher, I took on the roles of nurse, psychologist, social worker, confidant, and parent. I witnessed firsthand their struggle as Navajos in a country with historically abysmal policies affecting native life and education.

From these experiences, it became clear that education reform does not occur within a vacuum. Meaningful help for Mariano Lake Community School cannot be in the form of big goals, high expectations, standards, tracking, and a commitment to justice. Real reform for my students must address root issues associated with poverty and family life. My teaching experience under these conditions and false promises led me to conclude that TFA and an increased emphasis on testing will continue to purposefully ignore these aspects of education as they develop even more standards and bureaucracies that future TFA corps members will struggle to implement.

REFERENCES

Peters, J. (2014, July 3). New Mexico denies protest of Common Core–aligned testing contract. *Santa Fe Reporter.* Retrieved from http://www.sfreporter.com/santafe/article-8881-state-denies-protest-of-common-core-aligned-testing-contract.html

.

CHAPTER THIRTEEN

The Gaps Between You and Me: Being Gay in TFA

SUMMER PENNELL
Eastern North Carolina, 2009–2011

BIOSKETCH

Summer Pennell is a North Carolina native and was a Teach For America (TFA) corps member in Eastern North Carolina (ENC) from 2009 to 2011. Her experiences as a high school English teacher, particularly those with her queer students, motivated her to dedicate her career to queer students and teachers. She is currently a doctoral candidate at UNC–Chapel Hill, where her research interests include secondary English methods, queer theory and pedagogy, critical literacy, social justice education, intersectionality, and qualitative methods. She has an M.A. in folklore from the University of Oregon and a B.A. in English literature and interdisciplinary visual arts from the University of Washington–Seattle, and values interdisciplinary work.

NARRATIVE

Since its founding, Teach For America (TFA) has focused on the achievement gap: the difference in test scores between students in affluent schools and those in low-income schools. Corps members are taught to believe this gap can be closed through the perseverance of individual teachers. Yet, despite TFA's rhetoric, the organization itself ignores the gaps it created between the organization and its corps members, and between the corps members themselves. These gaps are the ones I fell through during my 2 years teaching in a small rural school in Eastern North Carolina (called ENC by TFA). TFA, as an organization, expects that teachers can individually effect change in their students through the power of teaching alone, as if teachers are in complete control of their students' lives and futures. This tunnel vision makes TFA staffers blind to differences between individuals that put results outside of their control. Working as a lesbian in the rural South, I was not a typical corps member. My local TFA staff was unwilling to see my needs as a problem and even less willing to see how my needs could affect my ability to teach.

Just Say Yes

I joined TFA when I graduated with a master's degree in folklore in 2009. The stock market had crashed, and the museum education jobs I had hoped for were being cut as quickly as my graduation was approaching. I saw a sign on campus for TFA and realized I had 2 weeks to apply for the last deadline. I was drawn in by their mission of serving underserved populations, and I thought that teaching in a public school would give me good experience for a later career in museum education. I combed their website, looking for information on how TFA handled LGBTQ issues, but found no information on how the organization supported these corps members or how they felt about teachers being out to their students. Yet, I remained optimistic and applied.

At the time, I was living in Eugene, Oregon. I was out and proud in all aspects of my life and couldn't imagine being any other way. When I received an offer to be a corps member in ENC, a rural region, I was hesitant. I immediately looked up the employment laws in North Carolina and found there was no employment protection for sexuality, gender identity, or gender expression. There was also a current battle in the state to include those designations in a law protecting students from bullying. This did not bode well, but I located an active gay community in the Triangle area (Raleigh, Durham, and Chapel Hill) though there was very little chance my teaching job would be in that area.

Meanwhile, TFA inundated me with phone calls, e-mails, and letters from regional staff and current corps members. I was told that my students needed me and were waiting for me in North Carolina. I found all this overwhelming, as I had not yet realized the extent of TFA's cult-like tactics. When the regional director called me, I was frank with her about my concerns. Having lived in small-town North Carolina until the age of 14, I had some knowledge of what I would be getting in to. In my small town, people who did not fit the norm were misunderstood and ostracized, and as an out lesbian I feared I would experience the same. As her ultimate goal was to get me to accept TFA's offer, she offered to put me in contact with a gay current corps member. I'm sure she chose him as she knew he would give me the answers I sought and would likely also speak positively about TFA. When I talked to the corps member on the phone, he was honest with me about his mixed feelings. He had been called a faggot by some of his students and was not getting a lot of support from his school administration, but he was satisfied overall with his decision to join TFA. I also talked to a non-TFA teacher in North Carolina who was a lesbian. Her main advice was to live in a county next to where you work to have more privacy. I was told by others that it takes a while to be accepted in small Southern towns, and that I should lie low my first year. I determined that I would make the best of the situation and be patient, and I was assured by my regional director that every effort would be made to place me within drivable distance of the Triangle. This seemed like the best I could hope for, so with a lighter heart I accepted the offer and prepared to move to North Carolina.

One of Us

My uneasiness returned at Induction, when the new cohort of TFA corps members meets in their region for orientation. The first night, an ENC alum spoke of how we should pay attention to our table mates, as he met his wife at this very event. This seemed strange to me: Was TFA pushing TFA marriages, to produce TFA babies? I had been wary of a cult mentality that first day (due to talk of how we were the best, the chosen ones), and this heteronormative declaration began to drive a wedge between the organization and me. I was already different from the typical corps member in that I was 27 instead of 22 (27 was ancient in TFA years), so now my aversion to dating coworkers, especially male ones, might also set me apart. It felt like the TFA staff members expected us all to be the same, with the same needs and expectations, ready to start our first real job. As this was not my first job, perhaps I was able to pay more attention to personal needs than the average TFA corps member, and consequently the support I sought was different. I did not feel that I was one of them, or at least not in the way they expected.

The cultlike atmosphere was also present at Institute, the 5-week teacher training period. I had joined TFA to gain teaching experience in a high school classroom and had not realized that some joined to be a part of a movement. Institute was full of forced-socialization attempts to bond everyone to each other and the organization, which I largely avoided by aligning myself with other skeptics: We called ourselves "the Snarky Old Folks." But there was one group I gladly joined, the LGBTQ Affinity Group. This group was a lovely break and gave me a chance to talk with a diverse group of queer corps members, in various stages of discovering their own sexualities. We met weekly and served as a support system for each other.

The rest of Institute was not as welcoming. During one of our diversity sessions, we listened to a recording of a former corps member talking about coming out to her students in the context of a class conversation. The Institute instructors were ambivalent about her situation. No one would discuss the organization's policy or even their own feelings about coming out to students, but the impression I got was that it was frowned upon. We spent another diversity session learning about a young boy who had recently committed suicide because his classmates perceived him as gay and teased him mercilessly. Everyone agreed this was a tragedy and that bullying should not be tolerated, though some corps members mumbled to themselves, unsure of how they felt about protecting gay kids or even kids who people thought were gay. How was this living up to the TFA motto of "One day, all children in this nation will have the opportunity to attain an excellent education?" It was clear that TFA did not count LGBTQ kids in that "all."

The LGBTQ affinity group discussed these troubling events, and we were glad to have a safe space to do so. Some group members from another region were experiencing discrimination from their own cohort and had taken it upon themselves to call a meeting to clear the air. I mention this not to speak for them, but to illustrate how an official TFA presence in this event was lacking. It was up to the corps members themselves to solve an issue that in other organizations would have been handled by human resources. There was no official position on LGBTQ issues, and I was appalled that TFA staff would be ambivalent about an issue that can cause real harm for students, both in school and in their personal lives. TFA staff loved to speak of education as the "new civil rights movement." I don't think we can draw simple parallels between complex social issues, but I found myself thinking, "What about LGBTQ rights? Does no one notice that movement?" It seemed that no one in TFA did, even though research has shown that discrimination based on sexuality, gender expression, and gender identity has a direct impact on what TFA cares about most: student achievement (Kosciw, Greytak, Bartkiewicz, Boesen, & Palmer, 2012).

Intersectionality was never mentioned in our diversity sessions. This shouldn't have been a surprise, as TFA's core values from 2009 were "relentless pursuit of results, the sense of possibility, disciplined thought, respect and humility, and integrity" (*The Fundraising Journal*, 2010). Working relentlessly without time for careful reflection was not a core value I shared. But it fit the TFA culture of working until exhaustion, because taking time for yourself meant taking time away from your students. Staff sometimes spoke of the importance of self-care, but the unstated implication was that if you needed too much of that you were selfish. And while "the sense of possibility" does have a nice ring of hopefulness, I would learn later that TFA staff would spout this core value to corps members who were struggling, stating that if they just kept that sense of possibility and expected the best in people, they would be fine.

We did, however, read Ladson-Billings's (2006) chapter, "Yes, But How Do We Do It? Practicing Culturally Relevant Pedagogy." I found it ridiculously contradictory that TFA encouraged its corps members to take their students' lives into account, while disregarding the corps members' own personal lives in their quest to "relentlessly pursue results." We were encouraged to live in the community we were teaching in to get to know our students and their families. Staff talked of giving students rides after school, organizing tutoring sessions at local fast-food restaurants, all from a teacher-savior perspective. These stories were in direct contrast to the advice I had been given to keep myself safe as an out lesbian in the rural South. The savior mentality was fed by Friday pep rallies where we were told we were the chosen ones, that students in our regions needed us, and that we could deliver them to salvation through our teaching. Some corps members thrived under this praise. I responded by wearing earplugs to drown out the chanting. I relied on my Snarky Old Folks friends when getting up at the crack of dawn, putting our lunches in our matching TFA bags, and riding on a school bus together to our training schools felt too much like a cult to bear.

Sympathy Is Not Action

After the 6 weeks were up (Induction and Institute), I went back to ENC. During Institute I was offered a job teaching English at a middle school within driving distance of the Triangle. Sadly, when the school's budget was finalized my position was terminated. A month later an offer came to teach English at a high school in a county that had newly partnered with TFA. This county was the most rural placement site in ENC, and 2½ hours away from the Triangle, making living there impossible. I did not immediately accept. When I told the ENC staff I was afraid to live in such a rural area as an out lesbian, they scolded me for making assumptions. They made it clear that not accepting would mean leaving the corps, and while I was willing to do that, they made a last offer to call the superintendent and inform him of my concerns. The ENC director reported back that the principal was supportive of me, and having researched the school and found it to be small and innovative, I accepted the position. Facing unemployment 2 months after moving across the country was not a realistic alternative. While I initially planned to look for an apartment in a neighboring town or county, as was advised, there was a room available in a house of corps members living in the town where my school was located—so in lieu of being homeless on my first day of work, I took the group up on their kind offer.

The community where I lived and worked was very small. It was at least an hour from any city, so my hopes for finding a nearby queer community were dashed. The county was mostly farmland and swamp. The largest store in the county was a grocery store, and one of the small towns was known for having an influential hellfire-and-brimstone-style preacher. Conversations in public seemed too risky, so I craved privacy. You never knew if someone nearby would tell everyone what the new teacher said. As an example of how fast the gossip train worked there, I once received a call from a parent who lived in Virginia who had heard about an incident regarding her child in my class earlier that afternoon. She heard of it not from her daughter, but from her cousin, who heard it from someone else on the school bus. Because of this local love of gossip, I never felt comfortable in public. Additionally, all my students knew where I lived, as did everyone in town. My house backed up to the swamp. The swamp was beautiful, and there was a short boardwalk through it that I found calming. But when I felt isolated, the swamp seemed more sinister, and I felt as if I were sinking.

My first semester was a magical golden time. I loved being a high school English teacher, loved my students, and loved being at a small school where I was the only TFA corps member. My coworkers were friendly, though I knew not everyone was comfortable with my sexuality. While I did not discuss it, my résumé screamed gay, and a few asked me sideways questions to try to figure out what my preferences really were. I did not let this bother me at first, for I was too busy enjoying my job. I escaped nearly every weekend to the Triangle, where I didn't have to worry about what I said in public and could keep my social life private, or at least away from my students and coworkers. I was building a support group for myself that was largely outside of TFA. Other than the Snarky Old Folks and my roommates, I did not build strong relationships with many corps members. It was difficult to build relationships with people who believed in an ideology I felt was fundamentally flawed. In retrospect, I wish I had tried harder to make more local ties. However, it was too taxing to fake a smile around people I feared would not accept me if they really got to know me.

That spring, things at my school began to change. These changes had nothing to do with TFA but made the stress of working in a rural location where I felt isolated more acute. There were rumors of my school closing, and I attended tense school board meetings where my coworkers and I feared our jobs were in jeopardy, only for our speaking time to be stricken from the meeting agenda. The superintendent had squandered the district budget, and that summer he was dismissed. A mentor at my school, frustrated with our principal's lack of consistent leadership, took a job in a neighboring county. Students and staff felt this stress. At that time, students suddenly became interested in my personal life as my novelty as a new teacher wore off. One coworker became increasingly nosy, asking pointed questions about my personal life no matter how much I deflected her questions. After she told me a student called me a whore and said he "didn't approve of my lifestyle," she succeeded in upsetting me, but she still learned nothing from me. That very weekend, at a TFA regional meeting I was "randomly" put into a diversity discussion group. When a Snarky Old Folk accompanied me to talk with our regional director about my fear of being outed in an unsafe environment, she was sympathetic but offered no real course of action or advice. Since TFA was not my employer, they could do nothing about my job insecurity or the discrimination I was facing, and they continued to spout their mantras of expecting the best in people and worrying solely about my students' achievement.

My friend Heather,[1] a fellow queer corps member working in my district, and I became our own queer support group of two. TFA had launched new online communities, and Heather e-mailed the organizers to say that as a queer woman in the rural South she needed support. They responded not with support, but with a general form letter saying she was now a moderator of a new LGBTQ online community. While at first it was just Heather and me talking to each other, gradually more corps members joined. Together, we discussed what we would like from TFA (a comprehensive policy on LGBTQ issues, training for TFA staff and corps members, basic acknowledgment of queer corps members as a group), any hard situations we faced in our classrooms, and what individuals were doing in their regions to improve things for queer corps members. One member shared a brilliant "manifesto" he wrote for his regional leadership. This group encouraged all of us, and we hoped that we would see positive change. Heather and I also planned to form a "Lavender Welcome Committee" for any incoming queer corps members so that they would have the support we lacked. Again, all support came from ourselves; we received no support or acknowledgment from the organization. While we were allowed to have our anti-TFA conversations on their website, we didn't know if anyone was listening.

In the fall of my second year, all homophobic hell broke loose at school. Our staff was diligently curtailing all public displays of affection between our students, and my coworkers asked me to handle the case of a girl touching another girl. Our principal's handling of discipline had become increasingly inconsistent, and we teachers had begun taking matters into our own hands. Thus, even though this situation should not have been my responsibility, I agreed to speak with Kelly as no one else was comfortable. I told her that while she could "play that way" (which is how she described her behavior), any touching between students is inappropriate. Soon afterward, the principal found out about another amorous incident between two female students. He called them into his office, demanding that they tell him the names of any other girls who had engaged in same-sex affection. After this queer witch hunt, he called all of their parents. Some were not out to their parents, and one mother came to pick up her daughter, Cindy. Luckily, the mother was upset she was getting a call from the principal rather than being angry about Cindy's sexuality. Later, Cindy and I had a long talk, and she told me her mother supported her. The next day, I confronted my principal, begging him not to out students again for fear they could be harmed, kicked out, or even killed by angry family members. He looked distressed at this idea, as he truly cared for the students, but I believe he let his own religious beliefs influence his decision. I reached out to TFA staff, and Heather and I met with three staff members at the regional office in Durham. While they were sympathetic, they confirmed that queer issues were not, and would never be, a priority to TFA. All suggestions for improving the lives of queer corps members or educating staff about queer issues in education put the burden on queer corps members. No TFA staff committed to working on the issue.

Next, parents started to complain about me. The principal called me into his office after school to tell me of two parent phone calls. Kelly's mother called, telling the principal "she just wanted her daughter to find out who she was, not have a teacher tell her it's okay to be gay." The previous year, Kelly had disclosed in a writing assignment that she was dating another girl, and it was common knowledge among the students that she identified as bisexual. It was clear Kelly's mom meant that she wanted her daughter to find out she was straight. Another parent, whose son Brian was in one of my classes, called to tell the principal I had posted on Facebook that I was going to come out to my students. This was false, and I explained to my principal that I had blocked both the mother and Brian from seeing my page. The principal confirmed my suspicion that the parent got her information from my coworker, Mr. Donaldson. Mr. Donaldson appeared to be an ally my first year, and previously had told me that Brian's mother was extremely homophobic, preventing her sons from seeing gay family members. Brian was widely perceived to be gay in the community, and I knew this was why he was combative with me in class, even if he was unaware of the reason. Since Mr. Donaldson had shared his concerns for Brian with me, he had changed. He was antagonistic, particularly to me and an African American female teacher, Alicia. The two of us became fast friends and confidants.

In my school district, stories floated in whispers of teachers who had been fired based on gossip alone, and nothing to do with their teaching abilities. North Carolina is an "at will" state, so being fired with little warning was entirely possible. I waited in fear for my phone to ring with a call from our new superintendent. My teaching record was good, but was it good enough to sustain threats from angry parents? I know my students suffered, as I couldn't pay attention to them when I was watching my own back. This was a situation TFA staff believed could not exist—one where my own needs were impeding my ability to "close the achievement gap" or have a "sense of possibility."

While I had no faith that the TFA staff would support me, I was encouraged by my friends and my girlfriend to reach out to them again. As my girlfriend pointed out, at the very least, I needed a record that I sought help in case things got worse. I emailed my corps member advisor (CMA), a woman who observed my classes and offered instructional support when needed. While she was sympathetic, she was at a loss for how to advise me, and wrote, "I know your number one priority will continue to be teaching your students and preparing them for college, and that is the most important thing for your students and their families." I was reminded that when things got tough, corps members' personal needs were never a priority.

I soon met with Chris, another regional TFA staff member. He was already planning to be in my town to meet with corps members at a local fast-food restaurant, but when I told him that was too public, he agreed to meet at my house. To my surprise, he listened with sympathy to my story. Even when I was frank and told him I was surprised he cared, since I had been told previously that issues of sexuality were not a priority, he wanted to help. He offered to talk to the superintendent, but I declined, as I did not trust him. He also offered to try to find me another placement, but this was unrealistic. The closest placement was an hour away, and breaking my lease or driving that far every day were not reasonable solutions. I stressed again that I wished the TFA organization, or at least our region, had a plan in place for when LGBTQ discrimination happened. When he left, I was at least encouraged that I had finally been heard. However, I wondered if he listened only because I had loudly protested their lack of a position on LGBTQ issues since I joined TFA. If this was the first time I brought it up, would I have been ignored or shushed?

One Day, Every School...

At the end of the year, I met with TFA staff for the last time. During my yearly review my CMA seemed distraught. She was upset about the events in the fall and felt terrible that she had not been able to offer more support. At this point, I felt better than she did, as I had one foot out the door and wasn't looking back. Later, I saw Chris at a corps member dinner in my county, and he mentioned that in early June the ENC TFA office would have training for supporting corps members. At his mention that LGBTQ issues could be included, I offered to help. He agreed, and I excitedly prepared a presentation, consulting the members of Heather's online group and other queer corps members from the region. Yet, as the day approached, my e-mails went unanswered. Finally, Chris replied that their schedule was too busy and they couldn't do any LGBTQ training. That was the last straw for me—I was tired of the burden of educating TFA staff about queer issues falling on the shoulders of corps members, only to have them ignored anyway.

The gap between TFA and me started early, but it eventually became too wide to cross, even if I wanted to. I wish I could believe that TFA would strive for not only "one day all (heterosexual) children" but also "one day all corps members." While I obviously think that an excellent education is important, I also hope that one day, every school will be a safe and welcoming place. Unfortunately, I do not think the cult of TFA will ever care about safety, especially the safety of its corps members. I do not think TFA is going away, but I hope they will learn to see their corps members as individual people with individual needs, needs that can't be controlled or overcome with a good attitude alone.

REFERENCES

Kosciw, J. G., Greytak, E. A., Bartkiewicz, M. J., Boesen, M. J., & Palmer, N. A. (2012). The 2011 national school climate survey: The experiences of lesbian, gay, bisexual and transgender youth in our nation's schools. New York: GLSEN.

Ladson-Billings, G. (2006). Yes, but how do we do it? Practicing culturally relevant pedagogy. In J. Landsman & C. W. Lewis (Eds.), *White teachers/diverse classrooms: A guide to building inclusive schools, promoting high expectations, and eliminating racism* (pp. 29–42). Sterling, VA: Stylus Publishing.

The Fundraising Journal. (2010). Organization spotlight: Teach For America. Retrieved from http://thefundraisingjournal.com/Archive/1004/Org_Teach_for_America.html

NOTE

1. Real name used by request. All other names are pseudonyms.

Section III:
TFA's Approach to Criticism and Critics

Good Intentions Gone Bad: Teach For America's Transformation from a Small, Humble Nonprofit into an Elitist Corporate Behemoth

WENDY CHOVNICK

Houston Summer Institute, 1998; Bronx Summer Institute, 2001; Washington, D.C. Corps Member, 2001–2003; Phoenix Staff Member, 2009–2012

BIOSKETCH

Wendy Heller Chovnick graduated from the University of Pennsylvania in 1998 with a degree from Wharton in public policy and a degree from the College of Arts and Sciences in urban studies. While studying in Philadelphia, she focused her academic and volunteer work on the topic of urban public education. Originally, Wendy was a 1998 New Orleans corps member. After coming down with mononucleosis during the summer training, she received an emergency release, and rejoined Teach For America as a 2001 D.C. corps member. She taught middle school math at Paul Public Charter School in Washington, D.C. and remained at her placement school for 4 years, 2 as a classroom teacher and 2 as the GEAR-UP coordinator. Wendy attended law school in Washington, D.C. and moved home to Arizona in 2008. She worked as the chief of staff to the Teach For America executive director in Phoenix from 2009 through 2012.

NARRATIVE

Teach For America (TFA) has a compelling mission and thousands of well-intentioned, hardworking, and intelligent corps members and staff members working towards its ambitious goals. Yet, how the organization functions and the questionable impact it is having, given its vast resources, are disturbing on many levels. I was a 2001 Washington, D.C. corps member, served as the chief of staff to the executive director in the Phoenix TFA office from 2009 to 2012, and have been dedicated to ensuring that "all children have the opportunity to attain an excellent education"[1] for nearly 2 decades. However, I no longer have much confidence in TFA as an organization capable of fulfilling its mission. The perspective I offer is further informed by my experience as a Jane Addams Fellow studying philanthropy and nonprofit management with the most transformative teacher I have ever had, Mr. Robert Payton. Specifically, this chapter discusses: (1) how TFA has changed over time, not always for the better; and (2) how TFA suppresses and ignores nearly all criticism levied against it, whether from inside the organization or from outside.

TFA: Then and Now

Having studied nonprofit management and philanthropic studies from 1999 through 2001 with Mr. Robert Payton at the Indiana University Lilly Family School of Philanthropy, I have high expectations for nonprofit organizations. Nonprofit organizations fill an important need in our society and in our democracy. To the extent that nonprofits accept state and federal tax dollars, they should be held to an even higher standard for outcomes and accountability. According to the 990 form TFA filed with the IRS in 2012 and the organization's 2012–2013 annual letter, TFA collected nearly $320 million from a variety of philanthropic and government sources in 2012. Notably, TFA changed its fiscal year in 2012. Thus, the 2012 numbers reflect an 8-month instead of a full 12-month year, and significantly underestimate the actual money TFA raises in a typical year. In addition, the organization reported endowment funds of nearly $200 million. With this much financial strength should come a great deal of responsibility. Unfortunately, based on what I saw during my time as an employee of the organization, TFA is not fulfilling its responsibility to use these extraordinary resources wisely. In addition, the existence of an endowment is troubling. The endowment suggests that TFA wants to exist in perpetuity; the strong implication is that the organization does not truly believe it can ever close the achievement gap.

There is no doubt in my mind that when Wendy Kopp started TFA in 1990, the organization began to fill a huge, unmet need in urban public education, notably by relieving teacher shortages and highlighting the need for great teachers. For me, and for many other college graduates, the organization also filled another very important need. There were a number of people graduating from elite colleges and universities who wanted to positively contribute to society. As Mr. Payton would tell his postgraduate students, "The only excuse for an elite education is a lifetime of service." There are many college graduates, both when Kopp started TFA and now, who have been privileged to receive an exceptional education and want to devote their lives to creating opportunity for others. TFA gave us a way to start on the path of understanding the many complex challenges facing low-income communities and what might be done to improve the education available to children growing up in those communities. However, TFA was a very different nonprofit organization in 2001, when I became a corps member, than it is now.

TFA has improved in some important respects over time. Specifically, TFA changed its recruitment strategy significantly and, to its credit, focuses enormous attention on encouraging people of color and people from low-income backgrounds to apply. A recent article by Perry (2014) highlights the success TFA has had increasing the number of staff members and corps members who identify as people of color and/or come from a low-income background. While this increased focus on the diversity of the organization is significant, I am not aware of current data that links this increased diversity to better student outcomes. Despite improvements like this, I believe TFA was in many ways a better, and more genuine, organization in the late 1990s and early 2000s than it is today.

As a 2001 Washington, D.C. corps member, I was surrounded with corps members, a very small TFA staff (4 staff members for 80 to 100 corps members), and fellow teachers who all felt a common passion to provide the best education possible for our students. Nobody thought that he or she had *the* right answer, and we were all striving to do our best for the students while seeking to understand the complexities and challenges facing the schools and communities in which we worked. Everything was about collaboration and working as hard as we could for our students and schools. There were few, if any, management layers, and all resources, both financial and human, went directly to the students and schools we were serving. In 2001, TFA felt like a grassroots nonprofit where everyone had a voice and each of us felt like we could have a positive impact. Everyone was accepted and valued simply for working as hard as we possibly could towards a common mission of providing an excellent education to low-income students. Admittedly, we were naïve. We started teaching with no formal education training and hoped we could make a significant impact on most, or even all, of our students. Our students' academic results were mixed and difficult to measure. As a corps member, you never truly know the impact you have on most of your students. You see them for only a year or two. Yet, I have had the privilege of keeping in touch with a handful of my students since 2002. They are now in their early twenties.

The most significant impact I have had on these students comes from keeping in touch with them for so many years, editing college essays, assisting with job applications, encouraging them, and being there to help them talk through and think through various challenges they face or life decisions they are making. Despite the uncertainty around the specific impact we were having on our students, when I was a corps member, there seemed to be a widespread sense of integrity, humility, authenticity, and a shared commitment to go above and beyond whatever we thought was possible.

Since 2001, management expanded exponentially within TFA. From 2009 until 2012, we had about 30 staff members in the Phoenix office and about 300 corps members working in schools throughout Phoenix. Thus, there were many more staff members supporting far fewer corps members than there had been in 2001. The number of management layers, both within the region and outside the region on the national team, was immense. In order to place 300 corps members (about 150 each year), we had an entire team of people dedicated to building relationships with schools and districts. We needed an entire team of people to fundraise for the region, and only about half of our staff members, mostly the managers of teacher leadership development (MTLDs), worked directly with corps members on a regular basis. For many staff members, especially those of us not working directly with corps members, it was difficult, or even impossible, to see how—or if—our work was having a positive impact on corps members or low-income students in Phoenix.

Even those staff members on the Teacher Leadership Development Team, whose main job it was to support corps members, spent countless hours each week in meetings and entering huge amounts of data. These time-consuming requirements, driven by management layers and management requirements, gave the MTLDs less time to work directly with corps members to help them improve their teaching. Another very real challenge is that most MTLDs stay in their roles for only 2 or 3 years. So it is common to have a brand new MTLD, with only 2 or 3 years of teaching experience and little or no experience providing professional development to new teachers, in charge of helping a new teacher learn. Further, it is common for MTLDs to be supporting corps members in content areas about which they have limited knowledge or expertise. The idea of corps members who are inexperienced teachers being supported by these MTLDs, who themselves often have limited teaching experience, is troubling.

As a result of the many management layers and many meetings that pervade the structure and culture of TFA, the vast majority of staff members and corps members, even high performing or highly effective ones, received an enormous amount of feedback on a weekly or even daily basis. This feedback, while intended to drive better outcomes, was often extremely harsh. Ongoing critical feedback was, and is, a large part of TFA's culture. Yet, I did not see this feedback translating into better results or outcomes for staff members, corps members or students. Notably, the support corps members and staff members receive is very inconsistent across regions. Neither management layers nor meetings were effective in ensuring that corps members or staff members received consistent, high quality support.

I witnessed a compelling example of TFA's failure to support its corps members, as a direct result of its expansion and excessive focus on management, during the 2013–2014 school year. A former student of mine who is now a TFA corps member started her second year of teaching in the fall of 2014. Her experience makes me question the structures and "support" TFA puts in place for corps members. My former student struggled significantly in her first year of teaching due to many factors, including an ineffective administration (the entire administration was replaced during the summer of 2014), a challenging student population with many unmet basic needs, and the fact that being a first year teacher is extremely challenging for anyone. So, she reached out to her MTLD for support. It was, and still is, my understanding that it is the role of the MTLD to help struggling teachers and to help all TFA teachers be as effective as possible in the classroom. Yet, it took months for her MTLD to make the time to actually visit the teacher and her classroom, in part because the MTLD had so many TFA-driven meetings and conferences to attend. According to this corps member, "It has been my personal experience that my MTLD spent less time coaching me and more time in retreats that were supposed to be beneficial to me. My MTLD only came to my school two times and her manager only came once. Both my MTLD and her manager did not know how to support me, which they admitted to me, partly because the school I am teaching in is so tough."

Back in 2001, if I had contacted my MTLD (called a program director then), she would have come to my class the following day or at least within a week to offer support and guidance. As a new teacher, I remember how helpful it was to have an experienced teacher observe my classroom and give me feedback or suggestions. It is unfortunate that TFA's significant growth, accompanied by a corporate structure filled with meetings and staff development conferences, appears to be getting in the way of providing some struggling corps members with the support they need and are explicitly requesting.

As I reflect on my time working with TFA, I attribute much of the negative change to the organization's misguided decision to change its core values in 2011, and to the organization failing to ask the right questions. When I started working with TFA, the core values were: Relentless Pursuit of Results, Sense of Possibility, Disciplined Thought, Respect and Humility, and Integrity. These values were clear and easy to understand, and could be both identified and cultivated in corps members and staff members. The current core values are: Transformational Change, Leadership, Team, Diversity, and Respect and Humility. These new core values are aspirational and unclear, and changed TFA as an organization as well as its overall attitude towards its work. The changes I witnessed were not positive. Instead of valuing hard work, a belief in others, and constant critical reflection to drive the actions most likely to help close the achievement gap, TFA now values transforming things above all else. While these new core values may very well be appropriate for the TFA alumni movement, I consider these core values for brand new teachers, and often inexperienced staff members, to be misguided and even irresponsible.

We would never ask anyone in a brand new field or a brand new job to be transformational from day one. Instead, we would expect those individuals to work hard and learn as much as possible so that they could one day become transformational leaders in the field. I often reflect on a line from a song by Common featuring Mos Def called "The Questions." In it, Mos Def asks, "How you got high expectations but got no patience?" This line highlights why I believe TFA is failing its corps members and its staff members, and failing as an organization. The only constant at TFA is change. Yet, the more things change, the more they stay the same and the farther TFA drifts from fulfilling its mission. TFA's flawed business model, where it is constantly innovating and changing, does not allow for any stability in the organization. A certain degree of stability is necessary for success. This type of constant innovation and change in a classroom would create a highly unstable environment for students that would result in an unproductive and unpleasant learning environment that would prevent students from succeeding. The same is true at TFA. This corporate model of constant change is failing at every level. TFA must have high expectations, but the organization must also learn patience, or it may never figure out what works and what does not. Ironically, after changing its core values and the academic outcomes corps members were working towards in 2011, TFA is currently in the process of trying to reinvent and re-envision these new core values because of the negative consequences they have had throughout the organization.

TFA staff members, corps members, and critics of TFA all have a sense of urgency about closing the achievement gap, and I believe we would all agree that high expectations are essential. However, expecting corps members to be transformational leaders and close the achievement gap in their first year of teaching is foolish. All of the transformational teachers I know have a deep sense of love and respect for their students and the communities in which they work. In addition, the vast majority of transformational teachers I know have either exceptional training in the specific subject(s) they are teaching and/or a consistent and long-lasting dedication to the students, schools, and communities in which they work, which lasts far beyond the 2-year TFA commitment. TFA should be much more reflective and cautious with the changes it makes and the results it expects. A return to the disciplined thought of the past would do the organization a lot of good.

From what I have seen in recent years, the many management layers and structures in place at TFA seem to be more of a barrier to providing corps members with adequate support than anything else. Over about a decade, TFA transformed from a small grassroots nonprofit where everyone mattered, everyone had a voice, and everyone was in it together, into a nonprofit that acts more like a high-powered corporate giant, with an extremely hierarchical structure, that is not adequately serving the needs of new teachers and is not set up in a way that allows staff members to provide the most helpful support and guidance to corps members. For me, it is an ironic and uncomfortable shift, given TFA's mission and orientation.

Despite the increased focus on diversity for corps members and staff members, the way in which TFA selects corps members and hires staff members felt very elite and elitist to me when I was part of the process of selecting corps members and hiring staff members from 2009 to 2012. TFA is constantly searching for *the* right fit and often fails to recognize a sense of possibility (one of the former core values) in its people. I witnessed this every time a manager took steps to "coach" another staff member out of his or her role. This meant a manager would convince the staff member that he or she was not a "good fit" for the role and should resign or, in some cases, the manager would put a staff member on an improvement plan that was virtually impossible to complete successfully. In these situations, TFA showed limited patience for what it considered to be struggling staff members, failed to carefully listen and consider the staff members' perspectives, and often encouraged great people who had made significant contributions to leave.

Even with well-intentioned efforts to be respectful and humble, the only former core value the organization retained, TFA's elitism, creates a number of very real tensions with low-income schools and communities. In some respects, TFA was a more elite organization back in 2001 simply because most of its recruitment took place at Ivy League schools. Yet, it didn't feel as elite then. It is ironic, and even sad, that this current, more diverse TFA feels far more elite and elitist now than it did a decade ago.

TFA and Its Unwillingness to Accept Criticism

In stark contrast to the harsh and constant criticism that TFA doles out to its corps members and staff members, much of what the organization has been doing in recent years—creating its own public relations machine—suggests a desire to be above criticism itself. During my tenure on staff, the organization created a national communications team whose job was to get positive press out about TFA and to swiftly address any negative press. My sense was, and still is, that TFA cares more about the public perception of what it is doing than about what it is actually doing to improve educational outcomes and opportunities for low-income students throughout the United States. I am a firm believer that all organizations, especially nonprofit organizations, must be open to critique and willing to engage in honest dialogue about limitations and how to improve. In my experience, TFA was more interested in sharing a good story than engaging in a public dialogue about really difficult questions facing the organization and facing education.

I would suggest that TFA's web page "TFA On the Record" provides an example of TFA's lack of openness to critique. As I will discuss in more detail below, "TFA On the Record" is merely a forum TFA created to "discuss" and comment on anything written about the organization that TFA believes to be misguided or incorrect. To me, "On the Record" is a compelling example of TFA's lack of openness to criticism and lack of a desire to engage in true dialogue, and evidence that TFA cares far too much about its public image. In addition, I believe that some of TFA's human resource policies are designed to quash and silence what could be valid and helpful criticism and insight into a very complex and multifaceted organization.

"On the Record" begins with an overview of TFA, its work, and its impact. It presents "6 Things You Should Know About Us." These "things" are no more than TFA putting a distinctly self-congratulatory spin on issues that deserve far more serious consideration and conversation. Here are just two examples of how TFA presents information in a way that seems less than forthright and disinterested in engaging in key conversations about important issues in education:

- The first point is, "Most TFA alum teachers work in traditional district schools, not charters." However, the numbers that back up this "fact" are that 48% work in district public schools, 42% in public charter schools, 6% in private schools, and 3% in other schools. Thus, TFA could have more accurately said "Most TFA alum teachers do NOT work in traditional district schools." With slightly less than half of alumni teachers working in public district schools, TFA clearly wanted to put its own marketing spin on the numbers. This "fact" also raises a key question of how TFA counts the teachers working in New Orleans public schools, where the district is 100% charter schools. Do the New Orleans alumni count as district or charter teachers? Instead of putting forth this questionable, and unhelpful, statistic, why not engage in a more substantive and meaningful discussion of the differences between public district and public charter schools, if any, as well as the equally important topics of access and quality?
- The second point (according to the "On the Record" site on August 6, 2014) was that, "TFA teachers return for a second year at a higher rate than new teachers nationwide." The numbers that back up this "fact" are: reportedly 90% of TFA teachers return for a second year as compared with 86% overall and 83% in low-income schools. Just below this seemingly positive statistic, the site explains, "We spend about $51,400 per corps member over three

years, starting with the recruitment year." For over $50,000 per corps member, I should hope that retention would be better for TFA teachers when compared with other teachers! Further, it strikes me that a small number of corps members quit during their second year. Thus, this statistic leaves me with more questions than answers. A far more helpful statistic would be one that compares the 2-year retention rates. Did TFA not highlight the 2-year retention rate because it didn't make TFA look as good? Where is TFA's acknowledgement that its retention rate should, in fact, be higher, because EACH corps member is provided with $14,000 in additional professional development over 2 years when compared with other new teachers?

TFA's first post to "On the Record" is dated June 24, 2013. Since that time, TFA has "responded" to 44 additional blog posts and articles in reputable publications, which include *The Atlantic, The Nation, Phi Delta Kappan,* and *Rethinking Schools.* TFA's responses fall into two main categories: They either clarify or correct a genuine misconception an author has about TFA, or they put what I call a "TFA spin" on an article that TFA does not consider to be "on message." In some cases, TFA takes the time and accompanying resources to post a response to articles that mention TFA only in passing.

My favorite example of what I would consider an unnecessary response from TFA occurs with an article in *Salon* magazine titled "White Supremacy Stripped Bare: What *Do the Right Thing* Tells Us 25 Years Later." The TFA post explains, "In an otherwise insightful essay…Brittney Cooper misrepresents TFA's program and mission." In reality, in Cooper's fairly lengthy piece, which I agree is both insightful and thought-provoking, the only mention of TFA is, "the TFA model, which has effectively deprofessionalized teaching, is at the center of the school reform movement. That same movement has increasingly privatized and gutted the public school system, creating even more inequality for black and brown youth." It does not seem to me that Cooper commented at all on TFA's program or mission. Instead, Cooper shares an opinion that could form the basis for a vibrant and important conversation about the role TFA has played, and is playing, in school reform. Instead of wasting time responding to this very minor point in Cooper's article, why not either let it go altogether, or invite Cooper to have a conversation with TFA staff about the school reform movement? I am deeply disturbed by TFA's attitude in "On the Record," and by the fact that the organization is taking time and financial resources to deflect and explain away critique instead of engaging with it. Not only does TFA too often refuse to accept criticism, but also, over the years, TFA has increasingly put on blinders, asking everyone to trust the organization and its leadership and not to think critically about the many ways TFA could be doing a much better job. My former student and current corps member summarized TFA's attitude towards criticism beautifully. She explained,

"Critiquing the organization is almost guaranteed to result in friendship suicide and employment suicide. TFA does not see criticism as an opportunity to improve. Instead, TFA uses anything that is not positive feedback as an opportunity to question your drive to close the achievement gap or your commitment to working with low-income communities."

Although I could respond to many more "On the Record" posts, I will comment on only one more. There was an article in *The Nation* in April 2014 about TFA's tumultuous beginning in the Seattle area. The article, by Alexandra Hootnick, is entitled "Teachers Are Losing Their Jobs, but TFA's Expanding. What's Wrong with That?" While I am relieved that TFA acknowledges the rocky start in Seattle, the reality is that TFA knew, or at the very least should have known, that there was little, if any, local support for its entry into the Seattle public schools. TFA Seattle opened while I was still on the Phoenix staff. Thus, I was privy to some of the conversations and great struggles TFA had throughout the process.

TFA's response to this article suggests that even though it admits that the opening of the Seattle region was problematic, the ends now justify the means. Specifically, the Seattle executive director comments that Hootnick's article "provides an incomplete picture of the successes our region has had since our launch." A corps member Hootnick interviewed for her piece, who has now been teaching at his placement school for 4 years, suggests he will make teaching a career, and was unhappy that Hootnick used a 2-year-old interview with him for her article. Still, TFA seems to be missing the real point of Hootnick's article and the most important questions she is raising: Should TFA have gone into Seattle in the first place? Was there a need for TFA in Seattle? Was there a teacher shortage? Hootnick suggests there was minimal, if any, need, as well as no teacher shortage. That leads me to another important question: Should TFA stay in Seattle? Will TFA strengthen the education system in Seattle or weaken it? These are important questions about which TFA should be ready and willing to engage.

TFA's entry into Seattle was a disaster on many levels. Had TFA been open at all to the immense negative feedback it was receiving, the organization would have, and should have, decided not to open a region there, at least until there was widespread community support. Ironically, during the time the Seattle region opened, we in Phoenix were receiving a lot of national pressure, and some pressure from funders, to expand to Tucson. Thankfully, we had a local leadership team, rather than a national staff member, that was ultimately able to determine that expanding to Tucson was not a good idea because there was not the necessary combination of need and community support in Tucson to allow TFA to open and operate there at the time. To its credit, TFA appears to have learned a lesson and stopped expanding for the sake of expansion. Still, for a number of years, one of TFA's goals was growth. That growth often lacked both an adequate sensitivity to community needs and a respect for key education leaders in those communities. This focus on expansion seems more akin to a corporate mindset than a nonprofit one.

One additional way TFA is silencing important critique and insight is with some of its human resource policies, notably its severance packages. Severance packages are common in for-profit organizations, and certain nonprofits use them as well. According to the Department of Labor, "Severance pay is often granted to employees upon termination of employment." At TFA, the employees I knew of who received severance packages were those who TFA had asked to resign. Lorraine Anderson King, the Senior Vice President of Communications at Teach For America, confirmed that the organization provides severance packages, "to the vast majority of staff members who exit for involuntary reasons in order to help support them in their transitions off of staff" and that those packages include a "severance agreement contain[ing] a non-disparagement clause…" (personal communication, January 2015). According to Jacobs (2011), severance agreements often contain noncompete or nonsolicitation clauses. Jacobs also explains that some include "a nondisparagement clause, which prevents you from saying anything negative about the company, even if it's true." As with most organizations, TFA's severance packages are confidential. Staff members who receive them are able to consult a few individuals, including an attorney if they wish, before signing one. Despite the secrecy that surrounds TFA's severance packages, in the 990 forms TFA files with the IRS each year, TFA publicly discloses how much money it has paid to key employees who received a severance package when they left the organization.

Specifically, in its 2010 filing, TFA reported that "Chief Development Officer, Lily Rager, and SVP, Teacher Preparation, Support and Development, Aylon Samouoha, received a severance payment of $63,424 and $96,023 respectively from Teach of [sic] America." In the 2011 filing, TFA reported that "Ellen Shepard received a severance payment of $65,323." Shepard was the "Chief Info Officer through Sept. 2011." She received a total of $221,638 in reportable wages in 2011. Thus, she received an upfront payment when she left that amounted to a number of months of her full salary as part of her severance package. I may be naïve, but these numbers are shocking to me, given that TFA is a nonprofit organization and that these significant severance packages were funded with philanthropic, or even government dollars. I, for one, would not want a donation I gave to a nonprofit organization going towards a severance package that includes a nondisparagement clause that forbids the employee from ever sharing his or her honest ideas, reflections, and criticisms about the organization after he or she leaves.

I was lucky. I left my employment with TFA voluntarily. Not only was I not asked to leave, but when I did not want to work a full schedule after giving birth to my second child, TFA would have allowed me to continue working a 60% schedule at 60% of my salary, because the organization wanted to retain me as an employee. Thus, I received no severance package and was never put in a position where I was asked to sign something saying I would never publicly discuss my opinions about the organization. I am disheartened by the many employees, both high-level ones disclosed on TFA's 990 and the many others we will never know about, who left the organization under a severance agreement and will never be permitted, under the agreements, to share their honest critique and feedback about TFA with the public. This distrust of critique is, to me, indicative of TFA's broad, self-interested, protectionist approach, which is completely contrary to a genuine commitment to do whatever it takes to improve public education.

CONCLUSION

The best teachers are often those who are constantly learning, always striving to improve their pedagogy, and open to well-intentioned critique directed at improving the effectiveness of and positive culture in their classrooms. As an organization with teaching and education at its core, TFA should, at the very least, model these characteristics.

Nonprofits like TFA could learn a great deal from taking to heart some of James Madison's reflections in his Federalist Paper 10. Despite Madison's focus on government, his insights ring true for nonprofit organizations as well. He wrote, "However anxiously we may wish that these complaints had no foundation, the evidence of known facts will not permit us to deny that they are in some degree true." I think that TFA would be a different, better, and stronger organization if instead of trying to point out the small things that are untrue or inaccurate, as it does with "On the Record," it would engage with the public, with its corps members, with its staff, and especially with its growing number of critics in the larger, more substantive critiques being levied against it that hold some degree of truth. I also think TFA would be a more genuine and possibly more effective organization if there were a way for it to regain some of the culture and characteristics, the feel of a smaller, more personal, less corporate nonprofit, from over a decade ago.

In a seminal book about the role of philanthropy and the nonprofit sector, Charles Clotfelter (1999), a Duke University professor, and Thomas Ehrlich, a senior scholar at the Carnegie Foundation for the Advancement of Teaching, explain that

> Too many of us working in philanthropy and the nonprofit sector believe that simply because we know we are doing good, the public should trust us. Not enough of us seem to recognize that public trust must not just be earned, but continually earned. The public is entitled to continued evidence that trust is warranted. (p. 514)

TFA has adopted a mindset that trying to "do good" is enough. Despite my criticism, I believe TFA as an organization, including most of its staff members and corps members, has good intentions. However, good intentions are not enough. To earn a wider degree of public trust, and to earn back the trust of many of us who were once avid supporters and have become critics, TFA should make it a priority to seek to truly understand, and even appreciate, the critiques being levied against it, and to communicate a more open attitude toward dialogue and critique.

A quote Matt Kramer, one of the co-CEOs of TFA, shared with me in a May 2014 e-mail exchange sums up why it is doubtful that TFA will ever open itself up to the type of criticism and honest dialogue that could make it a much more effective and honorable organization. Kramer wrote, "As Daniel Patrick Moynihan said, everyone is entitled to their own opinion, but not their own facts" (M. Kramer, personal communication, May 6, 2014). When one of the two top leaders of TFA believes that TFA is the one with the "facts," and the rest of us just hold "opinions," it seems clear that TFA is destined to remain an insular organization, uninterested in listening to critics, asking the right questions, and engaging in difficult but important conversations. This close-minded, corporate attitude is preventing TFA from realizing its mission of "One day."

REFERENCES

Clotfelter, C. T., & Ehrlich, T. (1999). The world we must build. In C. Clotfelter & T. Ehrlich (Eds.), *Philanthropy and the nonprofit sector in a changing America* (pp. 499–516). Bloomington & Indianapolis: Indiana University Press.

Conley, A. (2000, January). Philanthropy fellowship program attracts nation's best. *Research and Creative Activity, 22*(3). Retrieved from http://www.indiana.edu/~rcapub/v22n3/p16.html

Cooper, B. (2014, July 2). White supremacy stripped bare: What "Do the Right Thing" tells us 25 years later. *Salon*. Retrieved from http://www.salon.com/2014/07/02/is_black_life_expendable_what_do_the_right_thing_tells_us_25_years_later/

Hootnick, A. (2014, May 5). Teachers are losing their jobs, but Teach For America's expanding. What's wrong with that? *The Nation*. Retrieved from http://www.thenation.com/article/179363/teachers-are-losing-their-jobs-teach-americas-expanding-whats-wrong#

Jacobs, D. L. (2011, November 2). How to get the best severance deal. *Forbes*. Retrieved from http://www.forbes.com/sites/deborahljacobs/2011/11/02/how-to-play-your-hand-when-youve-been-fired/

Perry, A. (2014, August 11). TFA shows it's learned a lesson about diversity: Now, what's next? *The Hechinger Report*. Retrieved from http://hechingerreport.org/content/teach-america-shows-learned-lesson-diversity-now-whats-next_16993/

Teach For America. (n.d.). TFA on the record. Retrieved from http://www.teachforamerica.org/tfa-on-the-record

Teach For America. (n.d.). Teach For America's mission. Retrieved from http://www.teachforamerica.org/our-mission

U.S. Department of Labor. (n.d.). Wages: Severance pay. Retrieved from http://www.dol.gov/dol/topic/wages/severancepay.htm

NOTE

1. "One day, all children will have the opportunity to attain an excellent education" was TFA's mission for over a decade. Now, the mission reads, "One Day: Teach For America is growing the movement of leaders who work to ensure that kids growing up in poverty get an excellent education."

CHAPTER FIFTEEN

"I Confess, I Am a TFA Supporter. But…"

WALT ECTON
Metro Atlanta, 2010–2012

BIOSKETCH

Walt Ecton was a 2010 Teach For America (TFA) corps member, teaching high school social studies for 2 years at Booker T. Washington High School in Atlanta, Georgia. During his time at Washington High School, Walt coached girls' and boys' tennis, advised a number of clubs, and was named the principal's "Teacher of the Year." He also cofounded Emory Student Shadows, though which hundreds of high school students received a mentor at Emory University and had the opportunity to spend a day at the university one-on-one with their mentors, and the Policy Leadership Track, for TFA corps members interested in education policy. Before teaching, Walt earned his bachelor's degree at Emory University and a master's degree in peace and conflict studies at the University of St. Andrews. Walt currently serves as an associate director of member services at the Education Advisory Board, a best-practice research and technology firm in Washington, D.C.

NARRATIVE

I support Teach For America (TFA); allow me to explain. I believe TFA brings into the teaching profession bright young minds who wouldn't have otherwise considered the classroom. I believe TFA brings creative energy, excitement, and innovation into an environment where all are sorely needed. I believe TFA raises public awareness about the challenges of urban and rural education and the need for our country to invest more in our students and their future. I believe TFA brings passionate and intelligent leaders into the conversation about how to improve our nation's education system, in ways both large and small. From strictly anecdotal evidence, the TFA corps members I know perform well, for the most part, in the classroom. Although studies are sparse, they generally show that TFA teachers perform about the same as (or slightly better than) other new teachers at low-income schools (Clark et al., 2013; Xu & Taylor, 2011), though other researchers have cast doubt on some of the conclusions in those reports (Vasquez Heilig, 2013; Vasquez Heilig & Jez, 2014). This is an astonishing indictment of traditional teacher education and preparation programs in the United States. The critics of TFA are right—the preparation and training TFA corps members receive is woefully inadequate. That we, with our limited amount of training, are able to perform anywhere near the standards of those with traditional certification is shocking, and a true clarion call for reform of teacher education programs across the country.

While I have serious reservations about TFA, I also hope that there are a number of lessons that education and the teaching profession can learn from the program, its successes, and its failures. For all its positives and negatives, it would be hard to deny that over the past two decades TFA has built one of the most innovative programs to recruit and train new teachers. Education as a field and a profession *deserves* innovation, new ideas, and the new perspectives that corps members bring into our schools. Certainly, I would never suggest that TFA is the "answer," or even a roadmap for the future of teacher preparation, but I do think there are a number of positives, as well as a number of broader lessons to be learned from TFA.

As a TFA corps member and alumnus, I've often been asked, "Why did you want to join TFA?" My answer includes a wide range of reasons—from admiration for my grandfather's rise from poverty to an upper-middle-class life through hard work and education, to my own exposure to very unequal education systems in my home state of Kentucky, to a somewhat idealistic desire out of college to make an impact with my life, and a love of mentorship and working with those younger than me. However, the realization that TFA was a program in which I wanted to participate came from a quite surprising place—my college fraternity. Each semester, new members at Emory University's chapter of Alpha Tau Omega are asked to create a list of ten questions and to use those questions to interview every single brother in the fraternity. One of my questions I chose to ask read: "If money weren't a factor, what career would you choose for yourself?" Overwhelmingly, over the 70 or so interviews, the most common response was education. Repeatedly, my fraternity brothers talked about the desire to mentor, impart knowledge, shape young minds, inspire, and work with students who were eager and had their whole lives in front of them. For the most part, though, none of my fraternity brothers considered teaching a viable option, for some combination of reasons generally including the low salary, a fear of disappointing family members who had long expected their children to become doctors, lawyers, or businessmen, and the perception, held by many, that teaching simply wasn't much respected throughout society.

Eventually, though, TFA appealed to many of these individuals. With the exclusivity of its low acceptance rate, the intensive media campaign, and the messaging that this was a program for the "best and the brightest," teaching came to be seen as a viable option. Notably, TFA did not remove the first barrier many of my brothers mentioned—the salary. As TFA corps members were paid directly by their school districts with a standard first-year teacher salary, the pay was no higher than it would have been if we came through traditional teaching pathways. Clearly, salary (or at least, starting salary) was not an insurmountable barrier to consideration of the teaching profession. And TFA's marketing had somehow made TFA seem like a distinct career choice. When friends and family inquired about our post college plans, the typical response was, "I'm doing TFA," not "I'm becoming a teacher."

Over three graduating classes, about a fifth of my fraternity joined TFA; indeed, in Emory's entire graduating class of 2010, more graduates went to work with TFA than any other single employer. Today, many of my friends from college have left the classroom, but about a third remain into their fourth and fifth years. These individuals, for the most part, would have never considered teaching before TFA. Among those who are no longer teaching, my "TFA friends" are almost all working in roles that were clearly influenced by their time in TFA. Some are in medical school and plan to work in clinics for children and low-income communities, or even open school-based health clinics. Some are lawyers who work as child advocates. Some serve in legislative offices in order to influence education policy and policies impacting the students they taught (though there are fair questions to be asked about the policies promoted by TFA alumni, as I'll explore later). And some friends who went into the business world have stayed active by mentoring students and volunteering in community organizations.

A common criticism of TFA is that it is "something people just do for 2 years before moving on with their lives." While this may be true of some individuals, my experiences as well as TFA's own data show that even among those who do not stay in the classroom past 2 years, TFA does change the life trajectory of the overwhelming majority of its participants. More than in any other way, TFA plays perhaps its most significant role by molding a generation of young, talented, and ambitious leaders who now care deeply about education and other issues that impact low-income communities. While TFA's immediate impact on students in the classroom is certainly essential and deserves more rigorous evaluation and study, the importance of this secondary impact cannot be understated.

This impact is not limited strictly to TFA corps members and alumni. Instead, it extends to the entire personal network of each corps member. At dinners with friends and holidays with family members, TFA corps members tell stories of their time in the classroom. They tell stories of how dramatically underfunded their schools are, of how constrained they feel by policies that force them to focus too narrowly on standardized tests, and of the many challenges their students face due to poverty. Although TFA continues to make important strides in recruiting more people of color and more people from low-income backgrounds into the corps, many corps members are still neither people of color nor low income. In a society in which income inequality has become more stark and the gap between wealthy and poor continues to widen, TFA plays an active role in ensuring that these young adults across the socioeconomic spectrum have at least some exposure to poverty and diversity in the United States. It is my hope that this will play a significant role in creating a more empathetic, more understanding, more tolerant, and more aware society as my generation rises into positions of leadership and influence.

Recently, I attended a wedding in which I spoke with two older upper-class White women. After learning of my experience with TFA, they expressed horror at the thought of me working in such an environment. They began talking about how "sad" it was that "the poor" couldn't learn or work hard, and how there was "no hope" for education in the United States. It was clear these women had little to no experience in low-income communities. Because of the experiences of so many of my peers in TFA, this type of uninformed reaction and attitude towards education in low-income communities should become increasingly rare and should influence awareness across the socioeconomic spectrum of systemic challenges impacting urban and rural education.

Certainly, the long-term impact of TFA is and will continue to be particularly profound in the education policy and reform movements. With thousands of new corps members each year identified through the interview process as ambitious, intelligent individuals who have a desire to make a difference in their communities, it is only natural that TFA alumni will be active in educational policy and leadership. While corps members are certainly not monolithic in their opinions about education policy, I find the critique that TFA attempts to sway corps members' opinions in a particular way to be one of the strongest critiques of the program. In my own experience, for example, I felt almost indoctrinated around the topic of charter schools. Throughout my time in the Atlanta TFA corps, we were often exposed to excellent local schools, model teachers, or innovative principals—almost all from charter schools. There was a clear underlying message here—charter schools were good; public schools were bad (with a few exceptions, such as those public schools run by principals who were TFA alumni). For someone who came from a state in which charter schools did not even exist, and who had little awareness of the concept before joining TFA, I was never given the opportunity to question or think critically about whether there were any negative aspects or outcomes to the charter school movement. Not only did this influence the vast majority of corps members' opinions on charter schools, it also influenced the way they thought about the very schools in which they taught. If charter schools were the "good schools," then the public schools in which the majority of my TFA colleagues taught were the "bad schools."

This attitude that "education is broken" is so pervasive within TFA, both among staff and corps members, that there was often a sense that we (TFA) were "saving education." It naturally followed, then, that non-TFA teachers were the problem. TFA staff in Atlanta did take pains to celebrate teachers (including non-TFA teachers) through awards recognizing excellent teachers and student advocates. In a way, though, these awards merely served to highlight that the awardees were exceptions to the norm and reinforced the notion that most teachers were mediocre at best. While I don't believe this was in any way the intention of the awards (there was an honest desire to recognize excellent teachers), the practice did have the unintended consequence of reminding our corps that "most teachers aren't like *this*." Through our Summer Institute, TFA also led lessons about "respect and humility" towards non-TFA colleagues within the school. However, these lessons never seemed to go much deeper than lip service. A perfect example from the Summer Institute was the way in which we utilized our faculty advisors (FAs). These advisors, veteran teachers (mostly non-TFA), served as the teachers-of-record in the summer school classes corps members taught during the summer. They sat in our classes each day and observed our first weeks of leading a classroom of students. While the FAs were encouraged to provide us with feedback, there was no formal structure for this. Instead, the bulk of our feedback came from corps member advisors (CMAs), TFA-trained teachers who sat in on our classes only occasionally and (at my Summer Institute) had between 1 and 4 years of classroom experience. At the time, I remember feeling that my FA was not important to my development as a teacher, perhaps because of a bias I held that he was probably not very good at his job—in fact, he was probably part of the "problem with education" that TFA was seeking to fix. In retrospect, I missed an invaluable opportunity to learn from an educator with more than 2 decades of experience teaching in the same community in which I would go on to teach. While I regret that I did not take greater initiative here, I also wish that TFA had designed our training in a way that respected these teachers to a much greater extent.

TFA also relied so heavily on data in its instruction model that many of my colleagues fell into a trap of believing that data (in particular, data from standardized tests) was the only accurate way to measure student success and achievement. Certainly, this was not unique to TFA. I vividly remember the time my principal asked me to sit with a veteran (non-TFA) teacher who had been very successful at teaching to the state standardized test in my subject, U.S. history. As he reviewed my lesson plan about the end of the Civil War, he questioned why I had chosen to teach about Abraham Lincoln's assassination. When I responded that this seemed an important fact for any student of U.S. history to know, he told me "That is not your job. Your job is to prepare the students to pass the test, and Lincoln's assassination is not going to be on that test. If it's something they really need to know, they can learn it in college." While I didn't take this advice, I do worry that TFA's data-driven style of instruction can easily contribute to this "teach to the standards and the test only" mentality.

Perhaps my most significant critique of TFA, however, is that it promotes an entirely unsustainable style and approach to teaching, as evidenced by its high rate of attrition. While many TFA corps members leave after their 2-year commitment, having never intended to stay past 2 years, TFA could become significantly more impactful by retaining more teachers in the classroom for longer periods of time. Many corps members end their 2 years with a love for teaching and the classroom, a recognition of dramatic improvements in their own abilities, and an awareness that if they were to stay in the classroom, they would have an increasingly more meaningful impact on their students. Yet, they leave the profession due to intense burnout. While not unique to TFA members, the burnout challenge is exacerbated in TFA due a mentality central to the organization—one that places the success or failure of a student almost entirely in the hands of the teacher, and has little to no appreciation for any sense of work-life balance (Brewer, 2014).

For me, a student named Steven[1] was central to my burnout. When Steven dropped out of high school in March, I was devastated. Steven spent 2 years in my homeroom and 2 years in my U.S. history class he had failed the first time, and was 18 years old—but still technically a freshman after failing almost every class in his first 2 years of high school. Steven was a member of a gang, had just become a father for the second time, and struggled to read basic sentences.

As a TFA corps member, I felt it was my moral obligation to do everything in my power to turn Steven's life around. After all, why did I apply for TFA if not for students exactly like Steven? Over the course of 2 years, I tried everything I could with Steven. I read the textbook aloud to him after school; I gave differentiated homework that was closer to his reading level; I spent my lunch break with him several times a week reviewing lessons and preparing for tests and assignments; I even bribed him with candy for simply doing his work. After a year and a half, Steven started making progress. We would talk about life, sports, and music. I gave him advice on being a good father (though as a single, childless 23-year-old, I'm not sure I was the best person for that), and I felt that we had genuinely become close.

Steven's academic performance began improving. He turned in homework more regularly. He even earned a B on a test (not an easy feat in Mr. E's U.S. history class!). As he celebrated that B, dancing and showing off in front of the entire class, I beamed with pride. Steven was going to "make it."

But then, just a few short weeks later, Steven stopped coming to school. Calls went unanswered, texts never returned. One day while driving through downtown Atlanta, I saw Steven standing on a street corner. Excited, I waved and rolled down my window, "Steven, where you been?!" "You know, I wasn't getting nowhere with school, Mr. E…" After some failed attempts at convincing him to return, I drove off, dejected.

This was my fault. I had failed Steven. What should I have done differently? The second-guessing, questions, and blame haunted me for months.

In retrospect, of course, Steven's decision to drop out of high school was not my fault, and likely had very little, if anything, to do with me, but rather was the confluence of years of inadequate education, a challenging home life, and other factors in his schools and community. While nobody in TFA ever explicitly told me it was my fault, I certainly was never made to feel any differently. I understand and appreciate why TFA staff actively dissuaded corps members from blaming "external factors" (family life, poverty, etc.) for inadequate student success; after all, there's a great danger in lowered expectations, and a great power in the idea that a teacher can overcome any obstacle. Yet, by not recognizing the real impact of students' entire past and current lives outside of the hour and a half they saw us each day, the burden seemed to fall entirely on us. For me, that burden was crushing, on an almost daily basis.

Steven wasn't the only student "I failed," and at the end of 2 years, the burden and the guilt from my failures were too overwhelming. By any objective measure, I was a good teacher. I was named Teacher of the Year by my principal and Teacher of the Quarter by my colleagues, and I led my students to some of the highest "pass" and "exceed" rates in the district on state standardized tests. I started a successful AP U.S. history program and led the girls' tennis team to its first winning record in years. Along with two other TFA corps members, I started a mentorship program through my alma mater, Emory University, that served over 300 students by exposing them to college life, many for the first time. In the end, though, I still didn't feel that I was good enough.

It was "my failures" with Steven and others that weighed on me more than my successes. It was my utter exhaustion after 2 years of late nights, constant stress, and pressure from all sides (TFA, my school, and more than anything, myself). It was the fact that after 2 years, I felt disillusioned by my own inability to completely eliminate the achievement gap for my students—something TFA had made me feel was both possible and the bar by which I must measure myself.

I became another statistic in the large percentage of TFA teachers who don't last more than 2 years in the classroom.

My critiques of TFA are simply because I believe it can do better. In the debate over TFA, what often gets lost is that in any organization there are areas of strength as well as opportunities for improvement. Because few things are more crucial than the education of our youth, TFA can and must do better. I believe and hope that it will build upon its successes while learning from its failures. For all my criticisms of TFA, I still believe the organization makes a positive impact in the lives of its corps members as well as its students, and will make a profound and positive impact on future policies and the leadership of our country. The fresh energy and innovative ideas that large numbers of new corps members from diverse backgrounds and perspectives can provide a school and classroom have the potential to transform students' lives and school communities. The perspective and insights from alumni of the program have the potential to transform education and indeed our entire country.

REFERENCES

Brewer, T. J. (2014). Accelerated burnout: How Teach For America's academic impact model and theoretical framework can foster disillusionment among its corps members. *Educational Studies, 50*(3), 246–263.

Clark, M. A., Chiang, H. S., Silva, T., McConnell, S., Sonnenfeld, K., Erbe, A., & Puma, M. (2013). *The effectiveness of secondary math teachers from Teach For America and the Teaching Fellows programs.* Washington, DC: Institute of Education Sciences and Mathematica Policy Research.

Vasquez Heilig, J. (2013, September 23). "Does not compute": Teach For America mathematica study is deceptive? *Cloaking Inequality.* Retrieved from http://cloakinginequity.com/2013/09/23/does-not-compute-teach-for-america-mathematica-study-is-deceptive/

Vasquez Heilig, J., & Jez, S. J. (2014). *Teach For America: A return to the evidence.* Boulder, CO: National Education Policy Center.

Xu, Z., Hannaway, J., & Taylor, C. (2011). Making a difference? The effects of Teach For America in high school. *Journal of Policy Analysis and Management, 30*(3), 447–469.

NOTE

1. Pseudonym.

CHAPTER SIXTEEN

From 106th to 41st, One Chicagoan's Experience with Teach For America and Chicago Public Schools

RYAN GARZA
Chicago, 2011–2013

BIOSKETCH

Ryan Garza was born and raised on the South Side of Chicago. The son of a Chicago Public Schools (CPS) teacher and a city ironworker, Ryan quickly learned the importance of unions. After attending Chicago Public Schools for 17 years, he graduated from the University of Wisconsin–Madison with a bachelor's degree in political science. Ryan taught seventh and eighth grade social studies for 2 years at Bronzeville Lighthouse Charter School.

NARRATIVE

"Unions are the reason why our public schools are failing" were some of the first words out of my executive director's mouth on Induction night. Josh Anderson, the son of the senior advisor to Secretary of Education Arne Duncan, proceeded to rant about the diabolical nature of teacher unions, specifically the Chicago Teachers Union (CTU). From that moment until my final days with Teach For America (TFA), I was continuously intimidated, shunned, and criticized for my union beliefs and anti-charter sentiments.

TFA undermined my ambitions to be placed in a traditional public school from the very beginning—I was ultimately placed in a charter school. However, it became increasingly clear that it wasn't nonprofit bureaucracy that determined my placement, but rather a larger strategic neoliberal partnership between TFA and corporate interests that want to systematically replace traditional public schools with charter schools.

Growing up on the South Side of Chicago, I attended public schools for my entire educational career. Moreover, my mother has been a Chicago Public Schools (CPS) counselor for the last 26 years. I was privileged enough to attend Jane Addams Elementary School (where my mother worked since I was in the second grade). Jane Addams was a typical South Side school, with 92% of my classmates qualifying for free and reduced lunch, scarce resources, and overcrowded classrooms. Despite this, my teachers strived to provide a quality education. Since I was 13, it had been a personal goal of mine to return to my elementary school as an educator. This goal was the impetus for my application to TFA.

Exactly one day before the TFA "interview day," I approached Lauren Secratore, the director of placements at the time, and informed her that my former principal at Jane Addams wanted to hire me once I completed my TFA training. However, due to the CPS administration's failure to release budgets on time, she was not yet able to formally extend an offer to me. Secratore stated, "I know there will be room; however, I can't legally offer you a job." Under the TFA placement policy, until a formal offer had been made, I was required to attend the interview day and interview for other prospective teaching assignments.

My first interview was at Bronzeville Light House Charter School—a former traditional public school that had been closed down and reopened as a charter school. I was hired on the spot, and TFA obligated me to accept my first offer. If I had refused to take my first offer, TFA would have rescinded that offer and I would have been forced to quit TFA. Five hours later, my former principal from Jane Addams called to inform me that she was finally able to extend a formal offer. Elation rushed through my veins because, in my mind, I was one step closer to being able to fulfill my dreams of giving back to the school I had graduated from. I quickly e-mailed my manager of teacher leadership development (MTLD) and Secratore to inform them of the offer. Never in a million years did I think that TFA—an organization claiming to want to help students and empower communities—would reject the public school principal's offer.

TFA responded with an outright "NO." They stated I had already signed my commitment letter to my charter school, and they did not want to jeopardize their strategic partnership with Lighthouse Academies. Furthermore, since they said my potential position at Jane Addams would not be able to readily rely on data, they would not be able to let me teach there anyway.

What perplexed me was the fact that TFA championed community involvement; yet, they refused to let me teach in my own community. Rather than follow the lead of programs like Grown Your Own—a program that seeks to place teachers in their former neighborhoods and communities (Young & Berry, 2011)—TFA elevated their strategic partnership with Lighthouse Academies over students' potential growth and my historical connection to Jane Addams elementary school. Instead of me being placed a block away from my home, in a school that I had graduated from, and in a community where I knew the teachers, parents, and students, I was placed into a community I knew little to nothing about. After coming to the realization that I would not be able to fulfill my dream, I concluded that TFA's stance was more a matter of strategic partnerships than it was about community involvement.

Always Follow the Money

As my school year progressed, it quickly became clear that my placement in a charter school was a part of TFA's larger agenda to sustain and further its rapid growth beyond traditional public schools and into charter schools. As the year went on, I became increasingly curious about TFA's backdoor dealings and their funding stream. A friend of mine suggested that I do some research on the Joyce Foundation. Essentially, I discovered that TFA's agenda, coupled with the Joyce Foundation's neoliberal tactics, created a toxic environment for traditional public schools. It should be noted that both Barack Obama and Valerie Jarrett, Obama's political operative, sat on the board of directors of the Joyce Foundation (Shipps, Sconzert, & Swyers, 1999).

Eloquently stated by investigative journalist Steve Horn (2013), "With assets of over $900 million, [the Joyce Foundation] has helped in applying 'shock doctrine'–type 'venture philanthropy' to CPS, with tight-knit ties to the highest levels of the Democratic Party and the Obama administration." Horn further argued, "[A] group of corporate and civic leaders in the Chicago area believed they could help their home city do a better job educating its students, so they put their minds, financial assets, and talents together, and the result was The Chicago Public Education Fund" (2013).

On the matter of the Chicago Public Education Fund (CPEF), the right-wing organization Philanthropy Roundtable wrote, "The Fund's strategy is to serve as a catalyst and investment partner…to invest dollars and ideas into high-impact programs that will improve student achievement and school leadership system-wide" (Horn, 2013). Identified as a key contributor on the CPEF website, the Joyce Foundation invested $1 million to support its initiatives. In the words of former CPEF CEO Janet Knupp, "They [the Joyce Foundation] played a critical role in helping us forge relationships with larger foundations across the nation. They saw the value of our work on a local level but had enough of a national reach to start connecting us" (Horn, 2013).

However, the Joyce Foundation and its connection to conservative and neoliberal powerbrokers go far beyond contributions. Current CEO Heather Anichini worked for CPS's Office of Planning and Development under Duncan. In addition, Penny Pritzker, a close ally of Obama and the current secretary of commerce, was a member of the board of directors for CPEF and on the Chicago Board of Education.

What is most unsettling is the length to which these organizations will go to mask their anti-union and pro-charter agenda. For example, according to Steve Horn (2013), "Luczak's successor at Joyce's education program was Angela Rudolph, now policy director for Democrats for Education Reform's Illinois branch and vice chair of the Illinois State Charter School Commission." I, like Horn, vividly remember Rudolph's call to "'Put Students First' in fall 2012 to fend off the nascent Chicago Teachers Union strike" (Horn, 2013). Though, Rudolph told *Catalyst Chicago*, "What we have been most troubled by is this notion that we are anti-teacher or anti-union. We are a democratic organization and one of the cornerstones of the Democratic Party is unions" (Harris, 2012).

How is the Joyce Foundation connected to TFA? It is connected to the tune of $23.77 million given to TFA over the last 20 years. As I learned this, I began to think my placement at the charter school was far from a bureaucratic error. In 2013, 36 days after CPS closed 50 schools in the largest school closing in U.S. history, CPS increased TFA's budget from $600,000 to $1.58 million in hopes of hiring 570 new TFA corps members (Kugler, 2013). In effect, TFA got an extra million dollars while CPS was talking about its phony budget "deficit." As Horn (2013) elaborates,

> Since 2001, the Chicago Board of Education has doled out close to $6.6 million in contracts and hired 1,931 teachers from Teach For America, Board of Education contract records show. During that same period, thousands of CPS teachers got pink slips. The rubber meets the road in the relationship between the Chicago school restructuring movement's goal of creating CEO-type school principals and Teach For America's Principal Leadership Pipeline, which was launched in September 2007. The Principal Leadership Pipeline was a collaboration between CPS and Teach For America, financed by the Chicago Public Education Fund and the Pritzker Family Foundation.

Always Bring a Crowd

Clearly, at some level, my charter school placement through TFA was a part of a larger scheme to destroy public education. While I am not certain TFA was knowingly a part of this, they nonetheless perpetuated the privatization of Chicago Public Schools under the guise of mostly neoliberal "do-gooder" policies. This became crystal clear when I attempted to unionize my charter school by organizing a happy hour event for my colleagues so we could discuss unionization.

I received a knock on my door from my charter school's principal, Ms. Dotson, around 8:25 on a Friday morning in September 2012. My students were already in their morning routines. My first thought was, "That was quick." I expected a response from the administration, just not so soon after I forwarded the pro-union flyer to my coworkers. Next thing I knew, in the middle of homeroom, my principal came barging in demanding an explanation for my e-mail. I said, "It's my right to forward something during working hours." She said it was "poor judgment and lack of leadership." She said this was "bad for kids and a distraction." Ironically, this was said at the same time she barged into my room and stopped my class from learning.

At that moment, two things became clear to me: (1) that I had upset the administration; and (2) that it was not in my best interest to continue in a conversation with my principal on this topic—by myself. To the dismay and visible irritation of the charter network executives, I invoked my "Weingarten" rights, asking that this impromptu meeting be documented in writing. My principal openly denied that request, saying, "You don't need anything in writing."

During a review of my teaching skills, Ms. Dotson stated I was a great teacher but that my leadership and union beliefs were out of line. I demanded that those statements be put in writing and asked if that was official policy. As a result of these interactions with my principal, my charter school's position on unionization became clear, and it was surprisingly straight to the point: If we teachers unionized, we would be fired. Bluntly she told me, "If you try to join a union, you will lose your job." I simply smiled, requested that her statement also be put in writing, and asked if I was being formally reprimanded for my beliefs. She replied with a perplexed "No." When I asked if I had sent out information about a TFA happy hour, rather than information about unionization, would she be upset, she responded with, "Of course not."

In total, four teachers from my charter school ultimately attended the happy hour sponsored by CTU to foster "solidarity between charter teachers and public." Each of those four teachers were approached by our principal and were also told that if they unionized they would lose their jobs. Obviously, Ms. Dotson, a former TFA corps member herself, was adamant in her opposition to unions. She once asked me, "Aren't unions communist? I remember when I was in Cuba there were a lot of unions."

It became quite clear after TFA that Josh Anderson's statements that night at Induction were a strategic part of a larger scheme of neoliberal Democrats to privatize education. If I had known then what I know now, I would have told him so. Sadly, I'd bet my next week's wages that it wouldn't have done anything. Over the course of my 2 years I learned that TFA cares little about their members. They routinely care more about their partnerships with hedge funds, banks, and charter operators. And from my experience, this attitude carries over into practice for those TFA alumni like Ms. Dotson who leave the classroom and take school leadership positions.

REFERENCES

Harris, R. (2012, June 28). For the record: Democrats for education reform. *Catalyst Chicago*. Retrieved from http://www.catalyst-chicago.org/notebook/2012/06/28/20239/record-democrats-education-reform

Horn, S. (2013, July 9). Chicago school closings and the Joyce Foundation: The Obama connection. Retrieved from http://www.mintpressnews.com/a-closer-look-at-the-joyce-foundation-shows-obamas-ties-to-chicago-school-privatizations/164972/

Kugler, J. (2013, July 2). Teach for America gets an extra million dollars while CPS keeps talking about its phony "deficit." Retrieved from http://www.substancenews.net/articles.php?page=4364

Shipps, D., Sconzert, K., & Swyers, H. (1999). The Chicago Annenberg challenge: The first three years. *Improving Chicago's Schools, 1*(1), 1–60. Retrieved from https://ccsr.uchicago.edu/sites/defaul t/files/publications/p0b06.pdf

Young, V. C., & Berry, J. (2011, March 2). *Grow your own Illinois: An innovative approach to providing high-quality teaching in low-income communities*. Retrieved from http://www.growyourownteach ers.org/index.php?option=com_content&view=article&id=104&Itemid=128

CHAPTER SEVENTEEN

Can We Change? Reflections on TFA's Ongoing Internal Criticism

DERRICK HOUCK
Philadelphia, 2010–2012

BIOSKETCH

Derrick Houck is a math teacher at a charter school in Philadelphia and a 2010 Teach For America (TFA) corps member. He has taught courses in algebra 1, statistics, and advanced placement statistics at the ninth grade and twelfth grade levels. He worked as a resource room specialist at TFA's Philadelphia Institute in summer 2012. Along with his coworkers and the Alliance of Charter School Employees, he has been engaged in efforts to organize a union at their charter school. In addition to teaching mathematics, he helped found and continues to cofacilitate the school's music club, where he tutors students after school in piano and guitar. He has a bachelor of science degree in mathematics from Bucknell University, with a minor in education, and a master's degree in urban education from the University of Pennsylvania.

NARRATIVE

Teach For America (TFA) has had its critics since its founding in 1989, but only in more recent years have such voices found platforms in more mainstream media sources. A significant upsurge in this critical dialogue can be attributed to the 2013 gathering of TFA alumni at the *Free Minds, Free People* conference in Chicago, which sought to "[stage] a coordinated, national effort to overhaul, or put the brakes on, TFA" (Wells, 2013). This session was widely touted as the first initiative to specifically recruit alumni of the group to engage in criticism of TFA through various media outlets. Growing internal organization of critics from within TFA, in addition to fueling more media coverage, has also been prompting more direct responses by the organization's representatives to some of the critiques.

In this chapter, I detail some of the experiences I have had or have witnessed, as a 2010 Philadelphia corps member and alumnus, related to TFA's local and national handling of internal criticism. What emerges is a picture of an organization concerned with controlling its image in the media, fearful of and aggressive towards institutions that express disagreement with its philosophy of education, and unable and/or unwilling to acknowledge the depth of criticism that has arisen from resistance campaigns. These characteristics serve to promote the dismantling of democracy and democratic institutions in the regions where TFA operates, and thus further embolden and enable privatization efforts of the neoliberal reform movement.

Preparations in Dealing with Media

During my training in the summer of 2010, I was interviewed by my hometown newspaper regarding my decision to join TFA and my hopes for my first year of teaching. I was informed of the interview by TFA, as they request that all media outlets wishing to report on their members filter such inquiries through their offices. The staffer who contacted me asked to set up a time when we could prep for the interview, and we arranged to talk for 30 to 45 minutes by phone on a day close to the interview. The request perplexed me, because the interviewer was a local reporter from a small town with a population of around 4,000 people.

The piece that ran was, in fact, a local interest story wholly unconcerned with exploring any controversy around TFA. The prep with staffers from TFA's public relations department was a more intensive affair, involving several role-play exercises designed to ensure I could respond to any of the common critiques TFA was facing at the time. If I was to be asked about the effectiveness of requiring just a 2-year commitment of corps members, I was to focus on the fact that I was doing everything in my power at that moment to be the best teacher I could be for my students. I recall further preparation around the issue of the 5 weeks of summer training I was receiving, a facet of the TFA experience widely lambasted as insufficient for proper pedagogical preparation; I was to downplay the brevity of the training and again reiterate that I was working hard to learn as much as I could to do right by my students. My thoughts about the politics of TFA were relatively unformed at the time, and the reporter seemed uninterested in exploring any such controversies anyhow, so the story ultimately ran much in line with what I suppose TFA would have hoped.

I now regret having taken part in the interview, understanding that my responses to the interviewer's questions, by not actively challenging the preparation I received from TFA, served to endorse the odious "White savior" narrative, which holds that people of color require the intervention of Whites to achieve success or fix problems in their communities. Some popular films that have been criticized for promoting this narrative are *Freedom Writers* and *The Help*. Having been raised through high school in an overwhelmingly White small town, I came to implicitly accept that my upbringing and lifestyle was what should be considered good, normal, and worthy of striving for. Coursework at the liberal arts university I attended (which was predominantly White) helped me begin to investigate concepts of privilege and power, but I still entered TFA with an overconfidence that the academic success and leadership experience for which I was recruited would make me a great teacher in my first few years at the job. So, when asked by the reporter about what caused me to join TFA, I replied that at the time of my recruitment I thought of the organization as having "a noble mission," and that I personally enjoyed the "extra challenge" of working in a low-income community (Ellingsworth, 2010). To counter these self-serving statements laden with sentiments of superiority, I wish to be clear now that there was nothing "noble" about me seeking to fix problems I didn't understand in a community I knew little about. Furthermore, the "extra challenge" of working in Philadelphia, if such a challenge can even be said to exist, can be attributed to the need to work to overcome one's own ignorance and biases, which is, to be sure, an ongoing process.

My interaction with TFA staffers prior to the interview did not help raise my awareness of prejudices I might promote or harmful narratives I might play into during the course of the interview. In emphasizing the need to deflect questions about 2-year commitments and insufficient training, my preparation seemingly served only to protect the image of TFA. Obviously, ultimate responsibility for the things I said in the interview lies with me. I have provided context surrounding these events in the hopes of illustrating how TFA's proactive coaching of corps members in how to talk to media can perpetuate White savior narratives while deflecting criticisms of TFA's model of education reform.

In the next section, I detail ways TFA has promoted and defended its educational ideology when it has been challenged by individual corps members and in partnerships with higher-education institutions.

The Penn-TFA "Partnership"

Our training as TFA corps members in Philadelphia was two-pronged. TFA provided 5 weeks of summer training, coaching based on classroom observations (once every month or two, unless you requested more), and weekend professional development sessions held intermittently throughout the school year. The second prong involved the University of Pennsylvania, whose coursework during the school year was required for our certification at the end of 2 years' work and for a master's degree for those corps members who elected to take a few additional courses and pay extra money. In my experience, critical discussions around TFA and its role in local and national education issues were commonplace in Penn courses. During my first year teaching, I relished the opportunity to take graduate courses at Penn. In the midst of all the chaos that goes along with being a new teacher, these classes offered a space to step back and critically consider some of the bigger forces at play in the city in which we were teaching. Professors discussed with us the issues of class, race, politics, and poverty that affected the lives of our students in the classroom but often get swept aside when dealing with the daily barrage of paperwork and minutiae that eats up a teacher's day. Not all corps members found Penn classes useful, lamenting that the discussions were not practical enough to apply in the classroom in an immediate way; however, many of us found inspiration and newfound purpose in conversing about the difficult intersections of race, class, privilege, and poverty we were navigating each day.

Our training at Penn offered a more holistic view of education than that provided by TFA's behavior management techniques and "I Do, We Do, You Do" lesson planning structure. Penn administrators often explained this tension as two organizations offering their own perspectives, and it would be up to each individual teacher to decide where their beliefs lie. TFA was more reticent to acknowledge differences between its training and Penn's. The organization solicited feedback on our TFA and Penn trainings through an extensive yearly survey. During our Institute training, TFA surveys gained some notoriety among the corps when several recruits were called into one-on-one or small group meetings to discuss their responses that had not rated training sessions highly enough to satisfy the expectations of TFA staff. Corps member colleagues who attended these individual conferences got the impression they were there not to be heard out, but to be encouraged to speak out less.

Despite the feelings of intimidation surrounding TFA's surveys, the 2010 Philadelphia cohort, after our first year of teaching, submitted feedback that was upsetting to regional staff; allegedly, one of the questions that garnered unfavorable responses asked corps members to rate their level of agreement with the statement that Penn and TFA had similar visions for addressing issues of educational equity. Our responses had indicated a high level of disagreement with that statement. In response to the critical surveys, a series of initiatives were rolled out. Town hall–style meetings were conducted with our entire cohort and higher-level TFA directors, and a host of programmatic changes occurred in the Philadelphia regional offices, including changes in coaching protocols between program directors (the TFA staffers who observed our classes and gave us one-on-one feedback) and corps members. Most shockingly, a beloved coordinator in the Penn education department was reassigned to other duties, and rumors abounded that TFA had lobbied for her removal.

These events indicate that TFA uses feedback from discussions and surveys beyond its expected use in informing adjustments to offered services and employee duties. Comments and critiques are used to identify dissenters—who can then be individually addressed—or to ensure corps members are internalizing TFA's ideology. When corps members express disagreement with TFA's philosophy, their supervisors are held accountable, sometimes at the cost of their jobs, for their failure to impart the organization's beliefs. Penn clearly holds some responsibility as well, in allowing such a stifling of expression to occur. In partnering with TFA, Penn professors may be expected to sacrifice a degree of academic autonomy in order to hold back opinions that might challenge beliefs TFA holds dear, for fear of reprisal from Penn administrators who do not want to jeopardize the financial benefits the university collects from the partnership.

The next two sections of this chapter detail thoughts and experiences I had as an alumnus responding to speeches given by TFA's co-CEOs Matt Kramer and Elisa Villanueva-Beard at the first two Alumni Educators Conferences in 2013 and 2014. While I grew more ideologically distant from TFA throughout my experience as a corps member, I was never particularly vocal about practices I found problematic in training sessions or at other gatherings of TFA members. Leadership in this form of advocacy and activism came primarily from corps members of color, whose words and actions serve as continual inspiration to reflect on my beliefs and refine my conduct as a teacher. With a more critical bent than I had when I was in the corps, I traveled to Detroit in 2013 to attend the inaugural TFA conference for alumni who continued to work as teachers, as well as to connect with another alumnus currently working for a union that was organizing Detroit charter school teachers. (The connection was made possible by my involvement with similar organizing efforts at the school at which I was and am still working.) My intent in the following sections is to detail TFA's most recent responses to the growing public backlash and to examine how reforms within the organization are still failing to address the deepest ideological criticisms that TFA faces.

2013 Conference: Responding to New Critics

As I sat in Detroit's COBO center in the summer of 2013 at TFA's first annual Alumni Educators Conference, I felt twinges of the optimism and sense of purpose that had inspired me to join the organization in 2010. Elisa Villanueva-Beard, the then recently appointed co-CEO, was recounting how her feeling unprepared for college, and the stereotypes she faced as a Mexican American on campus, inspired her to join TFA as a 1998 corps member. Her remarks were bookended by allusions to the works of Dr. Martin Luther King, Jr., personal testimonies, stories about people pulling themselves up by their bootstraps, and civil rights rhetoric, which are hallmarks of TFA's recruitment and training. Hearing these familiar linguistic tactics reminded me in a regretful way how I was persuaded to join TFA, following what I thought at the time were the best of intentions.

The rest of Villanueva-Beard's remarks that evening were what I was most interested in hearing: the organization's response to recent criticisms in the press. Just a few weeks prior to TFA's meeting was the aforementioned *Free Minds, Free People* conference, which sparked widespread media coverage as the first effort to organize a critical contingent from within TFA itself.

The co-CEO's words in Detroit showed that TFA was feeling the pressure. Her speech labeled this new opposition as defenders of the status quo, going so far as to liken TFA's critics to the "moderate majority" of the civil rights era, whose complacency and inaction King targeted in his push for reforms. A representative line from Villanueva-Beard's speech was, "The enemy is the status quo—and for those who defend it the burden of proof is on them to explain to the parents of America's poorest children why it's better to do nothing than something" (Villanueva-Beard, 2013a). She introduced new initiatives TFA was taking in response to some of the criticisms she and co-CEO Matt Kramer had heard from current and former corps members on their "listening tour," including pilot programs in certain regions where some corps members could elect to spend up to a year prior to their teaching commitment in a more traditional student-teaching-type role in a local school (to address those who claimed 5 weeks' training was insufficient), and a commitment to hiring more corps members from racially and economically diverse backgrounds (to address concerns about an overabundance of recruits from White privileged backgrounds).

At this point, published criticisms of TFA were going far beyond calls to re-examine the 2-year commitment, to provide more robust training, and to recruit more diverse corps members, yet this is where Villanueva-Beard's acknowledgment of dissent stopped. At that very 2013 conference, a TFA staffer and panelist in one of the social justice–oriented sessions I attended cited White supremacy as a factor in the organization's inability to make progress towards its own stated goals regarding civil rights. Yet, in the CEO's address to the full membership of the conference, critiques that have identified TFA and its practices as colonialist or racist were given no response. Instead, those deeper criticisms were isolated to a room where a self-selected group of interested individuals could discuss them in a contained environment.

Furthermore, I continue to take umbrage at Villanueva-Beard's characterization of TFA's critics as people who think nothing should be done to reform the nation's education system. Activists around the country are advocating for local control of schools, fair funding formulas, and students' and workers' rights in nonunionized charter schools. I don't believe I've ever met someone who thinks "nothing" is a solution to the educational challenges our nation faces, and I can't imagine Villanueva-Beard has, either. I'm left to believe her intent was to belittle or marginalize voices that oppose the unchecked expansion of TFA in favor of more democratic means of reform by classifying critics as whiners and obstructionists.

2014 Conference: The Current State of TFA

I did not attend the 2014 Alumni Educators Conference, held in Las Vegas, but I watched online as co-CEOs Kramer and Villanueva-Beard gave remarks and then held a Q&A with prescreened questions from e-mail and Twitter, as well as live questions from the TFA alumni in attendance. I was curious to hear the conclusions they had drawn from their listening tour, the findings from their pilot programs with extended training periods, and whether they would acknowledge or respond to any of the institutional or systemic critiques they had skirted at the Detroit conference. Disappointingly, yet unsurprisingly, the tone and message of the 2014 meeting was much the same as the 2013 conference. Remarks lacked specificity as to the results of the pilot programs or what their newly stated commitment to "culturally competent training" would look like (Villanueva-Beard & Kramer, 2014). There was another increase in the percentage of incoming corps members of color or from low-income backgrounds but little acknowledgment of the damage that may already have been done in previous recruiting practices during the organization's 24-year history.

In looking forward to TFA's role in the education reform movement in the coming year and beyond, much emphasis was given to the need to build leaders in the education field from within the organization. Leadership has been a central focus of the organization since well before I joined, as evidenced by our training materials having been packaged under the title "Teaching as Leadership." TFA frequently talks about leadership and the need for its alumni to take on entrepreneurial roles to transform the educational landscape. As I watched the co-CEOs talk about these points again at the Las Vegas conference, I was able to understand better why I have found the intense focus on leadership troubling: TFA advocates for entrepreneurial leadership at the expense of democratic input from the communities they work in. In calling for new leaders to reform marginalized and underresourced communities, TFA fails to recognize the grassroots organizing and community leaders already at work. Sounding a need for outside agents to reform communities in which they may have worked for only 2 years plays into colonialist and White savior narratives about what is needed in urban education reform, especially when one is not likewise promoting the efforts of established education advocates.

Ultimately, I believe TFA's handling of internal criticism shows that, as an organization, it has been more committed to growing and improving the image of their brand than to taking meaningful action towards social justice, despite a growing number of dissenters among current members, staffers, and alumni. The organization proactively addresses dissent by coaching corps members in how to talk to members of the media, thereby perpetuating harmful and stereotypical images of helpless communities in need of intervention by privileged elites. TFA incessantly describes itself as a force for social justice while ignoring arguments that find the organization complicit in or actively promoting the spread of colonialist, racist, or classist ideologies. Its methods of handling dissent by isolating and thus silencing vocal critics—seen in the examples of one-on-one meetings to discuss negative survey feedback, and of sequestered social justice conference sessions where institutional critiques are ultimately confined to the rooms in which they are discussed—are mechanisms that oppose free discussion of ideas.

In stifling democratic expression in these ways, TFA finds itself a part of the larger neoliberal effort to turn public schools over to private operators with non-unionized staff, replace elected school boards with mayor- or governor-appointed boards, and promote the redefinition of democracy itself as choice in the marketplace of educational offerings (Lipman, 2011). These current popular practices within the education reform movement rob the communities in which TFA works of their voices by removing the accountability provided by public institutions and elected officials and school boards. Such tactics must be resisted and democracy within marginalized communities must be promoted if TFA's stated goals of social justice and educational equity are to be advanced. If it continues to evade dialogue and take meaningful action regarding its role in the promulgation of neoliberalism and its destructive effects on the communities it purports to serve, then TFA should be resisted in its efforts to grow, and questions must be raised about the need for the organization's existence.

REFERENCES

Cole, T. (2012, March 21). The White-savior industrial complex. *The Atlantic.* Retrieved from http://www.theatlantic.com/international/archive/2012/03/the-white-savior-industrial-compl ex/254843/

Ellingsworth, Jr., P. (2010, August 6). Barto native helps children through education. *Berks-Mont News.* Retrieved from http://www.berksmontnews.com/article/20100806/NEWS01/308069987

Lapayese, Y., Aldana, U., & Lara, E. (2014). A racio-economic analysis of Teach For America: Counterstories of TFA teachers of color. *Perspectives on Urban Education, 11*(1), 11–25.

Lipman, P. (2011). *The new political economy of urban education neoliberalism, race, and the right to the city.* New York: Routledge.

Strauss, V. (2013, July 17). A former Teach For America manager speaks out. *Washington Post.* Retrieved from http://www.washingtonpost.com/blogs/answer-sheet/wp/2013/07/17/a-former-teach-for-america-manager-speaks-out/

Villanueva-Beard, E. (2013a, July 18). "Fighting the wrong enemy." Remarks at the Teach For America Alumni Educators Conference, Detroit, MI. Retrieved from https://www.teachforamerica. org/blog/fighting-wrong-enemy

Villanueva-Beard, E. (2013b, July 31). How I define the status quo [Web log entry]. Retrieved from http://www.teachforamerica.org/blog/elisa-villanueva-beard-how-i-define-status-quo

Villanueva-Beard, E., & Kramer, M. (2014, July 18). Teach For America educators conference town hall: Video and speeches. Retrieved from http://www.teachforamerica.org/blog/teach-america-educators-conference-town-hall-video-and-speeches

Wells, M. (2013, July 10). Taking the organized resistance to TFA national at FMFP. *Free Minds, Free People.* Retrieved from http://www.fmfp.org/2013/07/taking-the-organized-resistance-to-tfa-national-at-fmfp/

Beyond Dupes, Disciples, and Dilettantes: Ideological Struggles of TFA Corps Members

TERRENDA WHITE
Los Angeles, 2002–2004

BIOSKETCH

Terrenda is an assistant professor of sociology and education at the University of Colorado–Boulder. She studies market-driven education reforms in urban communities and their cultural and pedagogical implications for classroom teaching and learning, including their impact on teacher professional autonomy and identity.

NARRATIVE

In this chapter, I share aspects of my own experience as a 2002 corps member and those of 10 fellow corps members of color,[1] whose inside stories I collected over several years. I use these stories to explore the ways in which Teach For America (TFA) corps members have experienced, and struggled against, the organization's ideologies about the causes of and solutions to educational inequality in the United States. Often, TFA constructs and endorses representations of corps members as a cadre of "super-heroic" (Trujillo & Scott, 2014) individuals with an extraordinary work ethic, whose dedication is superior to that of traditional teachers, and whose sheer will and efficacy alone is enough to fix dysfunctional urban schools and close academic achievement gaps. Indeed, my own first year as a corps member was documented by a major news network and subsequently used in recruitment materials by the TFA organization. Excluded in such depictions of our teaching are our colleagues and the veteran educators who work alongside us in urban schools. Also invisible are a myriad of important factors shaping the context of achievement and disparities between student groups, such as school segregation, unequal school funding, and the "taboo" subject of student poverty, as well as the tendency in the U.S. to concentrate and isolate poor children together over the course of their social and educational lives. Together, these issues create the context in which corps members teach, yet they sit unaddressed like 600-pound gorillas hungrily demanding attention by policymakers and reformers.

The stories below, however, challenge easy depictions of super-heroic individuals and reveal critically discerning young people who challenged the organization's ideology and its narrow approaches to reform. In particular, our stories reveal critical struggles about race and privilege, culture and pedagogy, and the broad educational and instructional needs of urban school children. These stories also reveal the value of experienced educators who were our informal mentors and models for teaching. Unfortunately, our stories also reveal the ways in which TFA representatives either silenced or failed to incorporate the views of its more critical members. Although those members were isolated, marginalized, and largely unheard by the organization, the narratives in this chapter give voice to those who refused to be dupes, dilettantes, or disciples in what has become a radical overhaul of the nation's public schools based largely on individualistic and market-driven rationales, in which TFA has played a key role.

Teach For America and Neoliberal Ideology

TFA has always boasted a two-pronged movement to impact classroom instruction within schools and education policy outside of schools. The first part of its mission is commonly identified with its recruitment of college graduates who complete a 5-week summer training program and are then placed in schools that serve low-income communities. The second part of its mission, however, is intertwined with distinct ideologies about the causes and solutions of educational inequality that are more obscure, not only to its broad bipartisan supporters but also to its more than 4,000 recruits who sign up each year.

In an effort to improve the nation's schools, policymakers in the past 30 years have offered a patchwork of reforms that include testing and accountability, elimination of teacher tenure, the weakening of teacher unions, merit-based promotion and pay structures for teachers, and market-based reforms involving choice, competition, and private management of public schools. Contrary to previous eras of reform that focused more on equalizing resources and inputs, current reforms share a focus on outcomes and the accountability of schools and individuals.

The focus of these reforms, moreover, fit within a dominant neoliberal ideology that favors individual competition, choice, and deregulation and privatization of public institutions as a way to improve services (Apple, 2006; Harvey, 2005; Lipman, 2011). In education, this ideology often shifts focus away from inequities that shape the structure and organization of public schools, and instead locates the primary source and solution of educational inequality with school actors, such as district officials, administrators, and schoolteachers whose dispositions and work habits are oftentimes viewed as deficient compared to private groups and entrepreneurs (Chubb & Moe, 1990). This view has shaped a political climate where teachers in urban schools, of whom many are veteran educators of color, have been blamed for the conditions and struggles of urban schools and have consequently lost their jobs in light of neoliberal reform efforts that have resulted in school closures and "turnaround" efforts (Buras, 2011). These efforts involve closing schools and turning them over to for-profit and nonprofit organizations that favor data-driven "no excuses" practices focused on test score production and competition, and which utilize flexible (i.e., nonunionized) and less expensive labor (Buras, 2010, 2011; Lipman, 2011). Hence, as the professional and pedagogical contributions of veteran educators have been denigrated, their schools have been infused with a cadre of "green" (i.e., novice) educators—including TFA corps members.

In light of these trends, critical policy researchers argue that TFA, and its alumni, are not simply bystanders or witnesses to the winds of current reform, but rather are part and parcel of the current storm that has gripped public education. Indeed, education historians have started to contextualize the social and political milieu of TFA's origin in the late 1980s and early 1990s. For example, Bethany Rogers and Megan Blumenreich (2013) noted important factors that laid the groundwork for the appeal of an organization such as TFA, including the politics of the Reagan administration, the collapse of communism abroad, and the seeming vindication of free-market capitalism (Rogers & Blumenreich, 2013). National and international politics of this era coincided with shifts in domestic social policies, including the growing isolation and "criminalization" of urban neighborhoods due to job migration out of cities and the re-segregation of schools (Rogers & Blumenreich, 2013). These broader policy shifts affected America's views of its public schools, and particularly its urban public schools. Ultimately, an emphasis on global competitiveness, government deregulation, and the freedom of markets abroad were offered up as rationales for improving social policies at home. While Reagan's promotion of the privatization of public schools (via school vouchers) failed to find broad support, the 1983 *Nation at Risk* report did, unleashing a criticism of public schools and a spirit of experimentation focused on performance and competition. Alas, this context helped to legitimize the advent of TFA (see Payne in Rogers & Blumenreich, 2013).

Due to worsening conditions in urban cities and the shifting political winds in the latter part of the twentieth century, TFA also benefited from bipartisan support for experimentation that focused on the quality and outcomes of schools. These reforms included standards-based education reform and autonomous charter schools that would exchange autonomy for accountability. By the 2000s, No Child Left Behind emphasized high-stakes testing and represented stronger political winds in the direction of school-based performance and student outcomes and a further drift away from policies addressing structural and systemic causes of educational inequality, such as inadequate school funding and racial segregation. Today, the political context in which TFA expands is full speed ahead in the direction of a market-based restructuring of public schools, emphasizing a cocktail of outcomes-based remedies to educational equity, including standards, testing and accountability, deregulation and privatization of school management, and choice and competition via charter schools.

However, not only is TFA situated within a broader climate of neoliberal reform, it is also an integral player in networks of neoliberal reformers. While the organization rarely advertises itself as embracing an explicit political or ideological framework about educational inequality, it does promote a core set of beliefs, including the "solvability" of educational inequity, the belief that "poverty is not destiny," the belief that transformational leaders and strong managers are essential, and the belief that acting with "high standards, urgency, and a long-term view" is important if change is to happen. While these principles are indeed laudable and work to garner broad appeal, particularly to idealistic college graduates, TFA's leadership and its alumni are often enmeshed in a network of partnerships whose reform activities convey a much more concrete political platform that is tied to explicit ideologies about the causes and solutions of educational inequity.

Indeed, recent research has identified the political and institutional impact of TFA's alumni whose actions outside of the classroom have helped the organization to expand its network of partners, funders, and affiliates, and most significantly, its network of private sector actors. This "education entrepreneurial network" (Kretchmar, Sondel, & Ferrare, 2014) includes a significant number of business executives, investment bankers, corporate foundations, and venture philanthropists. Convinced of the superiority of private management and the inefficiency of government bureaucracy, these groups have pushed to infuse education with neoliberal principles including market-based systems of choice and competition, deregulation and privatization of public services, and a scaling back of labor power via attacks on teachers unions and teachers' collective bargaining rights, the eradication of teacher tenure, and efforts to shift responsibility (and blame) for student performance to individual teachers themselves, using merit-based systems of evaluation, pay, and promotion. Hence, as a connective force at the center of an education entrepreneurial network, TFA has aligned itself with the network's reform activities and its endorsement of neoliberal reforms.

In light of the actions of leaders within the TFA organization, and despite the ways that TFA's appeal and expansion have been aided by the political winds of neoliberal hegemony in the late twentieth and early twenty-first centuries, how do we make sense of the swelling recruitment of young corps members—thousands of whom are seemingly "on board" the TFA vessel and are sailing, perhaps unknowingly, in the direction of neoliberal reform of public schools?

Speaking Out and Troubling the Waters: Voices of Corps Members of Color

Given the likelihood that TFA alumni will continue to play a prominent role beyond the classroom in much larger policy and advocacy efforts (Jacobsen & Linkow, 2014), it is important to understand the early socialization experiences of TFA corps members and to tease out the ideological dimensions and struggles of their training and development. To some degree, researchers have begun this work, but they tend to focus on TFA's leadership development programs and the ideological framework to which these leaders have coalesced (Trujillo & Scott, 2014). Yet, more research is still needed on the experiences of TFA corps members themselves, and particularly those who challenge the political and ideological dimensions of their training. In this vein, I share stories that highlight critical struggles among corps members who have rocked the boat and troubled the waters. What follows are narratives from corps members,[2] grouped thematically under the categories of "Feeling Duped," "Critical Disciples and Dilettantes," and "The Critically Determined."

Feeling duped. Some corps members described feeling misled about the nature of the "movement" they had signed up for. For many, the troubling surprise was related to lack of racial diversity and the need for more members of color. Yet, the overrepresentation of White corps members was only the beginning, as many stories below capture the deeper issue of "Whiteness" in terms of the social and cultural dispositions of TFA corps members whose race and class privilege were treated with "kid gloves" in ways that hindered the development of antiracist and inclusive instruction. Some corps members felt misled about the premise of the organization and their presence as novices in district schools. Reece's experience, for example, as both a corps member and later a program director, sheds light on how ideas about a "teacher shortage" shaped the organization's early messages, which then shifted to "closing the achievement gap." These messages were intertwined with subtle messages that seemed to denigrate the experience of veteran educators and pushed corps members to focus almost exclusively on results, and framed novices not as partners in improving education for urban students but as competitors driven to outperform and replace their non-TFA counterparts.

"A sea of White people": A movement steeped in White privilege.

A sea of White people. That was my initial impression. I did not fit the traditional mold. To an extent, I felt bamboozled, hoodwinked, and led astray. I had the impression that I would be joining a diverse movement, joining a group of activists from across the country... but there was little racial/ethnic and class diversity in my cohort or among the staff intended to support us. This created a climate in which my tenure with the organization was full of critiquing, organizing, and challenging the status quo. I have consistently been a critical friend to its mission, philosophy, selection process, and training. (Allison Richardson, 2004, Western Region)

I did my Institute in Los Angeles, California. So imagine, all of us working together for this mission of "One day" [all kids will have a quality education]. I felt that everybody was committed to that mission. And it was also nice to forge relationships with the other corps members in the other regions. But it was at Institute that I learned just how much the corps lacked diversity. For example, in my corps of Vegas we were roughly a corps of 50 and there were only a few members of color, but while the Los Angeles corps had 230 members, the LA corps had only 10 more people of color than ours! It made those racial disparities jump out even more. So even though we were all working toward education or trying to rectify educational inequity, there was still such a contrast or a vast disparity within our organization itself. (Keisha Grimes, 2004, Las Vegas)

I was grateful that TFA staff integrated mandatory workshops on issues of race and culture throughout the summer. But while the workshops did much to bring important issues to the surface, they also revealed the lack of knowledge that many prospective teachers held. Frankly, it was shocking to me that the TFA teachers gathered around me, who were headed off to work in our nation's most underprivileged schools in a matter of weeks, had little to no meaningful exposure to poor communities of color before joining the organization. It was obvious to me that my fellow corps members had lived in segregated worlds far from the communities in which they were slated to teach, almost wholly disconnected from the cultural and social worlds of Black and Latino communities. In stirring discussions I learned that many of them were reflecting on issues of race and racism for the first time! I wondered then, as I do now, what the consequences are for children of color taught by individuals with such obvious gaps in social and cultural knowledge. (Terrenda White, 2002, Los Angeles)

As a program director (PD), I learned early on that you had to treat White TFA members with kid gloves when it came to race. ... It was sort of like, "We can't make these White kids feel too uncomfortable because then they might quit!" So among the staff, it was a feeling of, "Don't be too mean to them." So there was always just this general reluctance to talk about the connection between race and education. Almost like race didn't exist. ...Yeah, we assigned them to read Lisa Delpit during Institute, but after that no one talked about race anymore. I can remember when I decided one year that I would start addressing race in my observations about discipline, such as, "You have six African American kids in your class, and do you notice that all of their cards are on red for talking? However, your Latino students are doing the exact same things, but you have not disciplined them in the same manner." The teachers would say to me, "Are you calling me a racist?" And I would say, "I'm just pointing out to you what I saw in your classroom." My fellow program directors would tell me to ease up on confronting corps members on things like race. So as a staff member, I never felt like I had a full license to call corps members on racial bias. ... In 2004, they fired me. I was the only one out of all the PDs I had started with who had not resigned. So instead, they fired me. I signed a waiver saying I wouldn't reveal what had happened, because TFA thought it would look bad. I promised not to talk to any media outlets about the circumstances. But when the day finally came for me to leave, it wasn't a surprise, and so I thought, "Okay, peace. I'm out!" (Reece White, program director 1988, Western Region)

In many ways, TFA made me into the "Angry Black Man." Before TFA, I was never that guy. I was racial, yes, and I had all the race pride, but I was never angry. But TFA sort of exacerbated all the racial problems I had trouble with, and by the end of Institute, I had gotten written up for so much ridiculous stuff. It was crazy. One time, they had to get the big boss lady, who was head of the whole Institute, to come and talk to me. She was telling me the whole TFA spiel, and she even told me that historically, the Black people or the people of color have always been written up more than the White folks at Institute! Well, I often spoke my mind, and they wrote me up for something like "lack of professionalism." Well, I collected a bunch of those reprimands, and I hung them all up on my door! (Marlon Simmons, 2010, Milwaukee)

As corps members of color, we were always kind of going against the grain, sitting there and knowing that some corps members were teaching with strong race and class bias. I felt that we always had to challenge those kinds of things and go against the grain. I think that because TFA is very inspiring, and because we, as an organization, expect such rigorous results, I found that it was hard for people to maintain humility on their quest for educational equity. And so my thing was just about encouraging others to keep themselves humble and to remind themselves of their privilege. (Keisha Grimes, 2004, Las Vegas)

"There's no shortage of teachers": TFA novices and the denigration of veteran educators.

Over the evolution of my experience from corps member to program director, I saw how the mission of TFA changed, which initially gave us the message that "We are here because of a teacher shortage." And it was often said that if we were not there, then there's only going to be permanent subs that aren't trained, or a revolving door of substitutes, and so forth. But I was on staff when the rhetorical shift came, from "We're here [because] of a teacher shortage" to "We're here to close the achievement gap," which was a very different message. And so now when I see how TFA is aggressively expanding, especially when I think about how teachers are being laid off, it makes me very uncomfortable. ... In general, I feel like the organization is setting itself up as though they're better than the average teacher [by focusing on test scores]. ... But to be honest, the organization has always had a sort of arrogance to it ... but I don't like that at all ... especially when I think about the people that helped me to improve the most as a classroom teacher... teachers who were from [my district], who would come by my room with stuff and check in on me and show me how to do things. And if you did not talk to older women in those schools, Black women teachers especially, then you couldn't understand what they knew about teaching poor children or Black children, or what they went through to even get jobs in teaching back in the day, and how unions were important to them to protect them. And I learned that their experience is tied to the history of women's rights and teachers' unions and to the fight for civil rights broadly. ... It pains me to see that TFA is putting itself in the "America's-teachers-suck-and-they're-entirely-responsible-for-our-failing-schools" framework. It's very disappointing. And the examples of TFA alum that get spotlighted are concerning. I, for example, do not consider Michelle Rhee a hero! And personally I feel like folks like her should know better. Particularly as a woman of color, she might not have even had a job back in the day if it weren't for unions." (Reece White, 1996, Western Region)

"Give me the data!": Cultural insensitivity and technocratic forms of instruction.

I feel that some of the insensitivity I witnessed at Institute was due to the way TFA re-cruited its members. Because TFA's recruitment process focuses so much on school/campus leaders, I think it lacks a piece for cultural sensitivity. And so they're just focused on getting results—people who leverage results in every aspect of their collegiate career. So it's really hard if the organization is so results-driven during recruitment and selection of candidates to also focus on the cultural sensitivity aspect that needs to accompany the organization. (Keisha Grimes, 2004, Las Vegas)

It was around 2003 or 2004 when we started the whole tracking and pushing for signif-icant gains. Why did we do that? I mean, we had a theory that if we could get teachers to track what they do with kids and pay attention to which students were on the edge of things, then they could identify what standards to focus on. But it's the worst thing now. I remember oftentimes there would be conversations I'd have as a program director with my corps members, who would be crying at the end-of-year meetings because they were close to getting their gains, but had just missed it, so perhaps their kids were at 78%, and not 80% significant gains. And then there was so much pressure on us, because our evalu-ations as program directors were based on whether our teachers made significant gains or not. So you were a good program director or not based on whether your corps members were on track to make significant gains and actually made it. (Reece White, 1998, Western Region)

I don't have a relationship with my TFA program director. The reason we've had trouble is because I feel that when she comes into my classroom for observations, all she really cares about is *data*, or results. I mean, when she came, her whole thing was "Give me the data, give me the data, give me the data." Well, I'm against that! I try to tell her that before she demands all of this stuff from the students, you have to really get to know them. Seriously know them. ... I told her that when everyone else comes into my room, they sit and actually talk to my kids and help them with reading, but when TFA comes in it's with their pads and stuff asking for data. You know, my kids are tired of White folks coming in and watch-ing them. They said that to me. These people come in and treat them like guinea pigs. This whole approach is *impersonal*, they're not even thinking about the curriculum itself or the content. (Marlon Simmons, 2010, Milwaukee)

Critical disciples and dilettantes. Not all corps members express deep misgivings about TFA. Indeed, some corps members express overall positive outlooks on their preparation and their experiences. Nonetheless, these members still offered critical insights about ways to support and improve the organization. In these instances, corps members are not simply contented disciples or dilettantes of TFA, but instead view themselves in the role of critical friends who seek change from within.

"Cleaning spots on rose-colored glasses": The role of critical friends in TFA.

I played the role of critical friend not only as a corps member, but also as a summer staff member. The last time I worked with the organization, I organized an impromptu, Institute-wide town hall so that new corps members and staff, primarily of color, could have their concerns heard, without disruption, from the local governing managing team and national chief of staff. I coded all of their concerns into analytic themes and insisted, along with partnering staff members, on institutional changes. (Allison Richardson, 2004, Western Region)

I grew up in New Orleans and I am a Teach For America teacher, but even with TFA, my perspective is quite different. You see, in 1990, New Orleans was one of the first cities TFA placed corps members in. And so, I'm one of few in the corps who was actually taught by a Teach For America teacher as a young child. My Teach For America teacher had a very profound impact on my education, so I tend to see the organization through rose-colored glasses. But even still, based on my experience as a corps member, there are a few things that I hope the organization must learn to do better. (Keisha Grimes, 2004, Las Vegas)

Teach For America did what it could to prepare me as a first year teacher, given its mission. Through Institute I learned about unit and lesson plans, the importance of the first 2 weeks of school, and behavior management strategies. In terms of teacher organization, I felt comfortable taking control of my first class. But, as I found out later, teaching is more than content, it is about real interactions with real human beings who are at the stage in life where they are developing skills and characteristics that will take them through life. …Teacher preparation programs do have the responsibility of preparing future teachers to understand the types of students they will work with. Teachers need to be prepared to teach a diverse array of students with different types of cultural, sexual, and economic backgrounds in addition to physical abilities. Not doing so is a great disservice. In that regards, as far as I remember, TFA lacked the preparation needed to tackle the issues of dealing with a diverse student body. So, if I had not brought with me my own experiences dealing with diverse individuals as an adolescent, I might have been less able to integrate into my TFA assignment, which was primarily comprised of Latino students. (Kimberly Johnson, 2002, Los Angeles)

Moving beyond dupes, disciples, and dilettantes: The critically determined. Lastly, despite the challenges and struggles voiced by former corps members, many conveyed possible next steps, for both themselves and the organization. Indeed, these aspects of their stories can serve as examples for current corps members and perhaps sow the seeds for transformative work to push the organization toward a more comprehensive approach to education reform.

"My success does not belong to TFA": Taking back control and power over one's work.

I told my program director not to call me anymore, and not to come into my class. I had a meeting with her and I told her…that her idea of teaching is not culturally relevant and it did not take the kids into consideration. And perhaps that's the fundamental thing I'm unhappy with, which is that TFA seems to have trouble understanding that kids [of color] often have to sacrifice culture to get a "marketable" education. So the message they give us teachers is that if we want our kids to be able to achieve in this system, we have to cut out all of the "Blackness," and just teach them all the bullshit. And I feel deep down that as an organization, and a brand, they simply want to use the results from my class; because I am successful with my students. But that's why I refuse to give them my numbers, they're not going to exploit me or my kids by using my the outcome data to say, "Look at what *we* did! Look at *our* success!" *No, TFA is not responsible for my success.* So I will not give them my data tracker [of students' test scores]. I will keep refusing. (Marlon Simmons, 2010, Milwaukee)

I left the TFA program. It was November of my second year. My friend and I decided that's it, we're leaving. By this time, several corps members like myself didn't fit with the organization's approach to teaching. So we came together and started an independent group that was focused on learning about antiracist, anticlassist, and antihomophobic teaching. We held regular meetings and get-togethers, and we even hosted training for new TFA corps members. But we wanted to be independent from the TFA brand. And eventually two of us decided to simply leave the program. Afterwards, a message came from our program director that said, "Since you've decided to leave the organization, I have to recommend that you both be released from your teaching responsibilities. TFA can no longer recommend you and endorse you to your principal." Imagine! We had good evaluations. We were doing all of our PD requirements for the district. And we participated in committees. We were also there for parents, and had a good reputation with teachers and community members. But here was TFA, whose approach we disagreed with, using its influence to recommend that we get fired. My friend and I were scared. We went to our principal and said, "Listen, we're no longer TFA." She said, "Okay," then grinned and said, "What now?" We told her that someone from the organization would call and recommend that she fire us. And she said simply, "Well, let them call me. Let TFA call me. There's no way I am firing some of my best teachers. So let TFA call." Finally, my principal gets the call, and boy did she let [the program representative of TFA] have it! She really had our back as teachers. We kept our jobs. (Enrique Rodriguez, 2001, Phoenix)

"Let's work on behalf of all teachers": Repairing a collective identity within the profession.

In reality, and with the rise of charter schools, the TFA mission went from changing things from within education, to just going off and starting our own thing. In this regard, I feel like our separation from other teachers shows that TFA has an inherent disregard for the teaching profession. But think about it, if the everyday teachers had what we had—a Saturday group called a learning team where they could go and get content or grade-level-specific knowledge; if they had someone observing them and saying, "Let's make a plan" for how to help your students, and someone to check back in with them to see how the plan was going, and to provide them resources to help them get there—if every single teacher had that, then oh my god! What would happen? That would be huge. If anything, TFA could position themselves to be a voice for that and to advocate for what all teachers need, instead of implying that throwing money at schools isn't the answer. But instead, said on behalf of all teachers, "Here's the things we've learned from our training Institute and here's how we can work *with* traditional schools of education." Instead, they act like a 5-week Summer Institute is the equivalent or superior thing. It's almost like the organization's insecurity, combined with its arrogance, does not allow it to truly collaborate with the rest of the profession. (Reece White, 1996, Western Region)

Today, as a more critical and experienced educator, researcher, and community member, I am troubled by the growing influence of TFA's professional model—a model that paradoxically privileges and dis-privileges poor communities by drawing needed attention to urban education in America on the one hand, while simultaneously "un-doing" the professional structures and intergenerational knowledge bases that can create structural, cultural, and institutionally sustainable solutions to those problems. Yet, looking back, I often question my complicity in such a model. As an African American woman with a high-status college degree and an emerging class privilege, perhaps I was lured by TFA's prestige and the "convenience" of a brief commitment to an altruistic cause. Regardless, I had little awareness about the larger political minefields gripping education reform, and I especially thought little about the importance of durable networks and relationships that create nurturing professional communities of teaching in schools and classrooms. Nonetheless, as a more critical educator and scholar today, the teaching and learning I endorse begins with the difficult challenge of telling the truth, of my own schooling experience as well as my observations in schools as an educator, distinct from and at times in collusion with current restructuring systems that often represent "changing-same" models of community oppression and domination. To speak to, and to testify with, other educators is to cultivate awareness and to begin the needed task of building and repairing the professional community of educators that some of us may have helped to un-do. (Terrenda White, 2002, Los Angeles)

CONCLUSION

The voices in this chapter, as well as the voices throughout this book, speak to countless yet nameless corps members who struggled to find their own voices, to speak against the organization's practices they found troubling. Some of them channeled their disillusionment into critical determination to work neither as saviors of urban students, nor as replacements for veteran educators, but as *partners with* families, teachers, and leaders in a common struggle for a more comprehensive education reform. Indeed, the former corps members in this chapter not only voiced their frustrations but also channeled them in different ways, as some of them have participated in organized resistance against TFA's practices and its expansions, while others are currently teaching or leading public schools of their own, and others are now teacher educators, university professors of education, and writers. Together, their insights raise important concerns about the need for a broader reform agenda on the part of TFA that includes not only high expectations and a focus on results, but also more resources and professional development to support all teachers and the conditions of their work, more critical educators adept at pedagogical approaches that are antiracist and culturally responsive, and a more stable teaching force that supports sustainable community-school relationships over time.

REFERENCES

Apple, M. W. (2006). *Educating the "right" way: Markets, standards, gods, and inequality* (2nd ed.). New York: Routledge.

Buras, K., Randels, J, Salaam, K., & Students at the Center. (2010). *Pedagogy, policy, and the privatized city: Stories of dispossession and defiance from New Orleans.* New York: Teachers College.

Buras, K. (2011). Race, charter schools, and conscious capitalism: On the spatial politics of Whiteness as property (and the unconscionable assault on Black New Orleans). *Harvard Educational Review, 81*(2), 296–387.

Chubb, J. E., & Moe, T. (1990). *Politics, markets, and America's schools.* Washington, DC: The Brookings Institution.

Harvey, D. (2005). *A brief history of neoliberalism.* New York: Oxford University Press.

Jacobsen, R., & Linkow, T. W. (2014). National affiliation or local representation: When TFA alumni run for school board. *Education Policy Analysis Archives, 22*(69).

Kretchmar, K., Sondel, B., & Ferrare, J. (2014). Mapping the terrain: Teach For America, charter school reform, and corporate sponsorship. *Journal of Education Policy, 29*(6), 742–759.

Lipman, P. (2011). *The new political economy of urban education: Neoliberalism, race, and the right to the city.* New York: Taylor & Francis.

Rogers, B. L., & Blumenreich, M. (2013). Reframing the conversation: Insights from the oral histories of three 1990 TFA participants. *Teachers College Record, 115*(6), 1–46.

Trujillo, T., & Scott, J. (2014). Superheroes and transformers: Rethinking Teach For America's leadership models. *Kappan, 95*(8), 57–61.

NOTES

1. The narratives were drawn from a larger project on alternative teacher education which utilized "counter narratives" emphasized in critical race theory.
2. All names (other than Terrenda White) are pseudonyms.

CHAPTER NINETEEN

Voices of Revitalization: Challenging the Singularity of Teach For America's "Echo Chamber"

BARBARA TORRE VELTRI

BIOSKETCH

Barbara Torre Veltri is an associate professor in the Department of Teaching and Learning at Northern Arizona University. Her research interests include teacher education, Teach For America, and collecting first-person narratives to inform the teaching of history. She is the author of *Learning on Other People's Kids: Becoming a Teach For America Teacher* (Information Age Publishers, 2010).

NARRATIVE

Teach For America (TFA) is viewed as a results-driven blueprint for educational reform (Alter, 2011; Will, 2011). The organization recruits and trains recent college graduates through a corporate-like model that espouses leadership and teaching-as-service (Brewer, 2012; Kopp & Farr, 2011). By design, TFA is highly competitive. In 2014, Teach For America accepted only 14% of its applicant pool (Teach For America, 2014). Teach For America instills its organizational truths to incoming corps members (CMs) (Kopp, 2001; Kopp & Farr, 2011). To this end, a singular, robust, and paternalistic socialization develops one's "thinking like a corps member" (Veltri, 2010, p.112). This collective mindset intersects with private sector, neoliberal, and neoconservative agendas (Hill, 2013; Kovacs, 2007; Lahann & Reagan, 2011).

Teach For America's Singular Voice

In 1994 TFA applied for, and assumed, the role of America's National Teacher Corps, a designation that enables the nonprofit to receive millions of dollars from the federally funded Corporation for National Community Service (CNCS) (Veltri, 2010). TFA's founder, Wendy Kopp, convinced policy leaders that "The only way to truly insure that all children have the opportunity to achieve is to inspire more determined, talented leaders to turn their attention to our nation's poorest regions" (Kopp, 2001, p. 144).

Teach For America's intent became its strategy: prepare its own TFA teachers, discount input from experienced educators, distance itself from education schools, procure funding from generous partners, vigorously recruit on college campuses and in social media, entice alumni to lead and grow programs, publicize achievement gains, align with innovation-oriented university presidents, lobby legislators for alternative licensure, and protect the brand through marketing, public relations, and media associations (Kopp, 2001).

Teach For America charges multimillion-dollar "finder's fees" to underresourced school districts that hire its corps of teachers. TFA's most recent IRS Form 990 (which covers a shortened calendar year, October 1, 2012–May 31, 2013) reports public support for the nonprofit over the 5-year period 2008 to 2012 to be greater than $1 billion ($1,157,020,068, per Schedule A, Part II, p. 2).

The organization notes focused efforts to maintain its highly coveted nonprofit designation: "TFA has processes currently in place to ensure the maintenance of its tax-exempt status" (Teach For America, 2012, Schedule D, Part XIII, p. 5). And, while the original mission of TFA initially brought teachers to hard-to-staff locations, alumni and researchers note that TFA corps have replaced credentialed teachers across the country (Buras, 2015; Hootnick, 2014; Kretchmar, Sondel, & Ferrare, 2014). Sondel, a TFA alumna, writes, "School leader autonomy, in conjunction with the growing presence of the TFA network in New Orleans, has resulted in schools with TFA corps members and alumni, or TFA affiliates, comprising upwards of 80% of instructional staff" (Sondel, 2014, p. 1). Moreover, it appears that TFA's finances and lobbying activities are directed towards influencing legislation (Buras, 2015; deMarrais, Wenner, & Lewis, 2013; Hill, 2013; Kovacs & Slate-Young, 2013; Kretchmar, Sondel, & Ferrare, 2014; Sommer, 2014).

This chapter examines the response to TFA's singular voice, agenda, and movement by TFA insiders, defined as those with direct personal intersection with the TFA experience. This study draws from a network sample of participants whose voices present perspectives that are not often encountered in the organization's public literature. These include, first and foremost, applicants to TFA, TFA corps members (CMs), TFA alumni, parents of corps members, faculty at universities who teach TFA, and district/state leadership.

Conceptual Framework and Data Analysis

The work of sociologist Zygmunt Bauman serves as the conceptual framework that chronicles how Teach For America's overarching directives are interpreted, deconstructed, and evaluated by insiders. Teach For America's messaging (both overt and covert) is interrogated through a frame that codifies insiders' experiences, subsumed under four categories that emerged from the data set of hundreds of e-mail and phone interviews and analysis of documents.

Pseudonyms used throughout this chapter maintain the anonymity of participants, lending authenticity and fidelity to both temporal events and circumstances experienced in real time, by those with insider knowledge of TFA. This longitudinal qualitative study: (1) defines the phenomena of Teach For America within its own echo chamber; (2) considers perspectives of TFA "insiders," (3) organizes and subsumes interviews and experiences under four distinct categories, and (4) considers the implications of these practices situated within the dialogue, beliefs, and actions of participants. Wolcott (2001) notes, "Informants do need to be given their voice," (p. 133) and, because many voices of corps members and alumni have been silenced by TFA, this chapter offers some of those perspectives. Wolcott (1999) reminds us, "The underlying purpose of ethnographic research is to describe what the people in some particular place or status ordinarily do, and the meanings they ascribe to what they do, under ordinary or particular circumstances, presenting that description in a manner that draws attention to regularities that implicate cultural process" (p. 68).

The Role of the Echo Chamber and Dissemination of TFA's "Knowledge"

Professor Zygmunt Bauman (2014) suggests that "the echo chamber" phenomena—whereby a singular voice systematically shuts out dissenting voices, by design—is prevalent in society as a result of social media and technological isolationism. According to Bauman, "When messages, information, or images are not to your liking and are ignored, minimized, deleted or turned off, you don't listen to what others have to say." One can infer that the echo chamber is, first and foremost, self-serving. It promotes messages of enculturation within a closed community. The oneness mindset puts forward an expectation that a singular, unifying belief will be commonly held as a prerequisite for success and belonging. Bauman refers to echo chamber communities as those having a unique way of disseminating information. Often, a barrage of messages is released to members as a means of reinforcing the organization's expectancies and communal bond.

Voices of Recognition

Insiders, adept at perceiving the contradictions of TFA's echo chamber "Truths," react by sorting through the rhetoric on TFA. There is a collective realization that recruiting promises don't amount to much:

> My decision is firm. I am the recipient of an international fellowship. You suggest that I teach, when I am not prepared to do so? Do you ever call students to congratulate them for becoming teachers or fulfilling their life's passion? Or do you only call to suggest that we accept TFA's offer to join? (College senior, reacting to call from the university president)

Insiders consider the original message of Teach For America, the one that enticed then to apply—"Teach For America aims to erase educational inequity by recruiting recent college graduates to teach for two years in urban and rural public schools...."— to be at odds with the realities faced by corps members, who expected that their TFA training would prepare them to teach. They note how CM placements are often erratic. Those assigned to special education admit to self-deprecation, a dilemma that intensifies as the academic year progresses and the echo chamber mantras continue: "Are you doing all that you can to eradicate educational equity? Have you submitted your test data?" For example:

> It's ridiculous that TFA qualifies for AmeriCorps money in my opinion, as they know nothing about AmeriCorps and de-emphasize the service aspect in their preparation of corps members. (Jackson)[1]

Then there are other insiders, who see through the TFA rhetoric and are compelled to deconstruct TFA's public statements:

> While I don't #resistTFA, I certainly don't take it at face value either. Also don't forget what Wendy Kopp, herself, said publicly in 2011, "We're a leadership development organization, not a teaching organization." Staying in the profession of teaching? It was never the point, is still not the point, and never will be the point. At least she can admit that now, although you won't find that quote on any of their marketing materials. (Vince)

The collective voices of corps members challenge discourse from TFA's echo chamber. Hootnick, a TFA alumna (San Jose) reports how insiders discount TFA's claims:

> TFA found itself pitted against a group of 47 alumni over whether recruits in California should undergo additional, state-mandated training to help new teachers meet the needs

of the state's large population of English learners. The alumni, who coordinated the first public rebuke of TFA from within its own ranks, wrote that the program's 5-week training was inadequate, and that to consider its recruits qualified to teach English learners "is a lie… While we deeply value our commitment to TFA, we must stand up for the 1.4 million EL students today struggling in California's classrooms." (Hootnick, 2014, p. 3)

Insiders' voices demystify the organization's questionable operating procedures. Teach For America not only directs funding towards lobbying but also expects corps members employed as full-time teachers to join them in that effort.

> Here's an example of (one of many) an email I received during my time in TFA. As you can see, I have to send a blind copy to my regional director, who keeps track that we CM's follow his directive. (Gerald)

Corps Members,

> *We are at the peak of our lobbying efforts again this year to receive a $1 million appropriation grant from the state of —. This crucial piece of funding enables us to bring more teachers [TFA teachers] to the state's classrooms. Getting the legislative approval for the funds this year is even more challenging in the face of mounting budget cuts. The appropriation has even made it to the top of our national priority list, and Wendy Kopp herself is flying in to speak with legislators to ensure that our appropriation remains in the budget. Please, add your voice to the cause! As both a constituent and a teacher, you have a unique chance to sway legislators with your thoughts and concerns.*

It might seem that insiders living within the echo chamber have no other choice but to comply with TFA's directives. But this group of insiders cannot reconcile the echo chamber's directives that: (1) TFA members are highly qualified; and (2) Teaching-as-service is truth-telling. TFA insiders point to the erosion of veteran educators and community-based teachers, and recognize that "Doing the Right Thing" begins with finding one's voice.

Voices of Disillusionment

Bauman (2014) asserts,

> If one is bored, or stops answering messages—which seem, on the surface, so safe; you just click on the message, and it's off your radar—there is initially no fear of communication reprisals that are immediate; within the confines of your own physical space, you believe that you retain complete control. But, with a social commitment, you make promises. Your personal identity is relegated to a secondary role. Community membership links you to a shared life with another group, where you are always within the radar of the echo chamber.

The voices of disillusionment admitted to feeling trapped; they could not even retain the privacy of their own thoughts. There was no time that corps members in this category felt that TFA's messages didn't haunt them:

> I think my roommate would describe his feelings as intense anxiety and never ending uncertainty. (Raul)

While receiving and sharing communication within the TFA echo chamber, community members are simultaneously jockeying for position within their peer group, assessing the "pragmatic considerations" that prompted their application to TFA in the first place, and considering alternatives.

According to Bauman (2014), "Whenever you've gained something, you lose something else. It's a zero-sum game." For many TFA insiders, the notion of never being alone is equated with loss of self:

> I, personally, wish I had done a better job making friends outside of my TFA circle during my time in [city]. (Hailey)

Advocating for one's self while promoting the community "truth" is acceptable. Self-efficacy for any other reason becomes a tentative construct. Insiders admit to inventing excuses. After a period of time, the community's message is viewed as forced, or an imposition:

> It really is fascinating to observe, at Institute, how the opinions corps members hold of TFA are capable of evolving so quickly. (Garrett)

Parents of TFA insiders shared the experiences of their corps member children, as CMs are reluctant to speak out after having witnessed the repercussions of others in their cohorts:

> My daughter's experience with TFA was, in a word, demoralizing. She was tenacious and a freethinking go-getter. Currently, she feels as though she not only lost her moral compass, but is in therapy. She finished the experience (because she couldn't quit), but is not a teacher, never was, and has no close associations with TFAers because they left for other pursuits, and few could be trusted in the first place. She is emotionally spent and was not prepared for her placement in elementary grades. (Mrs. T)

Another parent was also tentative about speaking on this topic because of residual repercussions linked to one's TFA experience:

> Now, my daughter has no job, doesn't want to remain in the district, because all positions are assigned by TFA alumni who run charter schools; she has no place to live, because three of her roommates already left town, and she's haunted by an inferiority complex and poor self-esteem that did not happen at any other time in her life, as a result of teaching for 2 years with TFA. (Dr. R)

Voices of disillusionment extend into the community, in spite of the echo chamber's public relations efforts. A despondent mother of a TFA teacher offered her voice to my sister, her medical doctor, during an annual visit. My sister called me, outraged, like I was responsible in some way for TFA's limited preparation and flawed placement model, to express her concern and echo the voice of her distressed patient:

> After 1 year with TFA, my daughter, assigned to teach elementary special education in Baltimore, returns with stage III lymphoma. If stress causes cancer, TFA did this to my daughter. (Mrs. McB)

Corps insiders recognize that they are commodified by the organization, yet they continue to conform (Brewer, 2012). Many accept this trade-off as the necessary part they are required to play over a particular time frame, usually for only 2 years in their postcollege early twenties, in order to reap the benefits of "good corps member" status (Veltri, 2010, p. 120). This outward compliance supports personal goals advanced after their TFA teaching career is successfully completed. Others, however, recognize that their individual worth serves a singular purpose—advance Teach For America's movement and grow its base to hardwire political and financial favor. And yet, they simply could not comply (Brewer, 2012; Rubinstein, 2011; Sondel, 2014; White, 2013):

> I remember my school director (at NYC Institute) insisting that CMs be more aggressive with distributing consequences to children they were teaching in summer school settings than was probably necessary. I believe this kind of "hypersensitivity" (as I would put it) to criticism is a reflection of TFA's failure to grapple with its own structural flaws. (Brandon)

Voices of Resiliency

Voices that fit this category respond in different ways. Some are pragmatic and self-serving, a high number are inwardly defiant and subvert privately, and a significant subset maintain an outward appearance of compliance while deconstructing the TFA messages through an array of predetermined actions. Others tend toward escapism. Bauman (2014) argued: "It's easy to cut yourself off from problems instead of taking on the difficult act of handling them." He terms this phenomenon "assuming life in the echo chamber."

Others counter-crusade surreptitiously, but do not lose themselves in the process. They recognize the flaws in the messaging, but in the short term they advocate for their own personal needs, and then the needs of their students. This group maintained their commitments because they assumed that their affiliations with TFA would provide them with the stepping-stone to something big: "Any career goal would be helped by one's association with TFA" (TFA recruiting speech, 2013).

But within a few short weeks, these insiders realized that they would have to learn who to trust, figure out teaching on their own, and support one another on many levels in order to complete their 2-year program and network. This group recognized, as one put it, that

> You can have these amazing goals, and can expect great things for our students, but if you don't give them the tools to succeed, and in that…I mean us. I see myself as a teacher that doesn't have a full toolbox; you can't expect children to compensate for what's lacking in my preparation.

Voices of Dissent

Another "truth" that bounces around the organizational "echo chamber" relates to Teach for America's alumni, a group whose socialization began during (corps training) Institute, continued during their 2-year teaching commitments, and appears to extend indefinitely. Teach For America maintains its base of alumni through personal outreach and social media. During fiscal year 2012 TFA reported that "alumni affairs activities superseded pre-service training as one of our three largest program services" (Teach For America, 2012, p. 45). Teach For America's echo chamber broadly advertises alumni-in-education retention data. "Approximately 80% of Teach For America's 28,000 alumni in 2013 were doing mission aligned work either in education or in other professions serving low income communities" (Teach For America, 2012, p. 44).

TFA collects alumni data annually, yet insiders know that the organization remains *data gatekeepers* who strategically determine which data is tucked away in an obscure location within the "echo chamber" and which information is beneficial to their growth trajectory. Alumni are targeted annually for their feedback. TFA's definition of the term *remaining in education,* on its website and in its publicly released statements, is loose and exaggerated. One insider explains:

> Staying in education, but not teaching, ranges from undermining public education in education-related roles … [to] moving into leadership roles and making a strong impact on schools and communities, and everything in between. Also, remember that the organization counts the alumni, on its staff of several thousands, as "staying in education," as well as the staff members in TFA spin-offs like KIPP, TNTP, and Teach For All. This means that the person who did operations work, coordinating the logistics of TFA conferences "stayed in education," as well as the person who was an administrative assistant in the office. (Diego)

While most insiders view the echo chamber messages seriously, there are many whose comments are tinged with sarcastic humor:

Basically, we have to find out which corps members are leaving—when they are packing up physically. Maybe we can get the data from the UHAUL companies in town, LOL. (Jeremy)

Voices of Self-Perpetuity

This group acted by choosing to sort through the rhetoric of TFA and were committed to locating their own niches in helping others and, ultimately, themselves, without taking on any "pressure" from TFA. As hundreds of corps members shared with me:

TFA didn't create the competitiveness, we all had that to begin with, but TFA had a way of bringing it out even more. (Stefanie)

Previously, the competitiveness seemed to be foremost among the students who boasted an Ivy League pedigree in their regional assignment, but they soon recognized that the realities of TFA and learning how to teach, on the job, with limited preparation, meant that all were basically on a level playing field, impeded by a huge learning curve.

Yet, in spite of one's unique dedication to kids—among first-generation college graduates, and especially minority corps members who wanted (for a short time, even if TFA was the only vehicle) to give back, support, or mentor children living in poor communities through education, without having the teacher training to do so—desire was not synonymous with teaching effectiveness.

There are advantages, however, in appearing to embrace the TFA echo chamber messages, at least on the surface, during and after one's 2-year TFA teaching commitment, without interrogating the messages' long-term effects. Corps members are well paid when they leave the classroom and work for Teach For America in some capacity.

The not-so-new pattern: Teach year 1 and 2; hang around and teach year 3; begin to criticize teachers and administration in the public schools during year 3, while you gradually move into TFA leadership as a MTLD (manager of teacher leadership development) and get an automatic $10,000 raise over your former teacher salary. To that, one may add the $5,000 stipend for supervising novice corps trainees over 5 weeks of summer work, too.

Voices of Revitalization

Hidden beyond the echo chamber are TFA alumni who entered education through Teach For America over a decade ago and continue their teaching work. Of those whom I have come to know personally, two earned national board certificates and remained in their urban school district for 10 to 15 years. Two others are principals in urban public school districts where they were first assigned to teach in 2001. After attending Harvard, another ran for public office in her Texas community where she was born and raised, supported by the Network for Public Education. Although she did not win her seat, she intends to seek public office on the school board in the near future. In the meantime, she and another colleague committed to public school education tutor and support high school students in navigating the college application process, because both were first-generation children of immigrant parents who succeeded in U.S. public schools.

Ten other corps members are currently teaching in high-poverty public schools in New York City, Buffalo, Chicago, Houston, and Mesa, Arizona, 14 years after they entered classrooms as TFA teachers. Alumni whom I came to know as corps teachers from 1999 to 2005 are now parents raising young children. Regardless of where they call home, across the U.S. or around the globe, none report that their children's teachers are TFA corps members.

While many support TFA financially, others opted to be removed from their e-mail lists and to deconstruct the messages of the TFA echo chamber. They recognize that only through dialogue can true understanding and collaboration take place. These voices of revitalization are committed to doing the right thing.

Implications

Teach For America reported $555,970 on its 2011 990 Schedule C: Political Campaign and Lobbying Activities (2011, p. 21) and $488,035 on its 2012 990 Schedule C (2012, p. 27) in attempts to influence foreign, national, state or local legislation expenses. Insiders note TFA's pervasive policy to keep their "image" untainted. To achieve this goal, the nonprofit often closes off access to researchers, teacher educators, and even alumni who seek certain types of information. Bauman (2014) described the *mind blind:*

> Those in power use the echo chamber, and if they do not like what they hear, they don't listen to what others have to say. They delete and turn off, and soon, one only dialogues with those who think like them, and agree with them. This results in a phenomenon whereby one is surrounded, not only in communication and social networking, but by images, ideas, research, documents, and media, that align with the voices of the echo chamber.

Teach For America operationalizes within an echo chamber mindset that has morphed into a hierarchical network. The brand, the message, and the imagery connote a singular prototype that has gained favor and financial support from powerful friends in high places. But there are those who resist, rebuke, and reconsider Teach For America's requests. What about the human resources superintendent who refused to hire Teach For America teachers in his district and noted,

"They don't stay; they don't know how to teach; and they cost money. What's the difficulty with that decision?" What about the TFA mom who refused TFA fundraisers?

> I received a phone call from TFA suggesting amounts for me to donate. I said, I already gave to TFA. … You have my daughter teaching for you. What more do you want? (Mrs. J, TN)

What about the corps member who shared TFA's deception with fellow incoming corps members when he recognized the sister of his college peer, an outstanding first grade teacher and a certified teacher (and my former Northern Arizona University student):

> I couldn't believe it when I saw her. Here we were, generally fatigued from long hours at Institute, trying to figure out how we're going to teach the kids; how we'd get our rooms to look like hers, and all of a sudden I realize… it was Kelly [pseudonym], and she was *not* like the rest of us, coming with only the TFA training we were going through. She was a certified teacher. And, in this video, TFA is holding her up to us incoming corps as the example of an excellent TFA teacher? Are you kidding me? I was wondering why would they deceive us like that. (Jared)

There are many TFA alums and corps members who don't negotiate with their souls. They know that "Doing the Right Thing" means that they speak freely, even when faced with economic and personal repercussions. Insiders who challenge the singular voice of the "echo chamber" through their own actions include university faculty:

> I'm on to the specific tactics that TFA employs to limit corps dialogue in graduate classes. Our university has a partnership with TFA. We cannot even communicate directly with TFA students because every message is copied to the TFA/university liaison. This truly impacts academic and personal freedom. TFA is trying to control the message and the messengers. (Professor J)

One university professor left one institution for another:

> TFA was imposing a strict module that included PowerPoints that faculty were required to use for their Teach For America graduate students. All an education professor had to do was insert their own name on the cover slide of the TFA prepared TFA methods class PowerPoint file. (Dr. K, VA)

CONCLUSION

Bauman notes that rather than engaging in the art of dialogue, where no one attempts to convince, pressure, or control another, TFA produces messages that are increasingly predetermined, and the rhetoric that is generated is designed to be exclusionary. While the singularly expansive ripple of TFA culture and the "singular voice" of TFA that counts as truth persists, insiders speak up, speak their truth, and admit that "TFA does not speak for me."

They share Kozol-like exemplars, raise questions, deconstruct untrue public-sphere educational reform policy statements, problematize the rhetoric of a singular Teach For America "echo chamber," and move, instead, towards a social justice of *revitalization*, as noted in Bauman's *The Art of Dialogue*, "where there is no assuming absolute right, no convincing, or talking to hear one's own applause" (Bauman, 2014).

In *The Art of Dialogue*, there are dual roles; participants assume the roles of teacher and pupil. Each can learn something from the other. There is no silencing of groups, people, or voices. The art of dialogue is informal and open; there is no predetermined agenda or rules. Rather, there is cooperation, and no one owns an absolute right position. "You purposefully meet and talk to each other. You talk and don't argue with people." Bauman concludes, "Dialogue is a matter of life and death to a democratic society. Everyone learns something from cooperation, and a real dialogue has no winners" (Bauman, 2014).

REFERENCES

Alter, J. (2011, June 3). Don't believe critics, education reform works: Jonathan Alter. Bloomberg View. Retrieved from http://www.bloombergview.com/articles/2011-06-03/don-t-believe-critics-education-reform-works-jonathan-alter

Bauman, Z. (2014, March 28). The art of dialogue: A meeting with Zygmunt Bauman at Arezzo [Video file]. Universita di Siena. Retrieved from http://www.youtube.com/watch?v=-YYjeYzqrUo

Brewer, T. J. (2012). Hyper-accountability, burnout and blame: A TFA corps member speaks out. *Education Week: Living in Dialogue*. Retrieved from http://blogs.edweek.org/teachers/living-in-dialogue/2012/02/hyper-accountability_burnout_a.html

Buras, K. L. (2015). *Charter schools, race, and urban space: Where the market meets grassroots resistance.* New York: Routledge.

deMarrais, K. P., Wenner, J., & Lewis, J. B. (2013). Bringing Teach For America into the forefront of teacher education: Philanthropy meets spin. *Critical Education, 4*(11), 67–80. Retrieved from http://ojs.library.ubc.ca/index.php/criticaled/article/view/184084

Hill, D. (2013). Class struggle and education: Neoliberalism, (neo)-conservatism, and the capitalist assault on public education. *Critical Education, 4*(10). Retrieved from http://ojs.library.ubc.ca/index.php/criticaled/article/view/184452

Hootnick, A. (2014, April 21). Teachers are losing their jobs but Teach For America's expanding. What's with that? *The Hechinger Report*. Retrieved from http://hechingerreport.org/content/teachers-losing-jobs-teach-americas-expanding-whats-wrong_15617/

Kopp, W. (2001). *One day, all children: The unlikely triumph of Teach For America and what I learned along the way.* New York, NY: Public Affairs.

Kopp, W., & Farr, S. (2011). *A chance to make history: What works and what doesn't in providing an excellent education for all.* New York: Perseus Books Group.

Kovacs, P. E. (2007). *Are public schools worth saving? If so, by whom?* (Doctoral dissertation). Georgia State University, Atlanta.

Kovacs, P. E., & Slate-Young, E. (2013, October 15). An analysis of Teach For America's research page. *Critical Education, 4*(11), 67–80. Retrieved from http://ojs.library.ubc.ca/index.php/critical ed/article/view/184138

Kozol, J. (1991). *Savage inequalities: Children in America's schools.* New York: Crown.

Kretchmar, K., Sondel, B., & Ferrare, J. (2014). Mapping the terrain: Teach For America, charter school reform, and corporate sponsorship. *Journal of Education Policy, 29*(6), 742–759.

Lahann, R., & Reagan, E. M. (2011). Teach For America and the politics of progressive neoliberalism. *Teacher Education Quarterly, 38*(1), 7–27.

Rubinstein, G. (2011, May 21). What happened to my TFA? *Teach for Us.* Retrieved from http://garyrubinstein.teachforus.org/2011/05/21/what-happened-to-my-tfa/

Sommer, C. (2014, January 7). How the corporate class is using Teach For America to turn K–12 teaching into a temporary, low-paying job. *Alternet.* Retrieved from http://www.alternet.org/edu cation/how-corporate-class-using-teach-america-turn-k-12-teaching-temporary-low-paying-job

Sondel, B. (2014, February 3). My many voices. *Critical Educators for Social Justice.* Retrieved from http://www.cesjsig.org/blog/my-many-voices-by-beth-sondel.

Teach For America. (2011). IRS Form 990. Retrieved from https://www.teachforamerica.org/sites/default/files/2011_990_fy12_3_.pdf

Teach For America. (2012) IRS Form 990. Retrieved from http://www.guidestar.org/FinDocuments/2013/133/541/2013-133541913-0a47efc5-9.pdf

Teach For America. (2013a). *Building a movement.* Retrieved December 5, 2014 from http://www.teachforamerica.org/why-teach-for-america/building-a-movement

Teach For America. (2013b). *Fueling long-term impact.* Retrieved from http://www.teachforamerica.org/our-mission/fueling-long-term-impact

Veltri, B. T. (2010). *Learning on other people's kids: Becoming a Teach For America teacher.* Charlotte, NC: Information Age Publishing.

White, T. (2013). *Teach For America (TFA) and the "endangerment" of communities: Counter-stories from TFA teachers of color.* Paper presented to American Educational Research Association Annual Meeting, San Francisco.

Will, G. (2011, February 27). Teach For America: Letting the cream rise. *Washington Post.* Retrieved from http://www.washingtonpost.com/wp-dyn/content/article/2011/02/25/AR201102250500 2.html

Wolcott, H. F. (1999). *Ethnography: A way of seeing.* Walnut Creek, CA: Alta Mira.

Wolcott, H. F. (2001). *Writing up qualitative research* (2nd ed.). Thousand Oaks, CA: Sage Publications.

NOTE

1. All names are pseudonyms.

CHAPTER TWENTY

The Grandfather of Alumni TFA Critics

GARY RUBINSTEIN
Houston, 1991–1993

BIOSKETCH

Gary Rubinstein was a member of the second cohort of TFA in 1991. He taught in Houston for 4 years, Denver for 1 year, and New York City for 11 years. He has also written two books about teaching, *Reluctant Disciplinarian* and *Beyond Survival*. Gary has been offering "constructive criticism" to TFA for over 20 years. He hopes that one day TFA will listen to him. He lives in New York City with his wife, Erica, and his two children, Sarah and Sam.

NARRATIVE

Excerpt from my blog (4/30/2013 "The Three Biggest TFA Lies"):

> The biggest problem with TFA is all the lying. Though the individual people I've known on staff aren't huge liars, themselves, the sum of all the lies add up to an organization whose lying is pathological. Really, they've elevated the art of lying to new heights, much the way Mozart elevated the concerto. Even people like Bernie Madoff who thought they were great liars can't help but marvel at TFA's techniques.

The lies began innocuous enough. They were just part of their PR, part of their advertising and fund raising efforts. Other lies they didn't even realize were lies until they were too embroiled in them, and still other lies they still don't seem to realize are untrue. If I could change one thing about the organization, this would be it.

...

Lies will not help America's children. Lies might make some charter operators rich which, I suppose, is good for the charter operators. But these lies are causing, around the country, schools to be shut down, teachers to be fired, and students to be scattered around looking for a new school after knowing that they got their old school shut down—and all because these schools, teachers, and students were not able to match the things that TFA has been lying about. (Rubinstein, 2013)

I can pinpoint the moment that transformed me from one of the most active and eager alumni in the history of Teach For America (TFA) to the person who wrote the blog from which the paragraph above is taken, and perhaps TFA's most tenacious and outspoken critic. It happened Saturday, February 12, 2011, at 5:15 p.m. at, of all places, the TFA 20-year anniversary summit.

I joined TFA in 1991, the second year it existed. I taught 2 years in Houston and then 2 more. In my fourth year I was voted the Teacher of the Year at my school. A few months later, in the summer of 1995, I was invited to share my wisdom with the entire incoming TFA corps. Standing at the microphone back then, I could never have guessed that 17 years later I'd be sitting at a different microphone in the NPR studios as the counterpoint in a segment called "Is Teach For America Failing?" The segment was inspired by a viral blog post I had written discouraging potential applicants.

The summer of 1996 was my first and last experience as a TFA paid staffer. Almost immediately, I had friction with some of my higher-ups, most of whom were a bit younger than me. The Institute director asked if I would represent the 1991 cohort at the opening ceremony with a short speech. After I submitted the speech, my school director called me aside and explained that I would have to remove the humor from my speech. I refused, and my lack of obedience was not appreciated. I didn't appreciate being told how to represent myself, and the two of us stopped talking to each other. To resolve the crisis, the director of operations of Institute, a young woman named Michelle Rhee, showed up at my school unannounced, requesting that I join her for lunch.

The 23-year-old Michelle Rhee had certainly not yet become famous for her moral crusade to fire "ineffective" teachers and principals. Even so, I felt a bit scared as she drove me, in silence, to the Mexican restaurant. To break the silence I asked her, "Are you driving me to Lake Tahoe to shoot me?" Whether she didn't understand my *Godfather II* reference or just didn't find it humorous—or perhaps it wasn't even funny—the question did not get any reaction from the woman who would one day be on the cover of *Time* magazine for her revolutionary idea that teachers have it way too easy. She asked if I thought I could try to get along with my school director, and I said I would try, and I stuck to my word and did manage to salvage the line of communication with my immediate supervisor.

Maybe because of these conflicts, my application to be a trainer the following summer was rejected. Since I wanted to continue to participate, I asked if I could volunteer to be a guest speaker at the Institute to present my workshop about what the first year is really like. This was an annual tradition for the next 11 years.

The workshops were popular and well appreciated by the new trainees since, as some wrote on their feedback forms, they "finally" got to hear the "truth." But by 2007 I was told that my volunteering was no longer needed. My advice, they said, was incorporated into the new training model. After 16 years, it seemed I was finished with my quest to improve TFA.

In 2011, when I signed up for the Teach For America twentieth year alumni summit, I had no idea that my organization—more of an alma mater to me than my college, for sure—was helping to fuel a destructive and, I believe, dangerous threat to education in this country.

Yes, I knew that the same Michelle Rhee who had taken me to lunch to discuss how I could improve had been hired and fired as chancellor in Washington, D.C., and that she had been on *Oprah* a few times. As a teacher in New York City, I was somewhat aware of the growth of the charter school movement and the "failing" schools closures that helped drive the charter growth. The founders of the most popular charter chain in the country, KIPP, Dave Levin and Mike Feinberg (also TFA alums), were friends of mine from my Houston days.

The twentieth anniversary summit was a charter school love fest. Many TFAers went on to start charter schools, and TFA was quite proud of them. But I still didn't get the big picture, though the fog was lifting throughout the weekend for me. Then there was that moment, when Secretary of Education Arne Duncan, whom I knew absolutely nothing about, made a speech in which he described the tough, but necessary, work of shutting down low-performing schools. He said that when he ran Chicago's schools, he shut down a chronically low-performing school, and in its place now was a charter school called Urban Prep. He was proud to announce that the school just had graduated its first senior class, and of the 107 graduates, all 107 got accepted into college. "Same children, same community, same poverty, same violence. [The students] actually went to school in the same building with different adults, different expectations, different sense of what's possible. Guess what? That made all the difference in the world."

As someone who had taught, at that time, for 15 years, something seemed wrong with this anecdote. Yes, I've seen some bad teachers in my day, and I have also seen some great teachers. On some days I've been both a bad teacher and a great one. But as important as a teacher is, the power of a teacher, I've learned, is somewhat limited, just as the power of a doctor is limited. The story just seemed too fantastic. This was my moment, Saturday, February 12, 2011, approximately 5:15 p.m.

When I got home from the summit, I did some research. I learned that Urban Prep may have had 107 seniors, but they had had nearly 170 freshmen 3 years earlier, meaning that over 40% of those freshmen were not part of the 107 mentioned in Duncan's speech. I also learned that Urban Prep had some of the lowest test scores in Chicago. I know politicians are infamous for stretching the truth, but for the secretary of education to do this, and to use this story as a justification for why it was the right thing to do to shut down that school and surely fire the teachers there, that was wrong. I wrote a blog about this and I e-mailed the famous 74-year-old education historian named Diane Ravitch.

I had known about Ravitch for a while. I had read a book of hers called *Left Back* (2000). I also had heard about her latest book, *The Death and Life of the Great American School System* (2010), which, from what I understood, exposed the lies about charter schools and about miraculous test score improvements in New York City. I wrote her a fan letter, which she responded to about 10 minutes later. I sent her my post about Urban Prep. A few weeks later, Diane Ravitch wrote to me to say that she would like to use my research in an op-ed she was writing for the *New York Times*. That viral op-ed, "Waiting for a School Miracle" (2011), was a big turning point in the fight to return decisions about education policy to people who understand education.

My status as a TFA alumnus helped establish my credibility. I could never be accused of being someone who had a chip on his shoulder from not getting into TFA. I guess like having an actual Vietnam War veteran protesting the Vietnam War, having a TFA veteran speaking out against TFA had some allure.

With Diane Ravitch tweeting out links to my blog posts, I suddenly had an audience cheering me on. Over the next years I tackled "miracle schools" anytime a politician held one up as proof that schools have the power to fix every problem every kid has, as long as our expectations are high enough. I tackled education research that supposedly proved, for example, that 85% of students who have an effective teacher 3 years in a row will pass the big test, compared to just 25% of the students who had three ineffective teachers in a row.

My most passionate posts, though, were about TFA. By far the most popular post I ever wrote summarized my feeling about TFA; it was called "Why I Did TFA and Why You Shouldn't" (2011). For 20 years my fight against TFA was a one-man operation. There were others who didn't like what TFA was doing, but those others did not waste their time doing anything about it. The publication of this post signaled to a lot of people who felt similarly that it was OK to expose TFA.

Other TFA alumni started blogging—suddenly, my cause had an army. Which was good, because I was getting quite burned out. Researching a miracle school took hours—hours I didn't really have, since I had a 3-year-old and a newborn at home at the time, and my diaper-changing skills and rocking-kids-to-sleep skills were definitely needed in my household.

In 2012 I got an idea to write a series of "open letters" to different people in high positions in education, leaders of the so-called "reform" movement. I wrote to KIPP founders Dave Levin and Mike Feinberg—no response. I wrote to my former lunch buddy Michelle Rhee—no response. For my final letter I wrote to the founder of TFA herself, Wendy Kopp. My letter and her response to me were featured in both the *New York Times* and the *Washington Post*, on the same day.

Excerpt from the January 31, 2013 open letter to TFA's founder and former CEO, Wendy Kopp:

Dear Wendy,

Hope you and your family had a happy New Years.

Without Teach For America there wouldn't be a "me," or at least there would be one but I'd likely be doing something very different and likely much less fulfilling with my life. And without you there wouldn't be a Teach For America. So in that sense you "made" me. To put this into pop culture terms, if I'm Luke Skywalker then you're, um, Anakin Skywalker.

I don't know if there are many people whose identity is as wrapped up with TFA as me. Starting twenty-one years ago I've pledged my time and my heart into this organization. I've been a corps member, a staff member, an alumni summit attendee, a volunteer recruiter, a workshop presenter, a keynote speaker, a panel member, a financial donor, a mentor, and a dinner host. And for the first nineteen of those twenty-one years, I was so proud to be a member of Teach For America. Anybody who knows me knows that my summer wardrobe used to consist primarily of Teach For America T-shirts that I've obtained over the years at various TFA functions. My wife, in fact, still uses the gray TFA tote bag as our main bag for transporting our kids' belongings to and from daycare.

And after nineteen years of being a proud TFA alum, for the past two years I have been somewhat ashamed of it. Though I am one of the few people to have attended the 5 year, the 10 year, the 15 year, and the 20 year alumni summits, I fear that I will not want to attend the 25 year unless TFA becomes again an organization I can identify with. And I don't mean this as a threat, really. There will be enough people at the 25 without me, but I hope that you see my current dissatisfaction with TFA as somewhat of a "litmus test." If an alum as gung ho as me is having doubts, surely there are many others too…

When you created TFA, one of the ideas, I think, was to tap a new source of people who could put their minds to the problem of improving education in this country. At the time, I doubt you ever expected that some of the alumni would become the leaders of a "reform" movement, while some other alumni would become huge critics of that same movement. And though I've recently seen some steps toward having more voices represented by TFA,

I feel like the fact that it took so long for this process to start, and that there still isn't enough of it, I get concerned that this is only a superficial type of inclusion.

Is TFA also proud of the reform critics? Are we not also part of the "best and the brightest"? Or is it that the alumni who lead the reform movement are "bester" and "brighter" than the critics? When your children are competing against each other in a sporting event, do you actively root for one over the other? (Rubinstein, 2012)

As I write this near the end of 2014, I've noticed that TFA has been trying out a new "messaging strategy." They are not as actively taking sides on controversial education reform issues, at least not publicly. Still, they are unable to conceal whom they side with when they invite certain distinguished alumni "leaders" to speak at their conferences and fundraising events. They may have softened their tone, but TFA continues to cause harm to the very students they claim to champion. The entire organization right now reminds me of the candy store that serves as an innocuous front to the illegal smuggling operation in the back room.

In the fight against reckless education "reform" I feel that I was certainly the right person in the right place at the right time. A math expert who could analyze wild claims, a TFA alum who could claim to be among the "best and brightest," like the Michelle Rhees of the country, and a writer who loves to prove he is right. This combination of qualities, together with the partnership of a little old lady with the mental wisdom and power of a Samurai—Ravitch—who knew exactly how my analytic skills can be applied to this vital cause, was what was needed.

When the war against the reckless reformers is ultimately won—they would implode eventually, even without all of this resistance, but the resistance is certainly speeding things up a lot—my personal contribution will likely not be remembered. But for me, I'll know that I played a part, and in doing so, stayed true to the thing that made me want to join TFA in the first place. I wanted to use my smarts to make a difference in the lives of children. Little did I know, TFA would ultimately provide me the opportunity to work towards neutralizing the havoc that TFA itself was wreaking on this country.

I close with a final excerpt from my blog,

If I were "America" I would have this to say to TFA: While I appreciate your offer to "teach" for me, I've already got enough untrained teachers for my poorest kids. And if teaching is just a stepping stone, for you, on the path to becoming an influential education "leader," thanks, but no thanks, to that too. I don't need the kind of leaders you spawn—leaders who think education "reform" is done by threats of school closings and teacher firings. These leaders celebrate school closings rather than see them as their own failures to help them. These leaders deny any proof that their reforms are failing and instead continue to use P.R. to inflate their own claims of success. We're having enough trouble swatting the number of that type of leader you've already given us. If you want to think of a new way to harness the brain power and energy of the "best and brightest," please do, but if you're just going to give us a scaled-up version of the program that tries to fill a need that no longer exists, please go and teach for someone else. (Rubinstein, 2011)

REFERENCES

Ravitch, D. (2000). *Left back: A century of failed school reforms.* New York: Simon & Schuster.
Ravitch, D. (2010). *The death and life of the great American school system: How testing and choice are undermining education.* New York: Basic Books.
Ravitch, D. (2011, May 31). Waiting for a school miracle. *New York Times.* Retrieved from http://www.nytimes.com/2011/06/01/opinion/01ravitch.html?_r=0
Rubinstein, G. (2011, October 31). Why I did TFA, and why you shouldn't. *Teach for Us.* Retrieved from http://garyrubinstein.teachforus.org/2011/10/31/why-i-did-tfa-and-why-you-shouldnt/
Rubinstein, G. (2012, December 31). Open letters to reformers I know. Part 8: Wendy Kopp. *Teach for Us.* Retrieved from http://garyrubinstein.teachforus.org/2012/12/31/open-letters-to-reformers-i-know-part-8-wendy-kopp/
Rubinstein, G. (2013, April 30). The three biggest TFA lies. *Teach for Us.* Retrieved from http://garyrubinstein.teachforus.org/2013/04/30/the-three-biggest-tfa-lies/

Index

Corps Member Advisor (CMA), 37, 40,
42–43, 47–49, 51–52, 67, 69, 136–137, 159
Critical Race Theory, 7, 85, 98
Criticism, viii, ix, 3, 5, 9–10, 32, 48, 51, 53, 72,
75, 80, 87, 107, 139, 142, 147–151, 153,
157, 162, 169–171, 173–176, 197, 205
Critique, vii, 3–5, 7, 9, 47, 51, 54, 56–57, 62,
80, 98, 112, 121, 148–149, 151–153, 158,
160, 162, 170, 173, 175–176
Cult, 130–131, 133, 137
Culture, 19, 22–23, 27–28, 47, 91, 96–98, 152,
180, 184, 188, 209
    of control, 4
    of fear, 4
    of compliance, 7, 92, 98
    of TFA, 113, 132, 144, 202
    corporate, 6, 8
    of heteranormativity, 8
    of poverty myth, 88
Curriculum, 6, 8, 21, 29, 33, 37, 40, 42, 49–50,
55, 61, 66, 69, 95, 99, 103, 121, 123,
125–126, 186

D

Deficit, 79, 87, 90, 98, 105, 166
    of mentoring, 6, 44
    views of parents, 7
    in relational trust, 41
    thinking, 57, 89–90, 92
Disability/Disabilities, 73–81, 123
Diverse/Diversity, viii, 5–8, 10, 27, 29, 33, 37, 42,
45, 56, 72, 83, 88–90, 92, 98, 105, 131–132,
143, 145, 147, 158, 174, 183–184, 187

E

Executive Director (ED), 108, 141–142, 150,
163
Experience, ix, 2–8, 15, 20, 22–23, 26–31,
33–34, 36–42, 45–48, 50–51, 56, 58–59, 62,
64–67, 70–72, 78, 80–81, 86–90, 92, 97–98,
100, 105, 112–114, 116–118, 121, 123, 125,
127, 129–131, 142, 144–145, 148, 157–159,

163, 167, 170–173, 179–180, 183, 185–187,
189, 192–193, 196, 206
Inexperience, 7, 22–23, 49, 60, 121, 144, 146

F

Faculty Advisor (FA), 40, 42–43
Feedback, 6, 23, 42–44, 69, 104, 144–145, 150,
152, 159, 172–173, 176, 198, 207

G

Gay/Lesbian, viii, 34, 39, 129–134, 136
LGBTQ, 130–132, 135, 137

H

Heteronormative, 5, 8, 131
Homophobic, 135–136, 188
Houston, 6, 9–10, 55–56, 58, 67–69, 141, 200,
205–207

I

Ideology, 63, 69, 71, 134, 172, 180
    achievement, 87–90
    neoliberal/market, 76, 78, 80, 180–181
    supremacist, 90
Impact, vii, 5, 18, 23, 25–26, 30, 34–36, 38,
44–45, 61–62, 73, 75–78, 86, 99, 117–118,
120, 132, 142–144, 148, 156–158, 160–162,
165, 179–180, 182, 187, 198, 201
Induction, 22, 58, 67, 102, 117, 122, 131, 133,
163, 167
Inequality, 29, 31–32, 64, 86, 97, 149, 158,
179–182
Institute, 2, 4, 6–9, 17–18, 20, 26–28, 31,
34–35, 38, 41–52, 58–60, 62, 67–68, 79, 89,
98, 102–103, 105, 107, 113–116, 122–125,
131–133, 141, 159, 169, 172, 184–187, 189,
196–198, 201, 206–207

ROCHELLE BROCK &
RICHARD GREGGORY JOHNSON III,
Executive Editors

Black Studies and Critical Thinking is an interdisciplinary series which examines the intellectual traditions of and cultural contributions made by people of African descent throughout the world. Whether it is in literature, art, music, science, or academics, these contributions are vast and far-reaching. As we work to stretch the boundaries of knowledge and understanding of issues critical to the Black experience, this series offers a unique opportunity to study the social, economic, and political forces that have shaped the historic experience of Black America, and that continue to determine our future. Black Studies and Critical Thinking is positioned at the forefront of research on the Black experience, and is the source for dynamic, innovative, and creative exploration of the most vital issues facing African Americans. The series invites contributions from all disciplines but is specially suited for cultural studies, anthropology, history, sociology, literature, art, and music.

Subjects of interest include (but are not limited to):

- EDUCATION
- SOCIOLOGY
- HISTORY
- MEDIA/COMMUNICATION
- RELIGION/THEOLOGY
- WOMEN'S STUDIES

- POLICY STUDIES
- ADVERTISING
- AFRICAN AMERICAN STUDIES
- POLITICAL SCIENCE
- LGBT STUDIES

For additional information about this series or for the submission of manuscripts, please contact Dr. Brock (Indiana University Northwest) at brock2@iun.edu or Dr. Johnson (University of San Francisco) at rgjohnsoniii@usfca.edu.

To order other books in this series, please contact our Customer Service Department:

(800) 770-LANG (within the U.S.)
(212) 647-7706 (outside the U.S.)
(212) 647-7707 FAX

Or browse online by series at www.peterlang.com.

CPSIA information can be obtained
at www.ICGtesting.com
Printed in the USA
FSHW020720081120
75715FS